The Romani Voice
in World Politics

The United Nations and Non-State Actors

ILONA KLÍMOVÁ-ALEXANDER
University of Cambridge, UK

ASHGATE

Published by
Ashgate Publishing Limited
Gower House
Croft Road
Aldershot
Hants GU11 3HR
England

Ashgate Publishing Company
Suite 420
101 Cherry Street
Burlington, VT 05401-4405
USA

Ashgate website: http://www.ashgate.com

British Library Cataloguing in Publication Data
Klímová-Alexander, Ilona
   The Romani voice in world politics : the United Nations and
   non-state actors. - (Non-state actors in international law,
   politics and governance)
   1. International Romani Union 2. United Nations -
   Non-governmental advisory organizations 3. Romanies -
   Politics and government
   I. Title
   323.1'191497

Library of Congress Cataloging-in-Publication Data
Klímová-Alexander, Ilona.
   The Romani voice in world politics : the United Nations and non-state actors / by
Ilona Klímová-Alexander.
      p. cm. -- (Non-state actors in international law, politics and governance
series)
   Includes bibliographical references and index.
   ISBN 0-7546-4173-2
   1. Romanies--Politics and government. 2. Romanies--Government relations. 3.
Romanies--Social conditions. 4. International relations. 5. United Nations. I.
Title. II. Series.

DX145.K55 2005
323.1191'497--dc22

ISBN 0 7546 4173 2

2004020406

Library
University of Texas
at San Antonio

Typeset in Times New Roman by Saxon Graphics Ltd, Derby
Printed and bound in Great Britain by A Rowe Ltd, Chippenham

Contents

List of Tables

Foreword

Mid 2004, the UN website lists 2531 NGOs in consultative status; 134 under the heading 'General', 1474 listed as 'Special' and 923 included in the 'Roster'. The explosive increase in the number of NGO's associated with the UN on the basis of article 71 of the UN Charter has triggered many publications on the role and position of NGO's within the UN. However, no publication has attempted to describe and analyze the efforts of one particular NGO as thoroughly as Ilona Klímová-Alexander's *The Romani Voice in World Politics: the United Nations and Non-State Actors*.

This is the third publication in this series, which focuses on the role and position of non-state actors in international law, politics and governance. Ilona Klímová-Alexander has touched upon of all of these elements in her description and analysis of the International Romani Union (IRU) and the relationship of this NGO with the United Nations. As this publication is difficult to classify in disciplinary terms, it perfectly fits in a series, which intends to exceed disciplinary boundaries.

The Romani Voice in World Politics demonstrates that the relationship between the IRU and the UN is a complex and multi-facetted one. Being only one NGO among 2530 others, the story of the IRU is a specific one, not necessarily exemplary for the experiences of other NGOs. The NGO world is too diverse to simply extrapolate the findings of this specific study to the overall relationship between the UN and NGOs under the UN's consultative status regime. Moreover, the IRU is an extra-ordinary NGO; voicing the needs of a people rather then advocating a particular public or private interest as most other NGOs do.

This book is a detailed account of successes and failures of an NGO to obtain consultative status and influence world politics; an account of the struggles of personalities; an account of lobbying and networking.

This study is the result of considerable field research and analysis of written documents. As a non-Roma, Ilona Klímová-Alexander has been able to obtain and retrieve information which was not previously available or which was not open to the larger academic and professional communities.

Ilona Klímová-Alexander's study not only presents the interested reader with the development and struggles of a NGO, it also invites the scholarly reader to question concepts like 'movement', 'NGO-strategy' and 'NGO-UN relationship'. *The Romani Voice in World Politics* demonstrates that the study of individual NGOs and their development as international non-state actors are necessary to further conceptualize the impact and status of non-state actors in international law, politics and governance. As such it is not only a valuable contribution to the ongoing discourse on non-state actors, but also a motivation to study the role and position of individual

NGOs in more detail and an incentive to increased comparative and interdisciplinary research.

Math Noortmann

Acknowledgements

Two people have acted as the main mentors during my research and manuscript preparation – Professor James Mayall from the Centre of International Studies of the University of Cambridge and Professor Thomas Acton from the School of Humanities at the University of Greenwich. I thank them both for all the support and guidance they provided in the course of this work. I also thank James for taking interest in my unusual topic, for help with securing fieldwork funding, and for a very personable approach which made me feel like an equal partner during our critical discussions. I owe to Thomas my first contacts with Romani activists, politicians and intellectuals. Among those, I want to mention three in particular: Nicolae Gheorghe, whose inquisitive and brilliant mind and intriguingly charming diplomacy inspired me throughout this project, Ian Hancock, who helpfully answered my frequent questions and requests for materials, and Peter Mercer who has been wonderful (informative and entertaining) company on many long drives to various meetings (saving me from complicated bus or train journeys).

Many other friends and/or colleagues, Romani and non-Romani, contributed to this book by providing ideas and materials. I am grateful to all of the people whom I interviewed, exchanged information with electronically and received materials from and who are listed in the main text and bibliography. Special thanks goes to Lynnaia Main, Grattan Puxon, Peter Vermeersch, Ephraim Nimni and Michael Stewart. Lynnaia and Grattan kindly shared all their research notes and materials and were a great source of support and encouragement. Lynnaia's master's thesis and Grattan's unpublished history of the Romani movement inspired my research and helped me to devise the structure of this book. Lynnaia's input was also invaluable in helping me relate my research to more general debates within international relations and related sciences. Peter introduced me to social movements literature and its relevance to the Romani case. Ephraim supported me in the last stages of the writing process, reassured me of the larger relevance of my research and encouraged me to seek a publisher for this work. Michael encouraged me to attend the Fifth World Romani Congress when others thought it impossible and insisted on meeting Nicolae Gheorghe. The Congress was an eye-opening experience and a leap forward in my understanding of Romani politics, and befriending Nicolae was not only an immense asset for this project but also a personal pleasure. The same goes for many friendships and acquaintances I developed in the course of this project with people I was unlikely to cross paths with had I chosen another research topic. The following friends and/or colleagues have read and commented on the draft of the book or its various chapters: Rainer Bauboeck, Geoffrey Edwards, Morag Goodwin, Will Guy, Lynnaia Main, Elena Marushiakova, Yaron Matras, Thomas Murphy, Ephraim Nimni, Vesselin Popov, Grattan Puxon, Bernard Stark, Nidhi Trehan, and Peter Vermeersch.

I am grateful to the editors of this series and to Ashgate for giving me the opportunity of contributing to the ongoing debate on the role of non-state actors in international relations and to Math Noortmann, the lead editor of this book series, for his helpful comments on the draft manuscript. For financial support I thank the following bodies: the Cambridge Overseas Trust, Central European University/Open Society Institute (Budapest), Centre of International Studies, Trinity Hall, and Board of Graduate Studies of Cambridge University, the Charitable Foundation of the British Federation of Women Graduates and the Faculty of Arts and Social Sciences at the University of New South Wales. I also thank my friends Věra Havlová, Amy Langenfeld, Manuela Rodriguez, Sarang Shidore, Charlotte Warakaulle, Alyn Ware and William Webster who helped me with accommodation during my fieldwork. The final editing of the book took place during my Visiting Fellowship at the School of Politics and International Relations at the University of New South Wales in Sydney and I thank Professor Marc Williams for this opportunity.

The biggest thanks however go to my parents, František and Blanka Klímovi, for their unconditional love and support, and to my husband Duncan Alexander who helped me to keep my sanity, happiness, health and confidence in my work in the most difficult phases of this project and provided much needed editorial support, translating my Czenglish into English and sharpening my arguments with impressively insightful questions for a materials scientist! He not only coped with all my difficult moods in the course of this project but still had the courage to propose at the end of it. Thanks for your faith, Duncan.

List of Abbreviations

Acronyms

BiH	Bosnia-Herzegovina
CAT	Committee against Torture
CEE	Central and Eastern Europe or Central and Eastern European
CERD	Committee on Elimination of Racial Discrimination
CESCR	Committee on Economic, Social and Cultural Rights
CHR	(UN) Centre for Human Rights
CIS	Commonwealth of Independent States
CoE	Council of Europe
CONGO	Committee on NGOs
CPRSI	Contact Point for Roma and Sinti Issues
CRC	Committee on the Rights of the Child
DIESA	Department of International Economic and Social Affairs
DPI	Department of Public Information
EC	European Commission
ECOSOC	Economic and Social Council
ERF	European Roma Forum
ERRC	European Roma Rights Center
EU	European Union
EUROM	European Romani Parliament
FRY	Former Republic of Yugoslavia
GA	(UN) General Assembly
GHM	Greek Helsinki Monitor
GIPSAR	the Assembly of Roma-Gypsies
HRC	Human Rights Committee
ICAT	International Convention against Torture and other Cruel, Inhuman or Degrading Treatment or Punishment
ICCPR	International Covenant on Civil and Political Rights
ICERD	International Convention on the Elimination of All Forms of Racial Discrimination
ICESCR	International Covenant on Economic, Social and Cultural Rights
ICRC	International Convention on the Rights of the Child
IFHR	International Federation of Human Rights
IGO(s)	intergovernmental organisation(s)
IGRM	International Gypsy Rights Mission
ILO	International Labour Organisation
IMADR	International Movement against all Forms of Discrimination and Racism

IRC	International Romani Committee
(I)RU	(International) Romani Union
ISCA	International Save the Children Alliance
JGLS	Journal of the Gypsy Lore Society
MFA	Ministry of Foreign Affairs
MRG	Minority Rights Group
NGO(s)	non-governmental organisation(s)
NTAG	National Traveller Action Group
ODIHR	Office for Democratic Institutions and Human Rights
OHCHR	Office of UN High Commissioner for Human Rights
OSCE	Organisation for Security and Co-operation in Europe
OSI	Open Society Institute
PER	Project on Ethnic Relations
PLO	Palestine Liberation Organisation
POS	political opportunity structure
PROROM	Proceso Organizativo del Pueblo Rom de Colombia
RANELPI	Romani Activists Network on Legal and Political Issues
RNC	Roma National Congress
RNN	RomNews Network
RSG	Roma Support Group
SRPS	Association of Romany Entrepreneurs and Private Persons in the Czech Republic
STP	Society for Threatened Peoples
SWAPO	South West Africa People's Organisation
TERF	Trans-European Roma Federation
TRP	Transnational Radical Party
UDHR	(UN) Universal Declaration of Human Rights
UK	United Kingdom
UN	United Nations
UNBisnet	UN Bibliographic Information System
UNDP	UN Development Programme
UNECE	UN Economic Commission for Europe
UNESCO	UN Educational, Scientific and Cultural Organisation
UNHCHR	UN High Commissioner on Human Rights
UNHCR	UN High Commissioner for Refugees
UNICEF	UN Children's Fund
UNIHP	UN Intellectual History Project
UNMIK	UN Interim Administration Mission in Kosovo
USA	United States of America
VPF	Vilnius Pedagogical Faculty
WB	World Bank
WCAR	World Conference Against Racism, Racial Discrimination, Xenophobia and Related Intolerance
WGC	World Gypsy Community
WGPM	Working Group on Protection of National Minorities
WWII	Second World War

Abbreviations

Aven Amentza	Roma Centre of Public Policies
CERD Recommendation XVII	CERD General Recommendation XVII on Discrimination against Roma
the Commission	UN Commission on Human Rights
the Division	UN Division of Human Rights
Romani CRISS	Roma Centre for Social Intervention and Studies
SATRA/ASTRA	Rroma Students and Youth Against Racism Alliance
the Subcommission	UN Subcommission on the Prevention of Discrimination and Protection of Minorities (renamed to Subcommission on the Protection and Promotion of Human Rights)
the Zentralrat	Central Council of German Roma and Sinti
169 ILO Convention	169 ILO Convention on Indigenous and Tribal Peoples

*To my parents and Duncan
with thanks for their love and support
and to all those who believed in this project
and helped me realize it*

Chapter 1

Introduction

What is the basis for collective representation in world politics? According to international law and practice, the answer is clear – the state. But is the answer the same if we rephrase the question in more normative terms – what should be the basis for collective representation in world politics? For many, the answer does not change. Yet for others, usually those who feel that states fail to adequately represent them, it does. The subjects of this book, Romani activists and their sympathizers, are among those. Claiming that states have failed to represent the interests of their people, the Roma, they have taken it upon themselves to represent 'Romani interests' in international decision-making fora. However, unlike ethnic or liberation movements, Romani activists do not seek the creation of an independent state for their people. In order to legitimize their representation, they argue that people should be represented in international decision-making on the basis of nationhood, not statehood. They are asking for recognition of the Roma as a subject of international law with the right to fully participate in international decision-making on the basis of being a non-territorial nation. Their three decades of attempts to represent the Romani people at the global level – through the United Nations (UN) fora – are the focus of this book. By analysing their specific efforts, this book aims to provide a contribution to the contemporary discourse on the role and position of non-state actors in a specific realm of world politics – the UN system. At the same time, this book is the first attempt to bring the Roma, Europe's largest transnational ethnic minority (or, as many of the activists, argue, a non-territorial nation), into the discourse of international relations, which has until now marginalized or ignored them.

I believe that Romani politics provide an interesting case study for international relations enquiries because it is precisely the Roma, more than any other group, who contest the foundations of the current international system and the state unity which are based on the congruence of people, cultures and territories. While diverse in customs, languages and dialects, religions, church affiliations and citizenship, the Roma can also be seen as members of a large diaspora which stretches over five continents but lacks a territory of its own and which is becoming increasingly bound by common political and cultural mobilization. On the one hand, they display a strong resistance to conforming to the bureaucratic state-centric international system, yet, on the other, also a willingness to use this system to their advantage. In order to find a niche for themselves within the framework of the nation-states dominated world, they have been engaged in the process of nation-building through elite political and cultural mobilization. The current Romani cultural mobilization includes promotion of folklore, festivals, education and publications in the Romani language, and language standardization. Their political mobilization brought about the formation of a state-like structure with its own constitution and embryonic government, parliament and diplomatic corps, established at the recent Fifth World Romani Congress (2000). However, they are not asking for a territory. Can they achieve an equal status and representation in the international community without building a territorial state?

Research Inspiration

This book was greatly inspired by Franke Wilmer's pioneering case study of international indigenous activism entitled *The Indigenous Voice in World Politics*. In this work, Wilmer suggests that the nature of the international system is changing towards being more open to various applications of self-determination for ethnic groups, and towards being more responsive to normative issues (1993: 27 and 199). This change allegedly allows actors who possess none of the conventional sources of influence which international relations literature accounts for (i.e. military strength, control of valuable resources, economic power, production or consumption/market power, recognized international standing or stable political and legal status, and scientific advantage) to exert significant influences on the global scale simply through the power of moral persuasion, as opposed to using coercive strategies (Wilmer 1993: 25). A similar argument has also been put forth by Margaret E. Keck and Kathryn Sikkink (two pioneers who have theorized transnational activism from the international relations perspective), who argue that the current international system allows transnational advocacy networks to exert influence on world politics through interpretation and strategic handling of information, which they use as a 'leverage to gain the support of more powerful institutions' (1998: 30). Wilmer argues that, as a result of this development, global indigenous activists have the 'ability to influence governments to pursue or change policies not clearly in the government's own interest' (1993: 2) simply through directly appealing to international decision-making institutions and indirectly attempting to influence world public opinion (1993: 25). She argues that '[a]fter five centuries of exclusion, the voice of the world's indigenous peoples has ... entered into the discourse of world politics,' albeit quite faintly (1993: 192).

If we extend Wilmer's logic, we could hypothesize that if, due to the changing nature of the international system, the world's indigenous peoples have managed to become actors in world politics without possessing any of the conventional sources of influence, other groups in a similar position should also be able to do so. An ideal case with which to test this hypothesis would be that of Romani transnational activism because no other is more similar to the indigenous. Both indigenous and Romani activism bring together groups of very diverse people united by their grievances. Both Romani and indigenous peoples are spread over several continents as citizens of dozens of states, speak a variety of languages and dialects and exhibit varied ethnic and cultural features. Both do not just direct their demands to nation-state political authorities, but also request that their rights are grounded in international law. Although there are some politically significant differences between Roma and indigenous peoples, these are outweighed by their similarities in regard to their (extra)legal status as encapsulated nations, social and cultural characteristics, forms of political organization, historical and current treatments by majority societies, and problems faced (for details of this argument see Klimova 2000). The dearth of literature on transnational Romani activism however precludes the testing of the above hypothesis with an analysis similar to Wilmer's. This book therefore aims to make a preparatory step for such an analysis, mapping out the interaction between Romani activists and the UN system as a ground-sweeping exercise for further, more analytical and theoretical research.

Objectives and Relevance

The book describes and analyses the attempts of the Romani activists to gain voice in world politics by interacting with the UN system and explores their capabilities and impact on international relations. The project has three objectives. Firstly, to introduce global Romani activism – its anatomy, history, political manifestos, goals and activities. Secondly, to establish the extent of the Romani voice or voices in world politics, what they call for and what influence they have had on the UN discourse on Roma, the UN's organizational structure and its activities regarding Roma. Thirdly, to establish the reverse influence – i.e. how interacting with the UN system has affected the organizational structure of global Romani activism and its discourse.

The book adopts a modified version of Bas Arts' definition of political influence: *Political influence is defined as the achievement of (a part of) one's policy goal with regard to [outcomes of inter-governmental agenda-setting, discursive commitments and procedural/institutional changes], which is (at least partly) caused by one's own and intentional intervention in the political arena and process concerned* (1998: 58). In other words, 'political influence implies that the policy outcome concerned is more in line with the policy goal of the player involved than would have been the case the latter not intervened [sic]. [Thus], the player did matter and has indeed made a difference' (Arts 1998: 59). Although this definition of political influence implies 'a causal linkage between specific outcomes on the one hand and specific player interventions on the other' (Arts 1998: 59), it does not imply that the player's interventions have been the main or sole cause of the outcome.

However, I do not aim either to test or develop a theory of political influence of non-state actors at this point. The analysis includes reflections on some of the sources and causes limiting the results of Romani activism, but given the dearth of available data and the methodological difficulties involved in defining and measuring success, I do not aim to hypothesize the chances of success of Romani activism in this book. Although I believe that there is a strong potential for using Romani activism as a case study for testing and developing theories of political influence of non-state actors, it would have been premature to take such an approach. As King, Keohane and Verba stress, '[i]t is pointless to seek to explain what we have not described with a reasonable degree of precision' (1994: 44). Thus we first need empirically strong case studies of particular aspects of Romani activism at various levels that outline some theoretical implications of the case and serve as a background for further, more in-depth analysis. The book thus largely concentrates on historical detail, using in-depth exploration and 'thick description'. Nevertheless, it does have a strong analytical component, scrutinising the relationship between an ethnic actor and an intergovernmental organizaton (IGO) and, therefore, contributing to the discourse on the role of non-state actors in world politics. In particular, it explores two propositions postulated by two different perspectives within International Relations theory – transnationalism and collective social action – which can be employed to study the influence of non-state actors. According to the transnationalism perspective, we can expect that

Romani activists are likely to be successful in gaining some political influence if they can provide quality expertise, display diplomatic and professional behaviour, acquire experience, reliability, integrity and prestige, and couch their demands in terms similar to those of existing regimes (as this increases the legitimacy of their demands) (Reinalda 2001: 37; Arts 2001: 208; Willetts 1996: 44–45). In terms of interacting with the UN system, non-state actors are likely to gain influence if they are tough, resolute, well-briefed, patient, adequately funded and led by individuals with vision, dedication to an ideal, and dogged determination, 'who identify an objective, who refuse to accept discouragement and who have the charisma to inspire followers to continue the fight until the goal is achieved' (Sankey 1996: 273–274). From the collective social action perspective, the activists' ability to instigate fundamental change will depend on the resources they can mobilize and the extent to which they can take advantage of the favourability of the political opportunity structure (POS) (Reinalda 2001: 37; Arts 2001: 208; Willetts 1996: 44–45). The book also explores a proposition which Reinalda and Verbeek suggest as an element of a prospective theory of non-governmental organizations (NGOs) in transnational and international relations. This proposition holds that the 'right to confer consultative status on NGOs is an important tool of influence of international organizations and national governments. ... Once NGOs have become recognized by international organizations, their room to manoeuvre will be limited with regard to the scope of their activities and their official positions' (2001: 152). Moreover, once NGOs have accepted the rules of the game of international politics and thus became players in it, 'international organizations will through their official procedures try to confine the role of NGOs in order to make them an instrument of intergovernmental problem solving and objectives' (2001: 155).

The relevance of this research is fourfold. Firstly, it looks at a case of political activism which has so far been neglected in political science and international relations literature (for the literature survey see Klimova 2003: §1.6.1). By making the first step towards closing the information gap about global Romani activism with a systematic study, it aims to both bring the Roma into the world politics discourse and stimulate further research. Secondly, it responds to calls from practitioners of international relations, including inter-governmental officials, for more information about the activities of Romani activists.[1] Concerns with the Roma, for example their east-west migration and asylum seeking, have already become a subject of intergovernmental negotiations (see e.g. Castle-Kanerova 2003; Pluim 2001). Governments and IGOs are turning to social scientists for policy advice, but end up consulting ethnographers because political scientists often know very little about the Roma. The science is therefore lagging behind the reality. Thirdly, by illuminating the interaction between Romani activists and the UN system and mutual influence in terms of discourse and organizational structure, the research contributes to some of the questions explored in the limited, but growing, literature on non-state actors. Finally, given the present lack of documentation and analyses of their own activities concerning Roma by both the Romani activists and the UN system, the information and analysis presented here offer a mirror to both the Romani activists and UN officials through which they can reflect on their activities in order to increase the effectiveness of their future actions.

Besides the primary findings (see Chapter 7), the material presented in this book also contributes to deepening our understanding of a number of issues in political science, international relations and sociology which were not the primary focus of the research. In relation to the modernity/tradition dialectic it portrays the struggle of certain Romani elites to adapt to 'modernity' by establishing a new identity, organizations and practices, so allowing them to integrate into the modern political society, with the opportunity cost being a greater distance between them and their communities (see e.g. Main 1994; Liegeois 1976). It shows how new elites are formed and reproduced through political socialisation and imitation and how they come to dominate the political process and nation-building through construction of 'imagined communities,' according to the Western model (see e.g. Anderson 1991; Chatterjee 1993). It also reminds us of the myriad forms of participation in the broader political process through recounting many different ways, successful and unsuccessful, in which Romani elites were involved in trying to modernize Romani identity, lobby a multitude of organizations, gain acceptance in mainstream political institutions, etc. It shows the extent of initiative involved in being part of the political process and the stamina needed to sustain these efforts and reap the harvest of these initiatives. In relation to the UN political process in particular, the book demonstrates the intricacies and frustrations of the UN system of political action and shows how much perseverance and energy is required to 'penetrate' it. In relation to the evolution of the roles and participation of NGOs in the international system, the book illustrates the wide range of means by which NGOs can participate in the UN political process, formally and informally. It delineates both the NGOs' progress in the past ten years in the UN system, and their continual marginalization within this system through 'fringe meetings' and other reduced forms of inclusion, lack of financial and human resources, etc. Finally, it presents a critique of the current concepts of nation and nation-state as primary political units in the international system.[2]

Scope

To overcome constraints of time, space and resources, the analysis has been limited to Romani activism at the global level, leaving out the local, nation-state and regional dimensions. Concentrating on just one level of Romani activism unavoidably leads to its partial portrayal. Although all the levels permeate each other, in some respects they differ significantly. For example, at the local and nation-state levels, Romani activists place a much greater emphasis on individual integration in the countries and municipalities, whilst global activism strives for equality through a collective recognition. Thus the data presented pertain to the global level and should not be generalized for other levels.

Although some might argue that the European level of Romani activism is more important than the global, the latter is preferred for the following reasons. Firstly, I want to emphasize the role of non-state actors in world politics through involvement at the global level (a phenomenon itself not yet sufficiently covered by existing literature). Secondly, the focus on the global level draws attention to the global dimension of the Romani plight and political mobilization. For, although Romani issues are most often discussed in relation to particular countries or Europe, the Roma are a globally dispersed people and their problems cannot *only* be addressed at the local, nation-state or regional levels. Thirdly, from a methodological point of view, the UN system provides a better framework for analysis than do European IGOs because the

UN system offers a clearly defined formal access to non-state actors. Although European IGOs have always taken more interest in Romani issues than the UN, and have had more interaction with Romani activists than the UN system, the interaction between non-state actors and the European IGOs often takes place on the basis of informal access, in the form of personal unrecorded contacts, and is therefore difficult to document. Lastly, the global level of Romani activism has so far been neglected in political science literature as researchers have concentrated their attention on the European level (see e.g. Barany 2002; Kovats 2001; Vermeersch 2001a; Vermeersch 2001b; Vermeersch 2002). This work ensures that the global level is also chronicled.

Determining the impact of Romani activism on world politics is limited to the analysis of what Keck and Sikkink identify as the first three stages of influence that non-state actors might have: agenda setting, discursive commitments and procedural/institutional changes within the UN system that relate to Romani issues. The last two of Keck's and Sikkink's stages of influence – affecting policy and actual behaviour of target actors (1998: 201) – would be premature to consider, owing to the novelty of the Romani issue within UN fora and the resulting absence of a coherent UN policy.

The book provides a brief historical background on the global Romani activism since the turn of the twentieth century. The analysis of the interactions with the UN focuses on the period from 1977, a year that marks the first UN resolution mentioning Roma *and* the beginning of negotiations between Romani activists and the UN, until the end of 2002.[3]

Constraints and Limitations

As in any other research project, I was faced with several constraints and limitations in acquiring and analysing data.[4] Firstly, there was a temporal proximity to the subject under consideration. Given the fact that some of the most interesting developments in the interactions between the Romani activists and the UN system only occurred during the course of the research, I decided to extend the time scope of the book until 2002, when the book was largely written up. Due to this proximity, the availability of some data was limited[5] and some of the information acquired has not been subject to public or academic scrutiny prior to my evaluation. While this contributes to its originality, it also challenges the quality of analysis. I have attempted to reduce this risk by triangulating research findings. Triangulation[6] (i.e. cross-checking) was also used to offset the constraints posed by the second limitation, which is the unreliability of some published data and the inaccuracy of some information gathered through fieldwork.[7] Secondly, the research results are somewhat constrained by the degree of success with which I managed to bridge what Martin Kovats calls a 'cultural divide' between myself and the subjects, the majority of whom are ethnic Roma, while I am non-Romani. There is a significant, historically-based degree of mistrust and misunderstanding between Romani and non-Romani communities in any part of the world, posing a challenge for any kind of interaction. On top of that, mistrust of researchers is even stronger. This sentiment mostly comes from the perception that non-Romani research on Roma is only conducted in order to control or harm them (as was Hitler's or, to a lesser extent, that of the Communist Party's scientists' research), or to make a personal material profit. However, the majority of the activists with whom contact was made most frequently are well integrated Roma used to dealing with the non-Romani world, which eased this limitation. In addition, I adopted a research methodology that, where possible, compensated for the cultural divide through confidence building measures (for details see Klimova 2003: §1.6.4.2).

Thirdly, several factors limited the availability of key actors for interviews. Romani activists are spread around the world, which does not allow for the conducting of a number of interviews within one research trip. I tried to use the opportunity of international gatherings for interviews, but often such circumstances (busy programmes and, at times, preoccupation with elections, lobbying and other political engagements) only allowed for brief encounters as opposed to lengthy interviews. Similarly, many of the key UN actors are based in academic and political institutions across the world, as opposed to being concentrated in the headquarters at New York or Geneva. In addition, the relatively long period covered by the project means that several people, who were important in the early stages of Romani activism, died before the project started or during its course. Similarly, many key UN actors had died, or had retired from their positions and were now difficult to trace. Finally, neither Romani activists nor (surprisingly) the UN has systematically archived data on their mutual interaction. With regards to the activists, this was due to limited organizational capacity and human and financial resources, while the UN had, until very recently, not considered Romani issues of enough importance to be recorded (van Boven 13 December 2002).[8] Therefore, I had to (metaphorically) dig around to unearth the data presented in this book. Consequently, much material may remain undiscovered.

Methodology and Sources

All the above-mentioned objectives, constraints and limitations were considered when designing an appropriate methodology for the project. Although one of the aims of the project is to determine whether Romani activists could have had any influence on agenda setting, discursive commitments and procedural/institutional changes within the UN system and *vice versa*, my ultimate goal is not causal inference (for description of causal inference see King, Keohane and Verba 1994: Chapter 3). Given the large number of independent variables (e.g. actions of UN members states and administration, non-Romani NGOs and media, increasing UN interest in human and minority rights issues, fall of Communism and rise of social problems in the former Eastern Bloc with immigration to the West as a consequence, etc.)[9] which would have to be considered, or controlled for, along with the actions of the Romani activists when trying to determine the causes of the relevant discursive and institutional changes within the UN system, reliable causal inference is not feasible at this stage. Instead I employ descriptive inference, to see whether a link can be established between these changes and the actions of the Romani activists (for description of descriptive inference see King, Keohane, and Verba 1994: Chapter 2).

The research combines data collection and background and interpretative reading with fieldwork techniques such as confidence building, formal and informal interviewing and participant observation. Face-to-face contact was crucial, not only for the confidence building, but also because a significant amount of material presented in this book consists of inaccessible documentation (such as the Romani and UN's internal pamphlets, correspondence, reports, minutes of meetings, etc.). By using interviews, participant observation, discussions with interested parties[10] and the available literature, I could triangulate the information from different sources (for details of methodology, including fieldwork techniques employed see Klimova 2003: §1.6).

Given the lack of secondary sources (see Klimova 2003: §1.6.1), the bulk of the book relies heavily on primary sources. These chiefly consist of journalistic accounts, news items, non-governmental, governmental and intergovernmental reports and documentation, and writings, documents and publications by the Romani activists. Some of the writings by the Romani activists and their sympathizers are often presented as academic pieces yet, although providing first hand accounts, they do not describe historical events in neutral terms. Instead, they present them in a light convenient for the creation of a Romani national history and mythology, and are therefore examples of political, rather than purely academic, writing (see e.g. Puxon 1975; Puxon 2000; Puxon 1981; Hancock 1999a; Hancock 1991a; Hancock 2002; Acton and Gheorghe 2001). Among the publications by Romani activists the most useful source was *Roma*, the official organ of the International Romani Union (IRU) published since 1974, and *Informaciaqo Lil e Rromane Uniaqoro* (Information Bulletin of the Romani Union), which supplemented *Roma* in the early 1990s. While these journals have to be treated with caution because they are effectively mouth-pieces of the IRU, they are an important, and often sole, written source of information on global Romani activism, because no official long-term archive yet exists. The use of electronic resources also proved indispensable in this project. Internet and E-mail have become one of the main mobilization tools for Romani activism – numerous Romani websites, news and chat groups have sprung up within the last decade (for details on the electronic sources consulted see Klimova 2003: §1.6.2). The research also relied heavily on archival sources, mainly belonging to Romani activists. Since, at present, no central, long-term and organized archive of global Romani activism exists, I had to collect archival materials from the personal collections of Romani activists (for details see Klimova 2003: §1.6.2). Of these, the Romani Archives and Documentation Center at the University of Texas at Austin, managed by Ian Hancock, comes closest to being a professional archive. This archive contains a wealth of Roma-related literature, including books, theses and student assignments as well as some official documents of the IRU (however mostly from Hancock's most active period as an IRU official during the 1990s). The current IRU President Emil Scuka also archives IRU materials, mostly since the 1990s, which were again consulted for this project. The archive of the Museum of Romani Culture in Brno, Czech Republic was a useful source of information on the co-operation between the Czech and Slovak Unions of Roma-Gypsies and the IRU, although, since the archive was only being professionalized and catalogued during the course of this project, many materials from this period had either been lost or were temporarily unavailable. In respect of personal collections, I obtained the most valuable materials from the following IRU officials: Grattan Puxon, Nicolae Gheorghe and Jan Cibula (Cibula's through the Museum of Romani Culture in Brno and through co-operation with Swiss history student Bernhard Schaer). UN and UN-related materials were obtained from the UN Archive in Geneva,[11] the NGO Department of International Economic and

Social Affairs (DIESA) file on IRU in New York[12] and the UN Dag Hammarskjoeld Library in New York.

While Part One of the book is limited to providing relevant background, Part Two is both empirical and analytical. This part uses the concept of POS as an organizing analytical framework. As the collective social change perspective tells us, the success of the Romani activists in instigating fundamental changes depends partly on the favourability of the POS and the degree to which they use it. The concept of POS helps us both to present the necessary information in an organized manner and to understand the access provided by the UN to non-state actors, identifying the limits and opportunities of the UN institutional political environment in which the Romani actors operates. Thus, it allows us to determine the extent to which non-state actors can influence agenda setting and discursive as well as procedural/institutional developments within the UN. According to social movement scholars, the degree of formal access within a political system is determined by the formal institutional structure.[13] When analysing the structure of collective action using the POS concept, this degree of formal access is one of the most significant variables (McAdam, McCarthy, and Zald 1996: 10). Neither the concept nor this particular variable have been greatly used outside of nation-state political systems. For instance, to my best knowledge, only three scholars have attempted to analyse the political opportunity provided by the formal institutional structure of IGOs – Florence Passy in her case study of the UN (1999), and Gary Marks and Doug McAdam in their case study of the European Union (EU) (1999). Passy applies a revised version of the theoretical framework by Kriesi et al. (1995) that has been adjusted for analysis at the international level in order to determine the degree of openness of the UN political structure towards challengers. Her framework concentrates on three main dimensions of the POS: the institutional structures of the political system which determine the degree of its formal access, the prevailing strategies traditionally adopted by authorities towards political contention which define the degree of their inclusiveness towards non-state actors, and the configuration of power which determines the possibilities for non-state actors to form alliances with established actors within the system. This book elaborates on Passy's analysis of the UN formal institutional structure as a background to the interaction between Romani activists and the UN.

Book Structure and Outline

Framed by the introduction and conclusion, the main body of the book consists of two parts. Part One provides background on global Romani activism (chapter 2) and on the UN system and its interest and involvement in Romani issues (chapter 3). Chapter 2 briefly introduces the history and anatomy of global Romani activism, presenting the actors involved, their political manifestos and ideological orientations, and goals and strategies. Chapter 3 provides an overview of the development of UN interest and involvement in Romani issues so as to identify key events/actions leading to UN agenda-setting, discursive and procedural/institutional changes.

Part Two, consisting of chapters 4–6, is the main empirical and analytical part, detailing the interaction between the UN system and Romani activists, using the POS organizing and analytical framework. Chapters 4–6 describe each of the POS dimensions in turn while illustrating how the activists used them, in order to gain an understanding of their influence within the UN system. Chapter 4 concentrates on the formal access offered by the UN to non-state actors. Chapter 5 studies informal strategies that were facilitated by the attitude of the UN towards non-state actors. Chapter 6 examines the UN configuration of power as relating to the activists' allies, while also detailing the activists' interventions at the UN for which allies were sought. The entire Part Two concentrates on the interaction between the activists and those UN and UN-related bodies that have shown significant interest in Romani issues as well as the events/actions leading to the agenda, discursive or procedural/institutional developments in relation to Roma that were identified in Chapter 3. Chapter 7 presents the findings of the study, draws conclusions from them and suggests a number of possible directions for future research.

Notes

1 Several state as well as international civil servants and politicians to whom I have spoken in the course of my research have expressed the desire to be better informed about Romani activism, its objectives and actions for the purposes of current or future co-operation.

2 I am grateful to Lynnaia Main for helping me identify these points.

3 A couple of references are made to events in early 2003 when these events relate to those started before the end of 2002.

4 The first two limitations are also acknowledged in the doctoral dissertation of Martin Kovats from which this book adopts the terms 'temporal proximity' and 'cultural divide' (1998: §I, chapter 3).

5 For example, a number of summary records of 2001 meetings of various UN bodies had not been issued by the beginning of 2003.

6 Triangulation as a research strategy refers 'to the process of multiple mapping, whereby a particular observation or finding is subject to scrutiny from more than one source' (Pinnock 1999: chapter 3).

7 For the difficulties involved in gathering accurate Roma-related data see e.g. Barany 2000; Siklova 1999. The problems with accuracy and proper assessment of first hand NGO information is also considered in Bakker 2001.

8 Where reference includes day and month, this indicates a personal communication in the form of an in-person or phone interview or electronic communication.

9 Note that some of these elements are mentioned in Main 1994: Chapter 3, PartIB2b.

10 For the characterization of the main actors with whom most frequent contact was maintained see Klimova 2003: 17, footnote 49.

11 File registry no. G/OR 340/118, Consultative arrangements and relations with non-governmental organizations, Romani Union.

12 NGO offices in Geneva and Vienna were also approached for information from their IRU files but refused access.

13 Doug McAdam has synthesized previous attempts at conceptualising POS and concluded that all authors have emphasized the importance of formal legal and institutional structure, although they were using different terms to define it: 'formal institutional structure' (Kriesi et al. 1992: 220), 'meaningful access points' (Brockett 1991: 254), 'access to the party system' (Rucht 1996), 'openness or closure of the polity' (Tarrow 1994). In his own work, McAdam uses the term 'the relative openness or closure of the institutionalised political system' (1996: 27).

PART ONE:
SETTING THE SCENE

Chapter 2

Introducing Global Romani Activism

This chapter briefly introduces 'the Roma' as the subjects of Romani activism as well as both the history and anatomy of global Romani activism, presenting the actors involved, their political manifestos and ideological orientations, and goals and strategies. Since a detailed description of these aspects is beyond the scope of this book, the information presented here is limited to establishing a pertinent background.

Who are 'the Roma' as the Subjects of Romani Activism?

'Roma' is a *political term* used as an umbrella name for all members of the Romani ethnic community.[1] Its usage in political and, sometimes, academic discourse (by both Roma and non-Roma) demonstrates a strong tendency towards treating the extremely ethnographically diverse Romani community or communities as a largely homogeneous group, overshadowing the various appellations preferred by the individual groups and subgroups (see Tables 2.1–2).[2] As the dominant discourse among global Romani activists has publicly promoted 'Roma' as an umbrella term for all of them since the late 1960s, this book accepts and uses it as such, yet without the implication that such homogenization is the correct approach. I am aware that from an ethnographic point of view, the Romani community is extremely diverse and all Romani groups, subgroups and metagroups have their own ethnic and cultural features (see Acton and Gheorghe 2001; Marushiakova and Popov 2001a: 33). However, discussing this diversity further is not the purpose of this book. It suffices to point out that, so far, the homogeneous Romani identity is a political project rather than a reality.

The definition of who the Roma are, as opposed to what is the term 'Roma', is more complex. In his doctoral dissertation, Peter Vermeersch provides a useful overview of three definitions, present in the academic discourse, of who the Roma are: 1) a historical diaspora (with common historic roots in the Punjab region in north-western India and common patterns of migration from this region to Europe and other continents), 2) a group characterized by a typical culture and lifestyle (nomadism, common cultural practices such as elements of religion, habits, rules of cleanliness, musical traditions and interpretations of the world through the lenses of *Romipen* – Romani values) and 3) a biological kinship, group or race (see Vermeersch 2002: 10–14 for the discussion of this overview). For the purposes of this book, Roma are those who are identified as such by the dominant discourse among global Romani activists. This discourse is however rather vague; within it, only the 'academic work' attempts to define Roma (see e.g. Hancock 2002). A few Romani political documents provide some loose definitions, usually under the influence of Hancock's work. They define Roma as 'a nation scattered throughout the entire

world' (UN Doc. E/CN.4/Sub.2/NGO/99); a diaspora of Indian origin, whose ancestors left India as members of martial troops and camp followers about one thousand
years ago (Hancock 1992); a racial group that shares 'cultural, linguistic and genetic
ties clearly traceable to tenth-century India'[3] (Gheorghe and Hancock 1991a); people
'known by various names such as Gypsies, Gitanes, tsiganes, etc'. whose 'history and
language are related with India and the Sanskrit-based languages' and who in their
own language identify themselves as Roma, Sinti or Manush (UN Doc.
E/CN.4/1991/NGO/51); people called Sinti, Lovari, Ashkari, Chorichani, Rumungre,
Vlach, Manush, etc.[4] (Acton and Klimova 2001, Appendix 2: International Romani
Union Charter); people of Indian origin (UN Doc. E/C.2/1993/R.4/Add.2, 16); a
legitimate ethno-linguistic population (IRU 1992); a distinct nation unified by the
Romani language, 'history, literature, culture and traditions, upon which they can
base their further development' (IRU 2000b); and a non-territorial nation of Indian
origin (see Romani thematic commission 2001). Based on the discussions among
global Romani activists, the current predominant identity frame is clearly that of a
non-territorial nation (PER 2003: 12). The numbers and geographical distribution of
Roma differ from document to document, mostly ranging from 10–15 million in the
world,[5] at times referring only to Roma in Europe and the Americas, at times pointing
out that unknown numbers of Roma also live in parts of Asia, Africa and Australia
(Fourth World Romani Congress 1990).

It is not the purpose of this book to provide background information about the
Roma. It is however important for the reader to note that they are amongst the world's
most disadvantaged, least integrated and most persecuted peoples. In most societies
they experience discrimination in employment, education, health care, administrative
and other services, and in many countries they are also subject to hate speech and
racist violence. Throughout the world and throughout history,[6] they have been dealt
with through the application of criminal law, with anti-Romani views being used to
justify systematic attempts at their collective exploitation, control, and/or elimination. In the twentieth century, officially sponsored policies ranged from extermination (most notably during the Holocaust)[7] to eradication of their traditional culture
through forced settlement and resettlement, ethnic cleansing, assimilation and sterili-
zation of Romani women (Fernandez Jimenez 1996: 7; van der Stoel 1993). As the
direct result of centuries of such discrimination, persecution and partly self-imposed
defensive isolation, depriving them of educational and vocational opportunities and
consequently of the social and economic benefits of modern societies, they often
belong to the lowest socio-economic strata and experience many related problems
such as acute and widespread poverty, massive unemployment, high rates of illiteracy, lack of formal education, substandard housing, inadequate health care and
cultural deprivation (RNN 1999; van der Stoel 1993; PER 1994: 3; UNDP 2003).

Contrary to the popular belief that the Roma are the parasites of society and
scroungers of the welfare system, who either try to improve their lot solely through
illegal means or passively expect to be taken care of, their leaders have been organizing to improve the situation of their people and attempting to enter mainstream politics since the beginning of the twentieth century, entering national parliaments in
some (mostly Central and Eastern European – CEE) countries as early as the 1960s,
firstly as mainstream politicians and then, by the 1990s, as declared representatives
of the Roma (Klimova 2002a: 108–115). At the international level, Romani attempts
for inclusion into IGOs are actually as old as these institutions themselves, with the

first Romani aspirations for international representation being directed to the League of Nations (see Klimova 2003: §5.2).

A Brief Account of the Origin and History of Romani Activism and its Globalization

Some of the crafters of Romani nationalist history argue that the roots of Romani activism date from the end of the nineteenth century, with early Romani attempts at institutionalizing their activities in the form of a regularly meeting permanent body, as well as *ad hoc* conferences (see e.g. Puxon 1975; Hancock 2002: 113–114; and Hancock 1999a). These early international congresses are, however, nationalist myths based on dubious sources and creative interpretation (see Hancock 2002: 113–114; Klimova 2002a: 108). Another phenomenon related to Romani activism, however, does have roots in the nineteenth century – the growth of non-Romani or pro-Romani (often religious) organizations that started to take an interest in the plight of Roma or were created to address directly their plight and lobby 'on their behalf'. The most recent such organization with an international reach is the European Roma Rights Centre (ERRC) which started to be active within UN fora in the last few years; its activities are thus accounted for in this book.

In some countries, Roma did in fact start institutionalizing their struggle for rights at the turn of the twentieth century, but only at local and nation-state levels.[8] Nevertheless, it was only since the 1920–30s that Romani organizations of a more collective form started to function somewhat regularly in several countries (Fraser 1992: 316).[9] At the same time, the first global aspirations occurred, in Poland and Romania. The leaders of the General Union of Roma in Romania (the Union)[10] fathered the idea of creating a permanent institutional international body in the form of an international pan-Romani Congress. This is verified in the Statutes of the Union, published by Hailey. According to these Statutes, the Union appointed its President Lazurica as a representative for the future international congress 'to be held in France or elsewhere,' decided to form committees and affiliated societies in every country, and planned to obtain travel grants for Romani delegates to attend international Romani congresses (Achim 1998: Chapter 4.2; Haley 1934: 186–190; Congresul Tiganilor 1933). Such international congresses never materialized in the interwar period, although legend maintains that one took place in 1933 or 1934 in Bucharest, with later international congresses looking back to this mythical event as their forerunner (see e.g. Remmel 1993: 131; Acton 1974: 101). In Poland, the global aspirations were directed towards the League of Nations, which was allegedly approached by a Polish Romani king[11] requesting a Romani homeland in Abysinia (see Klimova 2003: §5.2). Today these Polish attempts are seen as the roots of the global Romani activism, primarily embodied in the IRU (see Hancock 1991b). However, both the country-wide and global aspirations were crushed during the Second World War (WWII) when numerous Roma lost their lives in the Holocaust. Nazism left the nascent modern Romani activism paralysed for over a decade after the war, with Roma in many European countries, after barely escaping extermination, being reluctant to proclaim their ethnicity and organize along ethnic lines. Even so, some individual activities slowly started to appear in the period immediately following the war, with Roma in various countries founding new religious, political and cultural organizations, both locally and country-wide (Fraser 1992: 317).[12]

From the 1960s onwards, the UN has inspired the creation (although often only on paper) of a number of international Romani umbrella organizations that wanted to advance the interests of the world's Roma through UN discourse, instruments and structures (for details about these organizations and their activities see Klimova 2003: §2.3.1). These organizations enlisted mostly European but also some Middle Eastern and North American members. The main goal of the early organizations was to establish a Romani state with the help of the UN and through money to be gained by collective Holocaust reparations, or alternatively to at least win a recognized international status for Roma with the issuing of international Romani passports. Along with this goal, the organizations worked towards legitimization of Roma as a nation with the right to a state by creating and promoting national culture. Although the goals of improving living standards and cultural and moral uplifting of the Roma were usually declared, they have always remained secondary to the nationalist aspirations. By the 1970s these attempts crystallized into the First World Romani Congress held in April 1971, near London, attracting participants from Western, Central and Eastern Europe as well as Asia and North America, and the creation of the first durable global Romani organization – the IRU – by the time of the Second World Romani Congress in Geneva, April 1978. This transnationalization of Romani activism was concurrent with transnationalization of other movements and campaigns, a development that, according to Willetts, only started in the early 1970s (1982: 196). By then the controversial demand for state was officially dropped (although some Romani activists never gave up on the idea), while lobbying for Holocaust reparations stayed one of the main goals of global Romani activism. These transnational attempts then reinforced the growth of both local and country-wide Romani organizations in Europe (mostly Western as Romani activism in the Eastern Bloc was restricted by communist regimes) and some isolated attempts at organizations in North and South America, Australia, New Zealand and Asia (India and Pakistan). The boom of organizations in the former Eastern Bloc only occurred after the change of regime in 1989. At that time, the migration of many Roma from the Eastern Bloc to Western countries reinvigorated Romani activism in the West (Acton and Klimova 2001: 162–163), leading to the creation of new organizations, such as the Trans-European Roma Federation (TERF, uniting UK-based organizations – or rather self-appointed leaders – of Romani asylum-seekers from the Czech Republic, Romania, Bulgaria and Poland). The next paragraphs look more closely at the anatomy of global Romani activism, in terms of actors involved, their political manifestos and ideological orientations, and goals and strategies.

Actors Involved in Global Romani Activism

If, for the purposes of this book, we conceive of global Romani activism as activism targeting the UN system, we are principally left with one actor – *the IRU* – as the main Romani umbrella organization and the only Romani organization accorded formal access to the UN system by 2003 (see pp. 66–8). The other major Romani international umbrella organization – the Roma National Congress (RNC), functioning since the 1980s – is not considered here in detail because its lobbying concentrates mostly on the European, not the UN, level. However, the few RNC actions which did target the UN are accounted for in Chapter 5. In addition, a number of local and country-wide Romani organizations have at times been involved in interactions with the UN system, either under the auspices of the IRU or independently. Similarly, some interaction between organizations of non-Romani Gypsy and Traveller groups, such as the Irish Travellers or Banjara Gypsies, and the UN has taken place in relation to Romani issues. While their actions are recorded in this book, they do not warrant a detailed introduction here. However, one more actor must at least be introduced briefly. The *ERRC*, the only international pro-Romani organization (characterized as promoting Romani issues as its primary goal but not being primarily staffed and led-by Roma), was also accorded formal access to the UN, in 2001. Since the book is primarily concerned with the *Romani* voice and because its scope extends no further than the beginning of 2003 (by which time the ERRC had only just begun activities at the UN), it is not necessary to provide the same amount of background for the ERRC's work as for the IRU's; a brief description will suffice. The ERRC is an international public interest law organization which was established in 1996 to help 'the nascent Romani movement' to create 'internationalised human rights strategy initiative to monitor the human rights situation of the Roma and to provide legal defence in cases of human rights abuse' (ERRC 1996a and 1996c). Its goal is 'to give the Roma tools to combat discrimination and win equal access to government, education, employment, health care, housing, voting rights and public services' (ERRC 1996a). It

> acts to combat racism and discrimination against Roma and to empower Roma to their own defence by engaging in activities which include: monitoring the human rights situation of Roma in Europe; publishing information on human rights abuse of Roma and news about the Romani civil rights movement, ... legal defence, ... legal research, conducting seminars, ... advocating Roma rights in domestic and international governmental and non-governmental settings; maintaining a documentation centre of Roma-related, human rights and legal material; [and] offering scholarships and stipends to Romani students of law and public administration (ERRC 1996b).

The rest of the background in this chapter is limited to the IRU as the main actor of this book. The IRU is the resultant of the early attempts to establish a durable Romani international umbrella organization (see Klimova 2003: §2.3.1). Some organizational continuity of international Romani activism can be traced from the turn of the 1960s, starting with the World Gypsy Community (WGC), evolving into the International Romani Committee (IRC) and then the IRU. The main organizational feature of the IRU are its World Romani Congresses, which have so far been held in London (1971 under the auspices of IRC), Geneva (1978 where the IRU was formally constituted), Goettingen (1981), Warsaw (1990) and Prague (2000). I detailed the work of these congresses elsewhere (see Klimova 2003: §2.3.1.4–5). Each of these congresses was characterized by an increasing *attempt* at professionalization and towards more elaborate democratic procedures. At the fifth congress (2000), the IRU attempted to transform itself into a semi-governmental body with its own parliament, commissars responsible for various issues, a court of justice, etc. The IRU's work between the congresses mainly consists of infrequent meetings of its Presidium and/or commissions and occasional negotiations with various governments and IGOs. In addition, its branches in various countries organize educational and cultural events, including conferences and seminars. Overall, the IRU has been kept alive in between the congresses by just the work of a few dedicated individuals, often pursuing their personal interests such as Holocaust reparations, language standardization or the creation of Romani history. Many IRU meetings have taken place during various non-IRU international events at which IRU officials have gathered, later actually declaring such meetings as their own. Nevertheless, the IRU has, at least in theory, managed to establish itself as the only durable global Romani organization, gaining a consultative status with the UN Economic and Social Council (ECOSOC) that it has kept for over two decades (see pp. 66–68). Today, the IRU claims to have thirty-three member[13] and nineteen candidate countries.[14] Yet it is not really countries who are IRU members, it is local and/or nation-wide Romani organizations and individuals. IRU is the main organization promoting the concept of the Romani nation and its symbols, used as tools for unification and political mobilization, such as the umbrella term 'Roma', the Romani flag, slogan *Opre Roma!* (Roma Arise!), anthem (*Djelem djelem*) and national day (8 April), which were all adopted at the first congress (1971) (for details see Klimova 2003: 55).

Although there have been attempts to progressively bureaucratize transnational Romani politics in the form of the IRU,[15] lack of financial and human resources has been a major obstacle. At the local and nation-state levels, Romani organizations receive money from state and local authorities as well as domestic and international foundations and donors (especially since the 1990s); yet even at these levels there is an acute lack of financial resources (see e.g. Barany 2002: 227–230). At the international level, money from IGOs or foundations is generally available only for specific projects, yet the IRU lacks adequate resources to establish, man and sustain professional offices. However, since the late 1990s, limited financial aid has been available (for example) from the Council of Europe (CoE) budget earmarked for 'support for Pan-European Romani organizations' (Kempf 11 April 2002). Nevertheless, most of the IRU's work is, however, financed using money secured by its member organizations or even from the private pockets of individual activists. Emil Scuka, the current IRU President, for example, currently sponsors the IRU Presidium and Dragan Jevremovic, the current Chair of the Parliament, along with his organization Romano Centro and the CoE sponsors the IRU Parliament (IRU 2000f). There has been a long-term attempt to introduce membership fees for the IRU, with its current Charter stating that membership fees from individual members and organizations are the main source of income. In reality, though, few ever pay. The IRU therefore has to rely on other sources of income, which are identified as gifts, inheritance, and donations of nation-state and international organizations (see Chapter X of the Charter in Acton and Klimova 2001: 214).

All this significantly limits the IRU's potential for action. As Santino Spinelli, one of the IRU Parliament members, put it: 'We only meet when some money appears to organize an event like a congress, conference or parliament meeting, otherwise we're more a paper organization' (12 June 2002). The lack of funds also precludes attracting highly qualified Roma to work for the IRU. As Agnes Daroczi, 'a long-term organizer of government cultural, youth and education programmes in Hungary,' told the fourth congress (1990), 'if she was even assured the possibility of a small office somewhere, and the backing of a small executive committee who could really work together, she would have considered the position [of General Secretary]. But with no office, no money and a largely unwieldy international committee the task was impossible' (Nesbitt 1990). As of today, the IRU largely operates from the leaders' private homes or their local NGO offices. In 2002, the IRU opened its first lobbying focal point in Brussels, headed by Paolo Pietrosanti, within the office of the Transnational Radical Party (TRP, see p.141). The impact of its work for the IRU remains to be seen.

The Ideological Orientations and Political Manifestos of Global Romani Activism

Despite having functioned for over three decades, the IRU still seems to be in its nascent stage, characterized by a search for an ideology that can explain and justify its claims. As a result, its current ideology is somewhat incoherent and open to random influences (e.g. OSCE, TRP, see later in this section). It is often argued that the IRU is basically a nationalist movement (see e.g. PER 2001: 33–41). Indeed, it does exhibit many of the typical characteristics of a nationalist movement in the period of patriotic agitation, to use the terminology of Miroslav Hroch, a leading scholar of nationalism. Hroch identified three periods of the nation-building process of a nationalist movement: 1) the period of scholarly interest (the intellectual study of the language, the culture, and the history), 2) the period of patriotic agitation (denouncing the nation's disadvantaged situation, be it perceived or real, and starting to spread national consciousness) and 3) the rise of a mass national movement (participation of all classes and groups in the movement) (Guibernau 1999: 96–97). In the Romani case, the first period had its roots in the interest of non-Romani scholars in Romani culture, language and history connected to Romanticism at the end of the eighteenth century. While some scholars (e.g. Angus Fraser) argue that these scholars (most importantly Heinrich Moritz Gottlieb Grellman and George Borrow) restored the ethnic Romani identity by discovering Romani origins and/or studying their language, others (e.g. Wim Willems) believe that these scholars actually constructed a previously non-existing Romani identity by generalizing information about dissimilar groups which had only some traits in common (see e.g. Willems 1997: 293). What is important for this book is that Romani intellectuals, who started to emerge during the inter-war period and many of whom later gathered in the IRU, have embraced this ethnic identity, and by the 1970s had developed a nationalist discourse around it – so fulfilling all the tasks that Monserrat Guibernau, a sociologist who theorizes on contemporary nationalism, sets for nation-building intellectuals:

1) constructing a picture of the nation as a distinct community (which is different from the dominant nation in the particular territory) based on studying its history, culture, myths, language and specific traits,
2) (re)creation of the sense of community among group members by investigating the cultural and political history of the community,
3) constructing a discourse subversive of the current order 'which delegitimizes the state and its policies as a threat to the existence or development of the nation,' and up to a certain extent also,
4) offering an alternative to the current order of things (1999: 98).

As with other nationalist discourses, this one relies 'heavily upon the idea of a shared culture as a key element in the configuration of the group as a distinctive community with a set of characteristics, values, and a name which distinguishes it from other such communities' (Guibernau 1999: 93). IRU intellectuals emphasize the commonalities

between various Romani languages and dialects, traditions and values over the existing differences, and promote the name 'Roma' as an umbrella term for various
Romani and Gypsy groups (see Tables 2.1–2). Their discourse is also based on what
Guibernau considers to be an essential element of a successful nationalist discourse:
specific terms of disagreement with the current status of the nation. In fact, it contains
an element of all of the three categories of reasons that Guibernau lists as sources for
disagreement – moral, economic and political. The framing of the moral grounds
argument has passed through several phases since the 1960s, when the IRU's predecessors were formed. The following briefly sketches the various frames as presented
in the IRU's dominant discourse. It should, however, be noted that various more
marginalized frames and discourses have also existed in the IRU throughout this
time. In the first phase (1960s), the dominant frame (promoted most notably by Ionel
Rotaru) was based on the nationalist legitimation of a state arguing that people who
have developed a specific national identity have the right to establish themselves in a
state. In the 1970s and 1980s, upon the influence of leading IRU Yugoslav officials
(e.g. Saip Jusuf, Slobodan Berberski, and Sait Balic),[16] it moved towards arguing that
people with a specific culture different from that of the state where they live have the
right to be recognized as national minorities and to cultivate their culture with help
from the state. The early 1990s witnessed a shift towards the individual human rights
frame based on the principles of non-discrimination and equality upon the influence
of the OSCE Helsinki process (promoted primarily by Nicolae Gheorghe). The end of
the 1990s brought about a slightly contradictory frame morally based on the right of
all individuals to live in democracy, freedom, liberty and rule of law, yet arguing for
the collective right to be recognized as a non-territorial nation, with representational
rights at the UN (promoted by Scuka and Paolo Pietrosanti, see later in this section).
During the same period, the framing of the economic argument has changed little,
constantly arguing that the current political status of the Romani nation does not
allow for its full economic development because Roma are marginalized in all countries. The recognition of its status (first as a national minority and now as a nation) is
presented as a prerequisite to the economic development of the nation. On political
grounds, the IRU has always argued for representation in the UN on equal terms with
other nations[17] (although this demand became voiced most forcefully at the end of the
1990s), and its goal has been to become a fully-fledged world political actor.

Besides cultivating the nationalist discourse, IRU intellectuals have also been
working towards other nationalist goals such as transforming the 'low folk culture'
into a 'high culture' by standardization of the Romani language, publishing both
poetry and prose in Romani, writing and staging theatre pieces in Romani, translating
Romani works to other world languages and *vice versa*, etc. In order to preserve this
high culture and have it adopted by the Romani public, IRU intellectuals have
attempted to create a number of institutions such as Romani media, schools and
research institutes. While Romani traditions and arts are well alive in various Romani
communities, the constructed Romani high culture, including international variants
of the Romani language, has until now stayed foreign to the majority of Romani
public.[18] In other words, in most countries Romani intellectuals have not yet
succeeded in awakening, recovering or promoting the common history, culture and
language of their nation. Similarly, although the sentiment of dissatisfaction with
their current status is common to virtually all Romani communities, the emergence
and strengthening of a sense of solidarity and 'a feeling of some sort of extended

family among the members of the nation' (Guibernau 1999: 93) is not yet evident among the Romani public. The IRU therefore stays largely elite-oriented and concerned with the aims and interests of the intellectuals and the potential 'ruling elite', not those of the Romani majority. The global Romani mobilization has been elite-oriented from the start. At the nation-state level, whereas Romani activism in Western European countries actually has relied on street politics and mass involvement, in CEE it has largely been elite-oriented, mirroring the local political trends. This elitism permeated into global activism due to the significant influence of the CEE IRU leadership. At the same time, global Romani activism again mirrors the general global political trends of top-down common identity building through institutionalization and/or elite agitation. Neither has the IRU managed to incorporate into its goals the interests of all the different Romani groups spread across several countries, both settled and travelling, rich and poor. The IRU is still largely confined to Europe, with only isolated individual activism in North and Latin America, Australia, New Zealand, Asia and the Middle East. Not surprisingly, it is therefore copying a typically European modular form of nation-building of 'imagined communities' (on the concept of 'imagined communities' see Anderson 1991; on the argument about its modularity see Chatterjee 1993). It has therefore not reached Hroch's third stage yet. It remains to be seen whether it will reach it and thus develop into a successful nationalist mass movement. The alternative would be an elite-dominated comprador nationalism of the post-colonial type which, if successful in gaining political power, is likely to lead to authoritarianism, following the Arafat-style of leadership. While this might be a major obstacle to the success of Romani nationalism, history (especially post-colonial) teaches us that nationalist elites can achieve their state-building (or other) goals even without popular support from those that they claim to represent if they find support (or at least face no opposition) from other forces in the international system.[19] The failure of the Romani nation-building project, or its abandonment as a political strategy, are other possible outcomes.

At the moment, the IRU is not likely to follow the *typical* nationalist course because it denounces three of the seven core themes of the nationalist doctrine identified by Anthony Smith, a leading analyst of nationalism, all relating to creation of a separate territorial nation-state.[20] While at times the IRU's predecessors did entertain the idea of a Romani state (see Klimova 2003: §2.3.1 and §5.2), such a demand has not been seriously advocated in the public political sphere since the 1970s. Plans for a Romani territory (but not necessarily a homeland for the majority of the world's Roma) are, however, occasionally still discussed among the IRU members, for example in relation to the Romani suburb of Skopje Shuto Orizari in Macedonia or the possibility of creating a Romani enclave in Kosovo under the recent interim administration. Similarly, proposals for relocating Roma into depopulated parts of various (mostly CEE) countries (in the fashion of creating reservations for them) are still advanced by prejudiced mainstream local politicians from time to time. Thus, although it cannot be considered a classic case of a (a state-building) nationalist movement, the IRU (or at least some of its leading members) use the nationalist discourse to further both its identity-oriented and instrumental goals. In the first case, the nationalist discourse consolidates the movement, while in the second a social change is sought by redefining the dimension of nationalism as a legitimizing principle in international relations. While the principle that political status should be based on national criteria is reinforced, it is argued that an essential ingredient of the principle of political nationhood – territory – can be done away with. Indeed, since the late 1990s, the IRU (or its two main representatives at the global stage, Scuka and Pietrosanti) has promoted some kind of internationalist cosmopolitanism, arguing for a supranational structure in the form of a world government and world court of justice in which people are no longer represented on the basis of a state. This shows that the IRU's discourse is evolving alongside new (anti)international relations discourses.[21]

The latest ideas are embedded in the IRU's *'Declaration of Nation'* [sic] which is the only political manifesto of *global* Romani activism[22] so far and which was produced under a significant influence from the TRP ideas of Pietrosanti (see Klimova 2003: §2.3.1.5).[23] The two main ideas combined in this manifesto are a Romani claim for non-territorial nationhood and nation-state and international recognition, and a claim that the Romani nation offers to the rest of humanity a new vision of stateless nationhood that is more suited to a globalized world than is affiliation to traditional nation-states. The Declaration's demands are based on the premise that self-government and self-determination of peoples are now regaining extraordinary force in the international society, and that the aspiration of peoples, who share the tradition of speaking a common language, have the same origins and have experienced the same tragedies, to be represented as one people is universally recognized as legitimate.[24] Therefore, the Declaration argues the following. Based on the precedent of the Jewish and Palestinian nations, the Romani nation can ask for recognition from the UN as a nation or a state-like entity. The Declaration attempts to refute a rejection on the grounds that there is no room on earth for a new state, by emphasizing that the Roma are not asking for a territory. Its authors argue that, while such recognition (as a non-territorial nation/state) is a novel idea, it is not completely unprecedented since, for example, the Knights of Malta are recognized as subjects of international law entitled with diplomatic relations despite having no territory.[25] The need for such recognition and representation is justified by claiming that it is unthinkable that Roma would be represented by states that for the most part reject them and marginalize them. It is explained that the Roma do not want a territory, for such an aim is unsuited to their history and their culture – they want a recognized status. The Declaration claims that Roma have never wanted to create a Romani state [sic] and today do not want one, especially because the new developments in the social, political and economic realms are increasingly showing the inadequacy of the modern nation-state as a mode of organization which can successfully address the needs of individuals in the changing world.

The Romani nationalist claim is presented as benign and it is explained that an awareness of belonging to a nation is, in itself, not dangerous; the danger of violence and conflicts comes from the desire to make the concepts of a nation and a state come together in ethnically homogeneous nation-states, or in other words from the effort to unify citizenship and nationality. The Roma have, allegedly, paid for this tendency much more than any other people, in the forgotten pogroms which have often led the world near to the disappearance of the Romani nation (as such). The Declaration is based on the argument that the wars that rage throughout the world have broken out in places where nations or nationalities do not have representation; they are not represented by a state because there is no state, or because they are a minority in a particular state. It stipulates that the desire for the self-determination of peoples, including the right to dignity, recognition and representation, would not necessarily have to be directed towards the constitution of sovereign state powers (which brings about the violence) if the institutional framework of the world allowed different forms of power from those which now seem to be sought for and exercised.[26] It is claimed that, by seeing the suffering brought about until the very present by the tendency of making nation and territory coincide, recently most evident in the Yugoslav crisis and the breakdown of the Palestinian-Israeli peace process, the Roma are not asking for a territory. They want to achieve an equal status and representation in the international community without building a territorial state, and they challenge the existing international institutions to find a way of satisfying their demands. The message expressed in the Declaration is also that Roma do want to participate in international society[27] and its quest for improving peoples' lives on a basis of fundamental democratic principles. They want to live like everyone else and with everyone else regardless of nationality, religion or language, in a symbiotic system in which diverse nations aim to integrate through common institutions and rules without trying to assimilate each other. Moreover, the Roma want to participate in the creation of new and proper norms, institutions and forms of coexistence in an organized global society founded on legality. The Declaration claims that the Roma have survived for several centuries as distinct individuals and groups with a strong identity without creating a nation-state, so therefore, their example could help humanity find an alternative way to satisfy the need for identity without having to lock it to territorial boundaries. This is where the main appeal of the message addressed to the international society is meant to be found: the IRU does not frame their struggle in terms of the betterment of the Romani people, they believe that it is in the interest of humanity-at-large to find a way of ensuring peoples' rights and satisfying their need for identity that is less disruptive than changing current boundaries and population displacements. Thus they frame their cause as a struggle for the rule of law for each and every individual. This was well illustrated in Pietrosanti's oral statement, delivered to the 52nd session of the Subcommission on the Promotion and Protection of Human Rights (the Subcommission), drawing an explicit analogy to the movement led by Martin Luther King. His words were:

> In their recent world Congress [2000], the Roma declared they have a dream, the same concrete, political dream of Martin Luther King, who was able to push the great American democracy into further maturity, because he was not fighting merely for the emancipation of a minority, but rather or above all, he was fighting for the further and deeper implementation of the American Constitution, for the rule of law, for each and every American as single individual (Pietrosanti 2000).

The Declaration also offers the potential experience of the Romani nation as something that could contribute to the current debates about the need for a multi-layered and not strictly territorially bound governance in a world with increasingly porous frontiers (for academic ideas about world governance see e.g. Kukathas 1998; Bauboeck 2002; Hoeffe 1999; Beck 2002; Held 1995). It claims that the Romani experience testifies to the need for creating a 'truly global' international, not interstate, law,[28] because it shows that the international community has been unable to adequately implement either individual or collective rights when they are not mediated by states. It argues that the problem with the state being the guarantor of basic human rights and freedoms is that, so far, no modern nation-state has guaranteed these rights and freedoms to all people living within its territory. The laws of modern nation-states as we know them today are inherently inadequate for some individuals or groups, most notably the marginalized and minority ones. Therefore a transnational rule of law, supported by an adequate judicial system, is needed to assure democracy, freedom and liberty for each and all individuals, regardless of their nationality. This request is presented on the basis of the recent normative critique of the international system. It draws attention to the debate regarding the adequacy of the state for coping with the changing needs of a global society, a society that should not be organized exclusively from above. This debate allegedly involves prominent personalities in Europe and the entire UN community, both in academic and political circles (yet, these personalities are never named specifically) and revolves around the question of whether the existing international juridical systems and institutions are concretely able to guarantee freedom and liberty in a changing world, for each and every individual regardless of their nationality. The authors of the Declaration believe that the Romani request for representation as a nation which does not want to become a state could become a catalyst for the debate regarding necessary reforms of the existing international institutions and rules, in a search for a world in which the rights of all individuals will be ensured by laws enforced by adequate supranational institutions. The IRU critique is that the current limitation of international institutions is that they are founded on the rule of states and not on the rule of law.

To my best knowledge, neither the Declaration nor any other IRU's documents spell out what they envision under the institution of a non-territorial nation or state. However, some ideas were elaborated in a conference presentation by Sean Nazerali, Scuka's political advisor. Although the ideas in this paper are personal to Nazerali, they reflect the debate among the IRU's leading figures. According to Nazerali, what he calls 'a territory-less state' consists of a government and population, but no specific territory. Such a state is sovereign and autonomous, but shares sovereignty with a wide variety of institutions at other levels (country-wide, regional and global), according to the principle of personal autonomy. This principle allows communities (in this case the Romani state/nation) to regulate certain matters for all their members (determination of membership is left to voluntary self-identification), regardless of where they live (Nazerali 2001). In the original plans of Karl Renner and Otto Bauer, such personal autonomy is not limited only to cultural matters, it extends, for example, to administration of justice. Yet, most early as well as recent attempts to introduce such models have been limited to cultural affairs (see e.g. Eide 1998: 256). Nazerali's interpretation is closer to Renner's and Bauer's model because, although he states that only social and cultural matters would be administered through personal autonomy, he at the same time argues that administration of justice should also be largely taken care of by the national (non-territorial new-type state) units. (For more about the concept of personal autonomy see e.g. Bauer 2000; Bowring 2002; Coakley 1994; Nimni 1999; Tamir 1991.) In Nazerali's vision, the autonomous competencies are enshrined in special agreements/treaties with local and country-wide governments and intergovernmental organizations. The status of a territory-less state provides for negotiations on equal terms with territorial states, within the UN fora and elsewhere. This way the territory-less Romani state can not only draw attention to the violations of Romani rights at international fora, but, unlike Romani NGOs, it can also initiate legal proceedings by (for example) bringing petitions to the International or European Court of Justice or by referring the cases to the UN Committee for the Elimination of All Forms of Racial Discrimination (CERD). Nazerali argues that, with this scheme, the Romani 'state' could help strengthen international human rights mechanisms, which nation-states are reluctant to use fully. In addition, it could be an engine for creating transnational administration – e.g. world army, system of justice, taxes and electoral procedures. It would lead the way towards transforming the international system into a system where all social and cultural matters are left to nations (territory-less states) to be administered through personal non-territorial autonomy, while other matters are administered through territorial units. The territorial units would function on many levels (local, country-wide, regional, and global), depending on the nature of the issues (e.g. environmental and security issues would be delegated to the global level). People would be citizens of both their nations and territorial units (Nazerali 2001).

So far there has not been much of a discussion of this issue among academics. I am aware of only two academic reactions. The first one is a completely dismissive response of political scientist Martin Kovats, who argues that this call for non-territorial self-determination is nothing but 'the promotion of an authoritarian nationalist tradition in which a political community is constructed through the manipulation of vulnerable people, to secure the interests of an unaccountable elite' (Kovats 2003: 4). The second comes from Morag Goodwin, a Law PhD student, who takes the claims being made seriously but concludes that at the moment neither external nor internal self-determination can provide Roma with the sought recognition. She instead suggests that the revolution that the Roma should be agitating for is one towards an agonistic system of international order in which Roma (and other actors) 'would be allowed to determine the nature of their status at the table according to the terms of their own culture, through negotiations with other members of the world community' (Goodwin 2004: 64). If we take it that the Declaration argues that granting personal non-territorial autonomy for Romani communities is a necessary step towards addressing their problems, this argument actually does find support among contemporary political theorists (see Klímová-Alexander forthcoming 2005).

The Declaration can perhaps be best described as an internationalist manifesto, yet it is a curious mix of ethnic and liberal internationalism.[29] Reading the Declaration of Nation, one has the feeling that two different voices, the Romani (understand that of Romani leaders, most notably Scuka) and the TRP (understand Pietrosanti's), try to have their slightly contradictory demands heard in a common document, without making it completely internally coherent.[30] For Romani leaders, the document seems to be predominantly about declaring that Roma are a nation with the *collective* right to representation in IGOs. Pietrosanti seems to view the Declaration as a cosmopolitan document calling for a non-nationally-based way of representing *individuals* at the global level. Thus if this Declaration receives outside support, the Romani leaders can interpret it as a recognition of their nationhood, while Pietrosanti can take it as a support for a denationalized peoples' world government. The main bridge between the Romani (inter)nationalist aspiration and the TRP cosmopolitan aspiration is the claim that the territorial base of political legitimation (i.e. territorial nation-states) should be undermined. The controversy seems to be over undermining the cultural base of political legitimation. Traditionally, the Romani cultural distinctiveness has been asserted in contrast to the non-Roma. Throughout its existence, the IRU has been trying to gain recognition for the Roma as a distinct community with the collective right to representation, claiming that non-Romani politicians and institutions do not adequately represent their interests. Can such an attitude be converted into embracing the idea that we are all the world's citizens who should be represented as individuals?

Pietrosanti certainly does his best to make the ideas of cosmopolitanism attractive to the Romani leaders. He takes inspiration, for example, from the writings of Ulrich Beck (Pietrosanti 23 August 2001), one of the leading German sociologists, whose ideas could indeed be very appealing to some Romani leaders (for details see e.g. Beck 2002; Beck 1999a; Beck 1999b; Beck 2000; Beck 2002). For instance, Beck argues that it is in the states' interest to de-nationalize and trans-nationalize themselves (i.e. relinquish some sovereignty) in order to deal with their nation-state problems in a globalized world. Given that the international system is still dominated by nation-states, it is a wise strategy for non-state actors like the Roma to present the demanded changes as being in the states' interests. According to Beck, nation-states should turn into cosmopolitan states, who acknowledge the otherness of the others, allowing their self-determination, yet at the same time accept responsibility for them. Again, a very convenient notion for the Romani elites who want to represent their people, yet at the moment are unable to accept the responsibility of providing them with social and physical security. Furthermore, Beck believes that, similarly to secular states being the only ones that make the practice of various religions possible, only cosmopolitan states can guarantee a peaceful co-existence of various national and religious identities, and by implication guarantee the Roma dignity and security. In Beck's cosmopolitan world, '[l]iving together does no longer have to mean living geographically nearby. It can also mean living together across national [nation-state] borders and even across continents' (Zolo, Undated). How pertinent to dispersed peoples like the Roma! Finally, for Beck 'territory is *not*, as the era of nation-state makes us believe, an imperative for community life and society' (Zolo, Undated), supporting the IRU's claim that the Roma can constitute a non-territorial community/nation. As with Pietrosanti, Beck believes that '[t]he non-territorial social and political relationships and bonds which evolve in the cosmopolitan global society have yet to be discovered, affirmed and encouraged' (Zolo, Undated). Pietrosanti tries to plant their roots among Romani elites.

Embracing cosmopolitanism is in fact not unheard of among ethnic communities (see e.g. Forte 1995; Heilman and Cohen 1989). Rainer Bauboeck, leading theorist on transnationalism, stipulates that, while ordinary indigenous people lack a cosmopolitan consciousness, their activism is somewhat cosmopolitan[31] in its political orientation and mobilization. Yet, at the same time some indigenous leaders [as with Romani leaders] make use of 'the traditional vocabulary of nationhood that still buys legitimacy in our world'. For example, some indigenous leaders in North America insist on being called the First Nations (Bauboeck 2002: 132 and footnote 23). In Bauboeck's opinion, cosmopolitan governance could in fact occur as a result of endogenous development of liberal norms in response to the challenges raised by minority communities (e.g. right to self-determination, devolution of power to minorities, softening of borders between external minorities and their homelands, etc). Their demands could become the catalyst for a cosmopolitan transformation of democracy, even if these minorities usually lack a special cosmopolitan consciousness (Bauboeck 2002: 135). This actually seems to be Pietrosanti's aim, using the Romani request for representation as a non-territorial nation as a vehicle for far-reaching supranationalist reforms of the existing international institutions and rules.[32] The Declaration therefore must be seen in this light, as a document promoted largely by two IRU officers, Scuka and Pietrosanti, at a particular point in time and for a particular purpose. Its importance for the IRU should not be overstated just because it is its only global manifesto. It is still a very young document and its longevity and influence within the IRU and global Romani activism in general remain to be seen. Given the political fragmentation of the IRU, it could in fact be fairly inconsequential. Yet it is important for this book, for the historical record and as a background to the recent IRU lobbying activities at the UN.

In the opinion of the IRU leaders, the Declaration offers global Romani activism something that it has been lacking until now – a vision. It answers the question of what Roma want: 'a new status that would provide [them] with respect and their own place among nations – that is, a place within international organizations' like the UN or CoE (PER 2003: 34). The status would make Roma the subjects of international law[33] and 'entitle Romani representatives to conclude bilateral and multilateral treaties and agreements' (PER 2003: 34). Upon its release, the Declaration was a subject of criticism by various Romani activists, who argued that the potential dangers of this document might be larger than benefits, denounced its nationalistic tone and the IRU's (related) claim of being the only genuine representative of the world's Roma (PER 2001: 35–41). Yet, less than two years later, even many former critics surprisingly embraced the idea of a non-territorial Romani nation. In the IRU's opinion, an academic discussion about whether Roma are a nation is no longer needed; its Declaration of Nation has been presented to a number of governments and the UN Secretary-General with no objections being raised (see p.80). In addition, '[m]any international documents not only do not deny it, but actually strengthen the conviction among the Roma that they are indeed a nation' (PER 2003: 12). Note, however, that no intergovernmental document yet refers to Roma as a nation. The Romani convictions are mostly strengthened by NGO declarations or the statements of individual politicians (e.g. the recent initiative of the Finish President Tarja Halonen for a consultative assembly for Roma at the European level, see e.g. PER 2003: 28–31) (see also Klimova 2003: §8.2.3 and §8.4.2).

The IRU's Goals vis-à-vis the UN

The IRU's lasting declared goals are perhaps best reflected in the purposes of the IRU and Congress commissions.[34] One can find the best idea of the goals the commissions promote by reading reports of all the Congresses as well as the few reports that exist about the individual commission meetings.[35] Some recent IRU documents list the IRU's main goals but are less indicative of what the IRU really tries to achieve. For example the new IRU Charter adopted at the 2000 Congress lists the following as its main goals: to be the political representation of all Roma in the world; to develop favourable Romani qualities, traditions, culture and language; to respect human rights and fight for their implementation for all people; to help to preserve world peace and develop friendly relations among nations; and to work towards the improvement of economic, social, cultural, educational, and humanitarian conditions of the Roma in all countries (see Acton and Klimova 2001: 202). Alternatively, the IRU's program distributed at Congress5 lists, as the IRU's main aims, creating dignified conditions for Roma in their respective countries and providing 'opportunities for education, and thus offer[ing] the world educated Roma, capable not only of looking after themselves but also of assisting others' (IRU 2000a). This book is, though, concerned only with the IRU's goals declared to be or pursued in relation to the UN system, which are now discussed in more detail.

Promotion of Romani Identity and Cultural and Educational Rights

The IRU strives for recognition of a distinctive Romani identity that is based on Romani origins, history, traditions, culture, and language. On the one hand it has been lobbying the UN to pressure governments into recognising Roma as national minorities in their respective countries and providing financial and institutional support for the development of their culture and language. On the other hand, it has been trying to obtain financial and institutional support for Romani culture and language and education of Romani children and youth directly from the UN system, most notably the UN Educational, Scientific and Cultural Organization (UNESCO), arguing that states are unwilling to produce sufficient support (see pp.103–9).

Remedy and Prevention of Human Rights Abuses

The IRU turns to the UN with the hope that it will pressurize governments into ensuring the human rights of Roma living in their countries. It emphasizes that Roma suffer abuse because of being a minority in all countries. In addition, unlike many national minorities, they have no home country to lobby on their behalf. It therefore argues that the UN itself should take on the role of their home country. Pursuing Holocaust reparations (both symbolic and financial) has been an element of the lobbying for restorative justice since the times of IRU's predecessors. The IRU's most recent vision envisages the UN creating some sort of world court to which Roma could appeal when they experience prejudice or indifference in nation-state courts. The IRU aims to contribute to the remedy and prevention of human rights abuses of Roma by working towards the implementation of general as well as Roma-specific legal instruments (UN Doc. E/C.2/1993/R.4/Add.2).

Addressing Social and Economic Problems

Similar to the goals described in the previous paragraphs, the IRU seeks UN help for addressing Romani social and economic problems, arguing that these problems are both global and neglected by states. It asks the UN to pressurize governments into improving the standard of living of Roma as well as directly sponsor projects for such improvement (see e.g. IRU 2000a).

Recognition of Political Status

According to the IRU's ideology, all of the above-described problems (lack of cultural rights, human rights abuses, and social and economic problems) reduce to non-recognition Romani identity and the political status of Roma. It has therefore argued for recognition of Roma as a national minority in all countries where they live and also, more recently, as a nation with the right to a seat at the UN General Assembly (GA). The IRU strives for recognition as the representative of the world's Roma which would be entitled to hold the seat. According to its programme, its main political goal is to convince 'the world community of nations that the Roma are an integral and undeniable part of that community' (IRU 2000a).

The Strategies of Romani Activism

In order to address the problems and achieve the goals described previously, Romani activists has been using a variety of strategies typical to social movements. Wherever possible, they have been fighting for participation in decision-making at the local and nation-state, as well as international, levels. They have also mobilized resistance efforts, lobbied the media, local and nation-state governments as well as IGOs, carried out awareness campaigns and educational activities, co-operated with non-Romani organizations on issues of common concern, and litigated on behalf of their people. As the time and scope limitations of this book do not allow for the addressing of all of these strategies in detail, it concentrates just on the inter- actions between the activists and the UN system. It should, however, be understood that these activities are only one, rather small, part of the activities carried out by the activists.

Conclusion

In its brief historical overview, this chapter placed the beginnings of global Romani activism to the period when the League of Nations, the first 'global' IGO, was created. However, serious attempts at creating a durable global organization only occurred in the 1960s when the UN intensified its co-operation with international NGOs. A common factor of all these attempts was that Romani activists wished to advance the interests of the world's Roma through the UN discourse, instruments and structures. By the 1970s these attempts crystallized into the creation of the first durable global Romani body – the IRU –with the organizing of an international Congress, which became a recurrent event. The primary goals of global Romani activism became institutionalized through the Congress's commissions on Holocaust reparations, social status and issues, education, language and culture. Throughout the years, the organizational structure of the IRU has, at least in theory, become more elaborate, and with each Congress greater emphasis has been placed on the attempt to conduct democratic elections. As part of the IRU's attempts at transformation into a semi-governmental body, the main issues became embodied in the offices of commissars (for foreign policy, holocaust, human rights, Romani language and language rights, management and information systems, media and internal affairs, and economic, educational and financial and budgetary issues), which however largely exist only on paper.[36] In relation to the UN, the following were identified as the IRU's main goals: promotion of Romani identity and cultural rights, remedy and prevention of human rights abuses (including Holocaust crimes), addressing social and economic problems and recognition of political status. The last goal has recently been embodied in the first global Romani political manifesto – the IRU's Declaration of Nation, which espouses some cosmopolitan ideas but does not fully break with the IRU's nationalist aspirations. Although the goals of global Romani activism are pursued through a variety of strategies, the rest of this book is devoted to analysing only those strategies that are pursued within the framework of the UN.

Table 2.1   Romani Self-appellations. The Mosaic of Names used by Various Groups and their Primary Locations[37]

The main names used by various Romani groups originating in India and speaking, or having in the past spoken, a dialect of Romani

 Roma – original and most concentrated settlements are in CEE (and in small numbers also in Italy and Finland) from where they spread all over the world

 Rudari/Ludari/Lingurari Boyash/Beash/Banyash – Romania, Hungary, Bulgaria, Yugoslavia, Greece, former Soviet Union, North and South America, Croatia, Serbia

 Sinti[38] – Germany, Austria, northern Italy, the Netherlands, Belgium, eastern France (but also in small numbers in Hungary, Slovakia, Czech Republic, Russia and Yugoslavia)

 *Kale/Kaale* – Spain, Portugal, Latin America and the USA (and in smaller numbers also in France, England, Germany, Bohemia, Wales)

 Manush – France

 *Romanichal* – England, North America, Australia, France, the Basque country, Scandinavia, Crimea

Table 2.2 Other Groups of Interest to Romani Activism and Potential Candidates

Non-Romani Gypsy groups that have or might become subjects of Romani activism due to their Indian origin

Gypsy groups living in India	*Banjara/Ghor* and *Godolia Lohar*
Gypsy groups that (as with the Roma but at different times) migrated from India	*Lom* – Armenia, Georgia and eastern Turkey
	Dom – various Asian countries and North Africa

Groups traditionally considered Gypsy/Romani, embraced by Romani activists,[39] but recently claiming a separate identity

Egyptian identity		**Albanian identity or Ashkalije identity**	
Egyupti	Macedonia, Kosovo and Serbia	Some *Ashkalija*	in former Yugoslavia
Yevgi	Albania		

Non-Romani Gypsy groups of non-Indian origin that have or might become subjects of Romani activism

Irish and Scottish Travellers	Ireland, Northern Ireland, Scotland, England, USA and Australia
Woonwagenbewoner	Benelux countries
Quinquis	Spain
Jenische	Switzerland, Germany, Austria

Sources: Lee 1998; Bakker et al. 2001: 58 and 71; Marushiakova and Popov 2001a; Matras 2002. My chart was revised and corrected by Professor Thomas Acton, Elena Marushiakova, Vesselin Popov and Yaron Matras. All possible remaining mistakes are my responsibility.[12]

Notes

1 In reality, this term is used widely only in Central and Eastern Europe (CEE), and even there it is not the exclusive umbrella self-appellation. In other places it is used mostly among Romani political elites. In theory, the term should apply only to those groups who either speak, or used to speak, one or more of the various dialects of the Romani language, and use the word Rom/Romni (masculine/feminine singular) and Roma (plural) as an ethnonym. (Note that in some Romani dialects, 'Roma' only means 'husbands' and is not an ethnonym.) The adjective 'Romani' has, however, a much wider ethnonymic application than the nouns 'Rom/Romni/Roma'. The word 'Roma' is sometimes also used as an adjective. This, however, is less accurate linguistically; this book therefore uses it as such only in direct or indirect quotations and names of organizations. The words 'Gypsies' (Gitanos, Tsigane, Zingari, Cikani, Zigeuner, Ciganyok, Cingene, etc.) are also sometimes used as worldwide umbrella terms. They were originally coined by majority societies and may have been carried along by Roma to new countries where the majority may have believed them to be exonyms. They are now often considered pejorative by those who accept the self-appellation 'Roma'. Nevertheless, they are embraced by many who reject the term 'Roma,' with some groups or individuals using these terms interchangeably. Again, this book limits the usage of these words to quotations and names.

2 However, many use the term simply out of convenience, even if they recognise the heterogeneity.

3 Note that this definition emphasizes the exclusion of other marginalized groups with whom Roma are frequently associated.

4 Note that these are all Romani metagroups or subgroups.

5 The most recent IRU program puts the number at approximately 20 million in Europe, America, Australia and Asia (IRU 2000b).

6 For accounts of historical persecution of Roma see e.g. Crowe 1996; Hancock 1999; Fraser 1992.

7 For more about the Romani Holocaust see e.g. Kenrick 1999; Crowe and Kolsti 1991; Kenrick and Puxon 1995; Hancock 1991c; Fings, Heuss, and Sparing 1997.

8 For sources about this institutionalization in England, Bulgaria and the United States see Klimova 2003: 32, footnote 4.

9 For sources of information about these organizations in Russia, Bulgaria, Yugoslavia, Romania and United States see Klimova 2003: 32, footnote 5.

10 This Union functioned between 1933–1941 and 1945–1952 and held a number of local as well as country-wide congresses (Achim 1998: Chapter 4.2; Barany 2002: 148). Note that some authors claim that in the first phase it only functioned until 1938 or 1939 (e.g. Crowe 1996: 130; Liegeois 1986: 146) and that some incorrectly put the starting date of the Union to 1934 (see e.g. Barany 2002: 102).

11 For details about the office of the King of Gypsies in the mid-seventeenth century Polish Commonwealth and in the interwar period see e.g. Kaminski 1980: 133–136; Ficowski 1991: 15–22.

12 For references for Macedonia, Bulgaria, Poland, Hungary, Czechoslovakia, Germany, England, Switzerland and the United States see Klimova 2003: 34, footnote 11.

13 For the full list see IRU 2000c or Klimova 2003: 64, footnote 146.

14 For the full list see IRU 2000d or Klimova 2003: 64, footnote 147. Interestingly some previous long-term IRU members, such as India, USA and Australia, are not listed at all. All three of them were, though, listed among members before the 2000 Congress (see IRU 2000a). In addition, the IRU has an Australian Commissar for Australia and New Zealand and a regional office in India (see Acton and Klimova 2001: 200; IRU 2000e). Other long-term members with some of the largest Romani populations and most active domestic Romani politics, such as Hungary and Spain, were relegated to the status of a candidate country, also probably due to their absence at the 2000 Congress.

15 Following the modernization trend of bureaucratization of politics (see e.g. Weber 1947).

16 As well as Grattan Puxon, who was at that time living in Yugoslavia.

17 Understand nation-states.

18 There are, however, notable exceptions. For example, the Southern Slav variant of international Romani is gaining ground in Macedonia due to the well established Romani media outlets and due to the need for interaction between various Romani groups migrating from other parts of former Yugoslavia (Trehan 7 May 2003; Acton 14 May 2003).

19 On the discrepancy between West-inspired elite state-oriented nation-building (in the spirit of national liberation) and popular cultural nationalism of the masses in post-colonial states see e.g. Chatterjee 1993.

20 These themes are: 1) 'Nations can only be fulfilled in their own states'; 2) 'Loyalty to the nation-states overrides other loyalties'; and 3) 'The primary condition of global freedom and harmony is the strengthening of the nation-state' (Smith 1983: 21).

21 The last decade witnessed a growth of literature challenging the realist state-centric interpretation of international relations (see e.g. Arts, Noortmann and Reinalda 2001; Guibernau 1999; Keck and Sikkink 1998; Ryan 1995; Hall 1999).

22 While there are a number of documents detailing the European ambitions of Romani activism, such as the EUROM resolution, the European Charter of Romani Rights of the RNC or, in the EU, the Moral Charter of the Roma Nation of the Romani Activists Network on Legal and Political Issues, the Declaration of Nation is the only document with global aspirations. The EUROM resolution called for the establishment of a European Romani

Parliament as an autonomous political representation for and by European Roma, and declared a number of principles and goals (see Hancock and Matras 1990). The RNC Charter is a proposed legally binding document which would be signed by states, recognising the Roma as subjects of international law and safeguarding their rights and freedoms (see Klimova 1999: 69–70; RNC 1998). The basis of the Moral Charter is EU recognition of Roma as a nation without a compact territory, but with equality with other nations. It also establishes principles for regulating various aspects of the lives of Roma, such as definitions of Romani identity, mobility, living conditions, education, research, and representation (see RANELPI 2001).

23 The following discussion of the manifesto is based on my talk at the University of Greenwich (Klimova 2001d). This talk was prepared by synthesising information from the Declaration of Nation, recent interventions delivered by the IRU at the UN (see chapter 6) and Pietrosanti 1994.

24 Both the Declaration and the IRU's political strategy are clearly based on the principle of self-determination, although the IRU's President was at first conscious to admit it. By April 2002, self-determination was, however, (under significant influence from the PER) embraced as the guiding principle for Romani political mobilization (see PER 2003: 2 and 6). Pietrosanti maintains until today that the concept of self-determination is irrelevant to the Declaration of Nation, rather that the Declaration must be interpreted using the concept of 'the freedom to choose the democratic organization of cohabitation with others' (Pietrosanti 2003). However, as Goodwin points out, these concepts are intimately inter-related (Goodwin 2004: 58).

25 Note that this analogy does not completely work because, although the Sovereign Military Order of Malta has an observer status in the GA and does maintain official diplomatic relations with a great number of states, the UN took no action to recognize it either as a state or as a subject of international law (with the right to conclude agreements of international law). Being recognized as a subject of international law is another goal of the IRU, which in theory does not require achieving the status of a nation first. Such recognition takes place when 'power to exercise its own rights and carry out obligations under international law' is conferred upon an entity 'by way of an intergovernmental agreement (usually a convention or a statute) of States or an international agreement of other subjects of international law' (Simma 2002: 1080).

26 Similar arguments have in fact been advanced by a number of scholars who advocate non-territorial solutions as a means of preventing national and ethnic conflicts over territory, including Karl Renner, Otto Bauer, Yael Tamir, Gidon Gottlieb, etc. (see Bauboeck 2001).

27 Rejecting what some believe is the 'traditional' Romani approach of distancing themselves from non-Roma (see e.g. Hancock 2002: Chapter 11).

28 This seems to be conceptually the closest to the new vision of international law as not simply inter-state law but rather a 'law of humanity,' as theorized e.g. by Richard Falk (1995).

29 According to Norman Girvan, the Secretary General of the Association of Carribean States, ethnic internationalism is a *collective* movement amongst 'people victimised by social, cultural and economic discrimination' in support of international human rights law (Girvan 2002). Liberal internationalism demands that 'nations conform to a higher morality embodied in the doctrine of [*individual*] human rights' enforced by supranational bodies (Heywood 1998: 180).

30 According to Rainer Bauboeck, Pietrosanti's utopian project in fact distracts from the specific claims of Romani populations and is in fact counterproductive, if one of the main concerns is to secure full and equal citizenship for Roma in the states where they live (14 May 2003).

31 Here Bauboeck probably uses the term 'cosmopolitanism' in its more modest meaning of the 'goal of peace and harmony [and cooperation] among nations, founded upon mutual understanding, toleration, and, ... interdependence,' as opposed to its traditional meaning

of the goal of 'the obliteration of national identities and the establishment of a common political allegiance, uniting all human beings' (Heywood 1998: 181). Although the term cosmopolitanism is often employed to refer to the former, the term 'internationalism' would in fact be more fitting. For an overview of recent theories of cosmopolitanism see e.g. Vertovec and Cohen 2002.

32 Note that a similar attempt was made by the Bahai'i Kappenberger, another Romani sympathizer, ten years earlier, see p.133.

33 Note that Willetts argues that 'international NGOs recognised by ECOSOC may be considered to have acquired a legal personality' (2000: 206). Since the IRU is recognised by ECOSOC (see pp.66–8), this would imply that it does not need to seek a higher status in order to acquire a legal personality.

34 A number of commissions have existed since the 1971 Congress: Holocaust reparations, education and culture (two separate, at times as one commission), language standardization and social (and economic) issues. The work of the statutes commission has been very intermittent, meeting only around the 1971, 1978 and 2000 Congresses. An additional commission on Romani encyclopaedia was added at the 1978 Congress, surviving through the 1990 Congress but not the 2000 Congress. A media commission was added at the 1990 Congress and has so far survived. The 2000 Congress also added commissions on Kosovo, migration, and international politics and relations, but no commissar was elected to continue working on these issues. However, there is a lack of substance or results behind the work of these commissions.

35 See e.g. World Romani Congress Activities of its Presidium 1980; Report of the Third World Romani Congress 1981/82; IV World Romani Congress 1990/91; Acton 1972; Acton 1979; Daniel, Holomek, and Demeter 1979; Nesbitt 1990; Puxon 1975: Chapter 7; Puxon 1978/79: 32–72; Acton and Klimova 2001.

36 For a list of these commissariats and the office holders see Acton and Klimova 2001: Appendix I.

37 This chart is not meant to present a typology of Romani groups. Romani groups are further subdivided into metagroups and subgroups, each with a more specific name of its own, based on language, lifestyle, boundaries of endogamy, professional specialization, duration of settlement in their respective countries, religion, etc. (Marushiakova and Popov 2001a: 36). This chart shows only some of the most common self-appellations and their geographical spread. The maps indicate the locations in which people using these names are most numerous. Dark colour indicates areas of primary concentration and grey areas where the people are less numerous but still significant. Locations outside Europe are indicated only in the text and are not mapped. Note that variations of the same name (e.g. Kale and Kaale) are sometimes used by very different groups. The chart is only indicative, not exhaustive. While constructing a more exhaustive chart is a worthwhile task, it should be undertaken by trained linguists and ethnographers. Also note that the spelling of these names may differ from publication to publication, as a standardized international Romani orthography has not been embraced by but a few Romani intellectuals and non-Romani academics.

38 Sinti are the most vocal group in rejecting the umbrella term Roma; hence, for example the parallel usage of terms 'Roma' and 'Sinti' within the Organization for Security and Co-operation in Europe (OSCE) fora.

39 The IRU's charter, however, claims that for example Ashkalija are part of the Romani nation (see Acton and Klimova 2001: Appendix 2).

Chapter 3

Romani Issues at the UN

The aim of this chapter is limited to setting the scene for the analysis carried out in Part Two. The chapter provides an overview of the development of the UN interest in and approach to Romani issues in order to identify key events/actions leading to agenda-setting, discursive or procedural/institutional developments related to Roma. Within the UN system, significant attention to Romani issues has only been given within some subsidiary organs of the ECOSOC and some specialized funds, programmes and bodies; these are considered in turn. The links between the main events/actions, and the agenda-setting, discursive or procedural/institutional developments are established in the conclusions. Details of the key events/actions are elaborated in Part Two so as to establish whether there is a link between these changes and the actions of Romani and pro-Romani activists.

Romani Issues at the UN Commission on Human Rights (the Commission)

The Commission's interest in Roma in its fifty-six years of existence reduces to just the adoption of one Roma-specific and one Roma-mentioning resolution, and to some interest from three Special Rapporteurs and the WCAR. I discussed the WCAR in detail elsewhere (see Klimova 2003: Chapters 7 and 8), but the former two items are considered now. The Roma-specific resolution is *Resolution 1992/65*, entitled 'Protection of Roma (gypsies)'. This resolution is an amended version of a resolution proposed by the Subcommission (see pp. 41–2). It invites states to adopt measures for eliminating discrimination against Roma and to use the advisory service of the Centre for Human Rights (CHR) for this purpose. It also urges the Subcommission's Special Rapporteur on minorities to accord special attention to Roma and to provide information on their living conditions (see pp. 121–124). However, this task was peripheral to the preparation of a more general study on possible ways and means of facilitating the peaceful and constructive solution of problems involving minorities (UN Doc. E/CN.4/Sub.2/2000/28). The study only made fleeting references to Roma (see UN Doc. E/CN.4/Sub.2/1993/34), even though a number of governments had submitted information about them (see UN Doc. E/CN.4/Sub.2/1993/34/Add.1; UN Doc. E/CN.4/Sub.2/1993/34/Add.3). (Note that no NGOs mentioned Roma – see UN Doc. E/CN.4/Sub.2/1993/34/Add.2.) The recommendations of the study include one point on Roma noting the deterioration in their situation, but basically passing the responsibility onto regional organizations by suggesting that the OSCE and CoE should undertake Europe-wide measures to prevent discrimination and promote equality for Roma (UN Doc. E/CN.4/Sub.2/1993/34/Add.4).

Resolution 2001/9 on the right to development, adopted on 18 April 2001, is the first UN resolution that is not specific to Roma yet explicitly mentions them. No such mention was included in any earlier resolutions on development adopted by either the Commission or the GA. Paragraph 16 of this resolution recognizes Roma among vulnerable groups to which special attention should be paid in the process of the realization of the right to development (UN Doc. E/2001/23 and E/CN.4/2001/167: 73). It is unclear who initiated this reference. Although there was an intervention from an IRU representative during this session of the Commission, it did not relate to development (see p. 126). Roma were also not mentioned when the resolution was discussed (UN Doc. E/CN.4/2001/SR.62: 2–8). The reference probably resulted from these two factors: the attention that Roma received within the framework of the WCAR preparatory process (in full swing at the time this resolution was adopted), and the new interest in Roma shown by the UN Development Programme (UNDP) since the beginning of 2001 (see pp. 49–50 and Klimova 2003: Chapter 7).

Recently some of the Commission's Special Rapporteurs have started making brief mentions of Roma in their reports.[1] However, only three of them have paid more significant attention to Romani issues. The first one was Joseph Voyame, the *Special Rapporteur on the situation of human rights in Romania* (see also pp. 74–75). His first report (1990) contained just one paragraph on Roma, pointing out that they are subject to harassment, searches, confiscation of property and detention without trial or specific charges (UN Doc. E/CN.4/1990/28: 40). In comparison, his second report (1991) contained more detailed references to Romani issues. It pointed out that Roma are subject to defamation campaigns and public incitement to racial hatred which at times leads to violence, looting and destruction of houses. It cited, as an example, the statements by senior officials made in the media in June 1990, which were subject to a complaint lodged by the Ethnic Federation of Gypsies against the Director-General of Romanian Television. It also reported discrimination in the administration of justice against Roma and mentioned the 1990 Kolganiceanu incident in which 200 Roma were left homeless after their houses were wrecked and burned. The local authorities made no attempt to prevent or redress the incident because they viewed the Romani community as deviant and criminally inclined, and thus they in fact tolerated or even encouraged expressions of hostility towards the Roma. The conclusion of the report stated that the Romani community is very marginalized and isolated from the rest of society by distrust and prejudice. In Voyame's opinion, this constituted an important minority problem to which the Romanian authorities should devote attention (UN Doc. E/CN.4/1991/30: 27 and 30). The third report (1992) devoted yet more attention to Roma. The summary of events of interest to the Rapporteur cited several examples of wrecking and burning of Romani houses and a racially motivated murder of a Romani man. It also drew attention to some positive developments, namely the establishment of Romani political parties and civic associations; plans to train teachers in the Romani language, prepare appropriate textbooks and develop experimental programmes for the vocational integration of Roma; and a project for rebuilding houses burnt in a pogrom. The report concluded that, although the Romani community is still very marginalized and ill-protected by the police, the Romanian authorities are taking serious measures to improve the community's education and to enable it to assert its identity (UN Doc. E/CN.4/1992/28: 5, 6, 26, 33 and 299). Voyame's last report on the same topic (1994) was mostly a summary of reports submitted by other bodies. It included the Romanian Government's report regarding the implementation of Commission Resolution 1993/72, entitled 'Situation of human rights in Romania', which included the Government's concern about social integration of the Roma, its report of a Snagov seminar on Romani issues organized in 1993 and its account of the 1993 Hadareni 'pogrom'; the findings of the International Labour Organisation (ILO) Commission of Inquiry regarding Roma and their consideration by the Committee of Experts (see pp. 51–52); Amnesty International and Romanian Helsinki Committee reports about the 1993 Hadareni 'pogrom' and cases of inter-ethnic conflict involving Roma; and an International Human Rights Law Group report about discrimination against the Roma and biased media reporting (UN Doc. E/CN/1994/76: 14–25).

Maurice Glele-Ahanhanzo, the *Special Rapporteur on Contemporary Forms of Racism, Racial Discrimination, Xenophobia and Related Intolerance* from 1993 (when this post was created) until 2001 also turned his attention to Romani issues. He published annual reports, in which Roma had become a recurring item by 1997. Most notably, upon field visits, he addressed Romani issues in his recommendations to the Czech Republic, Romania and Hungary, concentrating on community building measures, segregation in education, improvements in anti-discrimination law, tolerance and information campaigns, involving Romani organizations in decision-making, and police attitudes towards Roma. In his work he relied upon information provided by NGOs, including the ERRC (Rooker 2002: 251–254, see p. 17). His missions were prompted by reports of systematic discrimination (particularly in education, employment and housing) against Roma in these countries and of frequent acts of violence against them by members of extreme-right organisations and the police (UN Doc. E/CN.4/Sub.2/2000/28). It remains to be seen whether Doudou Diene, the current Rapporteur, will continue to give attention to Roma in his reports, as none were available by the end of 2003.

The last Rapporteur to take an interest in Romani issues was Miloon Kothari, the Commission's *Special Rapporteur on adequate housing as a component of the right to an adequate standard of living, and on the right to non-discrimination*. He devoted an entire section of his report on his mission to Romania (14–19 January 2002) to housing and living conditions of the Roma, whom he identified as a vulnerable group. He called attention to how their poor housing conditions led to increased health risks among children and warned of evictions caused by inappropriate structural reforms. He cited an attempted segregation case at Piatra Neamt as an example of good practice of intervention by the civil society and the central Government regarding discrimination in housing. He commended the actions of a Romani NGO, the Roma Center for Social Intervention and Studies (Romani CRISS), regarding this case and urged 'the Government to continue monitoring of the situation of Roma and to act firmly against any discriminatory practices affecting Roma, including by local authorities and private owners, that negatively affects the enjoyment by Roma of the right to adequate standard of living including adequate housing' (UN Doc. E/CN.4/2003/5/Add.2: 17). He recommended that: '[t]he needs of vulnerable groups such as Roma ... should be integrated into national housing sector policies' (UN Doc. E/CN.4/2003/5/Add.2: 10–11); existing human rights norms and standards, including General Comments Nos. 4 and 7 of the Committee on Economic, Social and Cultural Rights (CESCR) and CERD General Recommendation XXVII on discrimination against Roma, particularly its paragraphs 30 and 31 on housing, should be born in mind when further elaborating and implementing strategies on housing for Roma;

Romani men *and* women should be engaged in a meaningful process of consultation for this purpose; 'the State should make additional effort to raise public awareness among the Romas [sic] and to facilitate their obtaining proper identity documents ... [and] ratify relevant international conventions on statelessness' in order to further facilitate the integration of the Roma (UN Doc. E/CN.4/2003/5/Add.2: 18). He furthermore urged for a review of eviction laws, policy and practice to ensure that 'no individual or group, whether Roma or non-Roma, suffers disproportionately therefrom' (UN Doc. E/CN.4/2003/5/Add.2: 15). A couple of his points from this report were reiterated in his general report on housing (see UN Doc. E/CN.4/2003/5: 10–11). (See also p. 75.) His other small contribution to promoting the Romani cause was a dialogue into which he entered with the Government of the Federal Republic of Yugoslavia (FRY) about alleged threats of evictions of Roma (UN Doc. E/CN.4/2003/5: 12).

Romani Issues at the Subcommission on the Promotion and Protection of Human Rights (the Subcommission)[2]

The Subcommission was the first UN body to take an interest in Romani issues, with a 1977 report by its Special Rapporteur to carry out a study on the rights of persons belonging to ethnic, religious and linguistic minorities. This led to the passing of two resolutions – Resolution 6 (XXX) of 31 August 1977 and Resolution 1991/21, entitled 'Protection of minorities'. However, it was only in 1992 that the Commission actually delegated the task of addressing Romani issues to the Subcommission. Since then the Subcommission has addressed Romani issues within the framework of prevention of racial discrimination and protection of national minorities (UN Doc. CERD/C/SR.1422), with the Special Rapporteur to carry out a study on the rights of non-citizens paying attention to them in his work. At the end of the 1990s there was an initiative for appointing a Special Rapporteur specifically on Romani issues, but this has been blocked by the Commission. The work of the above-mentioned Special Rapporteurs and the resulting resolutions are now introduced.

Francesco Capotorti, as the *Special Rapporteur to carry out a study on the rights of persons belonging to ethnic, religious and linguistic minorities,* referred to Roma several times in Chapters 3 and 4 of his study (UN Doc. E/CN.4/Sub.2/384/Rev.1). He mentioned (for example) their distinctiveness, their disadvantaged educational position resulting from the impossibility of studying in their mother tongue, illiteracy problems and programmes to address these problems, and the obstacles to maintaining their customs. He also pointed out that the use of customary Romani law is allowed in the private sphere in some countries, although traditional Romani marriages are not recognized by the state (see e.g. paragraphs 258, 380, 381, 384, 352, 481 and 516 in UN Doc. E/CN.4/Sub.2/384/Rev.1). However, he made no Roma-specific recommendations (see also pp. 40–41, 74).

In 1998, upon recommendation from the CERD, the Subcommission entrusted David Weissbrodt with preparing a working paper on the rights of non-citizens, which he presented on 31 May 1999 (UN Doc. E/CN.4/Sub.2/2001/20: 3). Amongst other things, Weissbrodt pointed out that there had been no systematic UN effort to understand the situation of the Romani minority in Europe, and that there had not been a thorough study addressing the ways in which Roma suffer discrimination and of methods to improve their situation (UN Doc. E/CN.4/Sub.2/2000/28). He identified Roma as posing 'a special problem in areas of race and non-discrimination' because 'their citizenship rights are often not recognized' (UN Doc. E/CN.4/Sub.2/1999/7: §76). The Subcommission then decided to recommend that the ECOSOC authorize the appointment of Weissbrodt as the *Special Rapporteur to carry out a study on the rights of non-citizens*. This decision was supported by the Commission and Weissbrodt was appointed in 2000. In 2001 he submitted his preliminary report, repeating the findings of his working paper and providing a summary of various international legal standards and the jurisprudence relevant to the rights of non-citizens, mentioning Romani cases several times (see UN Doc. E/CN.4/Sub.2/2001/20; UN Doc. E/CN.4/Sub.2/2001/20/Add.1). His 2002 progress report and his final report no longer mentioned Roma specifically, but their Addendums 1 and 2, which provided an update on UN and regional activities, both did (see UN Doc. E/CN.4/Sub.2/2003/Add.1 and Add. 2).

Recently there was an initiative for appointing a *Special Rapporteur on the rights of the Roma*, but this post was never approved. On 26 August 1999, the Subcommission discussed Romani issues under agenda items 3 and 8 ('Comprehensive examinations of thematic issues relating to the elimination of racial discrimination' and 'Prevention of discrimination against and the protection of minorities'). These issues were also raised in the working paper on the rights of non-citizens (se above). Consequently, the Subcommission decided to entrust its expert Yueng Kam Yeung Sik Yuen with the task of preparing a working paper on the human rights problems and protection of the Roma. This was to be submitted to both the next session of the Working Group on Protection of National Minorities (WGPM) and the Subcommission, thus allowing the Subcommission to decide on the feasibility of a study on the subject (UN Doc. E/CN.4/SUB.2/DEC/1999/109).

During its next annual review on 14 August 2000, the Subcommission discussed Romani issues in detail. During the afternoon session, Sik Yuen presented the findings of his paper. He described the discrimination Roma experience in many areas, arguing for tougher anti-racism laws and for the prosecution and punishment of perpetrators of attacks on and discrimination against the Roma, including the police. He also urged states to take responsibility for protecting the Roma, ensuring effective remedies, providing assistance to Romani victims, and establishing communication and trust-building programmes with the Roma. He also pointed out that in South America the Roma have had relative success in participating in civil society and proposed that this successful adaptation required an in-depth study. Another expert opined that Roma is one of the most delicate subjects to be taken up by the Subcommission in twenty years, and that it was high time that the Subcommission started paying more attention to their rights. He recalled that in the past, when the issue of Roma had been raised by NGOs and others, it had never managed to sustain the international community's attention for long. Another expert pointed out that solving the problem of the widespread discrimination and violence against Roma throughout Europe required a concerted effort by governments, NGOs and Romani leaders. The suggestion to conduct a study was supported by many of the Subcommission's experts speaking that afternoon. Also during this session, Paolo Pietrosanti of the TRP spoke 'on behalf of the Romani nation' (see p. 129). The Subcommission concluded that Roma were subject to pervasive racism, violence, and social and economic problems (UN Press Release 2000a). The discussion continued during the evening session, with a number of NGOs addressing Romani issues (see pp. 130–2). At this session, one expert argued that Roma were a special case of minorities who wished to have the same rights as others without wanting to change their lifestyle, and that special attention should be accorded to studying such a non-traditional form of integration. A representative of the Czech Republic asked that the future study on Roma recommends 'best practices' for addressing Romani issues and strengthening Romani self-identification. A representative of Slovakia pointed out that Roma bore some characteristics of both national minorities and indigenous peoples (UN Press Release 2000b).

On 17 August 2000, the Subcommission decided to recommend that the Commission adopts a decision asking the ECOSOC to authorize Sik Yeun as Special Rapporteur on the human rights problems and protection of the Roma (UN Doc. E/CN.4/SUB.2/DEC/2000/109; for full text of the draft decision see UN Doc. E/CN.4/2001/2- E/CN.4/Sub.2/2000/46). The Commission reviewed this request at its 2001 session but did not approve it. This disapproval is not made explicit in the resolution covering the review of the request (see resolution 2001/55 Rights of persons belonging to national or ethnic, religious and linguistic minorities in UN Doc. E/CN.4/2001/167: 246–249). Instead, the request is ignored and, in another resolution, the Subcommission is reminded to concentrate on studies specifically recommended by the Commission (see resolution 2001/60 Work of the Sub-Commission on the Promotion and Protection of Human Rights in UN Doc. E/CN.4/2001/167: 260–263).[3] The Subcommission's Chairman announced that

> [s]he had been slightly disappointed by the resolution adopted by the Commission to the effect that the Sub-Commission should not continue its work on the Roma. If that issue was considered too political for the Sub-Commission, perhaps it should be taken up by the Commission itself, since it was a matter of considerable importance in both Eastern and Western Europe (UN Doc. E/CN.4/Sub.2/2001/SR.17: 11).

Nevertheless, the Subcommission did not reiterate its request for the appointment of the Special Rapporteur in either 2001 or 2002 (see UN Doc. E/CN.4/Sub.2/2001/40; UN Doc. E/CN.4/Sub.2/2002/46), despite a request to do so from the RomEurope – Human Rights Coalition (comprised of Medecins du Monde International, the Save the Children Alliance, the International Federation of Human Rights Leagues, the International League against Racism and Anti-Semitism, the National Union of Social Institutions for Gypsies and the Gypsy Research Centre) during the 2001 session (UN Doc. E/CN.4/Sub.2/2001/SR.17: 8). At the seventh session of the WGPM in 2001 Sik Yuen again spoke about violations of the rights of Roma. He deplored that the Commission had not agreed to the Subcommission's proposal of appointing a Special Rapporteur on the topic (UN Doc. E/CN.4/Sub.2/2001/22). Some mitigation is that his working paper was used as background material for the WCAR (see UN Doc. A/CONF.189/PC.2/19). It remains to be seen whether the request for his appointment will be revived.

Resolution 6 (XXX) – the very first UN resolution referring to Roma was passed by the Subcommission on 31 August 1977, when Capotorti's study was discussed (see above). The issue of Roma had been raised by Benjamin Whitaker, UK Subcommission member, who, at the 31 August 1977 meeting, suggested that, since the Subcommission members had no territorial or national/nation-state allegiance, they should focus on this particularly alarming transnational case. He reminded the

Subcommission members of the Romani Holocaust and of current discrimination (UN Doc. E/CN.4/Sub.2/SR.795: 5–6). At the same meeting, Romani representative Puxon delivered an oral intervention (see p. 127). At the afternoon session Ram Bhagat, Indian Subcommission member, introduced the draft resolution E/CN.4/Sub.2/L.670 on 'gypsies,' saying that it was humanitarian in nature, aiming to assist the Roma to reach equal social and economic development with other people while respecting their particular traditions and aspirations (as suggested by Capotorti's study which concluded that assimilation would be met with resistance). One member of the Subcommission suggested that one of the paragraphs – recognizing that Roma had historic, cultural and linguistic ties of Indian origin – would be put to vote separately as his knowledge did not confirm this supposition. Several other members stated that they did not have the knowledge to decide if this paragraph was correct. Bhagat said that the Roma themselves claimed to come from India and supported this with linguistic evidence. He was nevertheless willing to delete the paragraph if his co-sponsors agreed. Another expert argued that giving special rights to Roma would be discriminatory to other people; to dispel his objection the resolution was amended to call for 'all the rights enjoyed by the rest of the population'. Other experts argued that the resolution should be addressed only to those countries that actually discriminate against Roma and consequently a phrase 'if they have not already done so' was inserted after the reference to according rights (UN Doc. E/CN.4/Sub.2/SR.795, 5–6).

When one looks at the objections closer, the base line was that individual Subcommission members, although supposedly having no nation-state allegiances, believed or were instructed to argue that in their countries (e.g. Romania and the Soviet Union) Roma had the same rights as other citizens. Whitaker supported the resolution most strongly, reminding that this was the least the Subcommission members could do for the Romani victims of Holocaust, who had been denied any compensation. He also pointed out that there was no evidence contrary to the paragraph on Indian origin and that both the Roma and the Indian government supported it. There were three votes for and three against deletion of the paragraph, with fourteen abstentions. The Chairman therefore decided to cast his vote in favour of deletion, which was carried out. The rest of the resolution (UN Doc. E/CN.4/Sub.2/399),[4] as amended by the discussion, appealing to those countries that have not yet done so to accord Roma all the rights enjoyed by the rest of the population, was adopted without a vote (see UN Doc. E/CN.4/Sub.2/SR.796: 8–10). In its preamble, the Subcommission noted that Capotorti's report found that there are gypsies (Roma) within the borders of many countries (E/CN.4/Sub.2/384/Add.6, annex III).

It took fourteen years before the Subcommission considered another resolution on Roma – *Resolution 1991/21*, entitled 'Protection of minorities,' which was adopted on 19 August 1991 (UN Doc. E/CN.4/Sub.2/1991/SR.33: 10). It expressed awareness that 'in many countries, various obstacles exist to the full realization by persons belonging to the Roma community of their civil, political, economic, social and cultural rights and that such obstacles constitute discrimination directed specifically against that community, rendering it particularly vulnerable' (UN Doc. E/CN.4/Sub.2/1991/L.9 in Danbakli 2001: 265–266). It also expressed concern about manifestations of racism, prejudice, intolerance and xenophobia against Roma, and recommended that the Commission adopts a resolution to alleviate this situation, urging the Special Rapporteurs to accord attention to Roma, inviting states to adopt and implement measures (in consultation with Romani communities) guaranteeing equality and protection to Roma, and emphasising the need for the UN to provide advisory services to states for such a purpose (UN Doc. E/CN.4/Sub.2/1991/L.9 in Danbakli 2001: 265–266). The Sub-Commission wanted the Commission to adopt such a resolution because, as Theo van Boven, the Dutch Subcommission member, pointed out, 'it was for the Commission, not for the Sub-Commission, to accord special attention to the specific conditions in which the Roma (gypsy) communities lived' (UN Doc. E/CN.4/Sub.2/1991/SR.33: 9). (See also p. 128.)

Romani Issues at the Working Group on Protection of National Minorities (WGPM)

The Subcommission's WGPM has concentrated on Romani issues since its inception in 1995 (UN Doc. CERD/C/SR.1422). So far it has considered Romani issues during all of its annual sessions (see UN Doc. E/CN.4/Sub.2/1996/2; UN Doc. E/CN.4/Sub.2/1996/28; UN Doc. E/CN.4/Sub.2/1997/18; UN Doc. E/CN.4/Sub.2/1998/18; UN Doc. E/CN.4/Sub.2/1999/21; UN Doc. E/CN.4/Sub.2/2000/27; UN Doc. E/CN.4/Sub.2/2001/22; UN Doc. E/CN.4/Sub.2/2002/19), with the most attention being given in its seventh session (see UN Doc. E/CN.4/Sub.2/2001/22). During this session, the WGPM adopted the following recommendations in relation to Roma: No. 7 recommending that the OSCE and CoE 'intensify their work to ensure that persons belonging to the Roma are not subjects of discrimination and can enjoy their minority rights in all fields, including education and language' and No. 10 recommending to treaty bodies that 'attention be given, in particular, to the situation of the Roma and the Sinti in the countries where they exist, taking into account that they appear to face special difficulties in many countries' (UN Doc. E/CN.4/Sub.2/2001/22). These recommendations were to be forwarded through the Subcommission to the relevant bodies. However, at its eighth session, the WGPM decided that although it appreciates the ongoing work of OSCE and CoE, it would continue its own consideration of ways of preventing discrimination against Roma and protecting their minority rights. It also reiterated its recommendation no. 10, which had not yet been fully implemented, and requested that the UN High Commissioner on Human Rights (UNHCHR) bring it to the attention of the relevant treaty bodies (UN Doc. E/CN.4/Sub.2/2001/22).

Monitoring of Romani Rights by UN Treaty Bodies

Five of the six UN human rights treaty-monitoring bodies have taken some interest in Romani issues. They are:

1) Human Rights Committee (HRC), supervising the implementation of the International Covenant on Civil and Political Rights (ICCPR);
2) CESCR for the International Covenant on Economic, Social and Cultural Rights (ICESCR);
3) CERD for the International Convention on the Elimination of All Forms of Racial Discrimination (ICERD);

4) Committee against Torture (CAT) for the International Convention against Torture and Other Cruel, Inhuman or Degrading Treatment or Punishment (ICAT); and
5) Committee on the Rights of the Child (CRC) for the International Convention on the Rights of the Child (ICRC).

Only the Committee on the Elimination of Discrimination against Women has not (as of yet) paid significant attention to Romani issues. The interest of three of these – HRC, CESCR, and CERD – in Romani issues is well documented (see Rooker 2002). All of these bodies have obligatory reporting procedures, although CESCR has no mechanism for complaints. Complaints to HRC and CERD can be raised using individual complaint procedures, provided that states recognize the competence of those bodies to receive them, and through inter-state complaints (for details of monitoring, reporting and filing of complaints, see Rooker 2002: 79–84). Under HRC, neither an inter-state complaint nor an individual complaint has ever been lodged regarding Roma (Rooker 2002: 83–84). Under CERD, no inter-state complaint has ever been lodged, but in October 2002 two individual complaints regarding Roma were made. The first of the Romani cases was closed by CERD in favour of the Romani victims (for details see Rooker 2002: 137–139) while in the second it was found that Slovakia did not violate ICERD. CERD nevertheless recommended legislative improvements to Slovakia (see Miroslav Lacko v. Slovak Republic 2002).

The available analysis of the interest of the treaty bodies in Romani issues only pays attention to the issues of racial discrimination and violence against Roma, education of Roma and minority status and collective rights (for the summary of these findings see Klimova 2003: 106–107, footnote 68; for the full analysis see Rooker 2002). It demonstrates that all the three committees in question have, since their inception, been concerned with Romani issues to at least a limited extent, and have devoted considerable attention to them since the 1990s (Rooker 2002: 370). It is beyond the scope of this book to carry out a detailed research into the work of the other two treaty bodies that have shown an interest in Romani issues – CAT and CRC – but a preliminary probe suggests that their attention to Romani issues has also increased since the 1990s (search of the treaty-bodies database has yielded a number of results in relation to Roma, see also pp. 77–8).

As the recommendations of these bodies usually concentrate on situations in individual states, their work is not of primary interest to this book. One exception to this is the *CERD General Recommendation XVII on Roma* (27 August 2000). This is the most elaborate general UN document on Roma today; its adoption is therefore now discussed. It is the only Roma-specific recommendation adopted by any treaty body. In fact, it is very exceptional for CERD since it is the first time that they adopted a General Recommendation on a specific theme or group (Rooker 2002: 370). The recommendation urges States to adopt measures to protect Romani communities against racial violence and to improve their living conditions. It calls upon states to adopt and implement nation-state strategies and programmes, to express determined political will and moral leadership, with a view to improving the situation of Roma and protecting them against discrimination by state bodies or persons and organizations, and to respect the wishes of Roma as to the designations they want to be given and the groups to which they wish to belong. Furthermore, the recommendation calls upon states: to ensure that legislation regarding citizenship and naturalization does not discriminate against members of Romani communities; to take all necessary measures to avoid any form of discrimination against immigrants or asylum seekers of Romani origin; to take appropriate measures to secure effective remedies for members of Romani communities and to ensure that justice is fully and promptly carried out in cases concerning violations of their fundamental rights and freedoms; and that measures be taken to acknowledge and compensate WWII 'wrongs' done to Romani communities by deportation and extermination. It also urges the UNHCHR to consider establishing a Focal Point for Romani issues within her Office and for the then forthcoming WCAR to take account of the Romani communities as some of the most disadvantaged and discriminated against in the world (UN Press Release 2000c; see also p. 45).

This recommendation was a result of a two-day *thematic discussion on racial discrimination against Roma* during CERD's 2000 session. A year earlier the CERD had decided to hold this discussion, because the consideration of periodic reports had made it realize that some Romani concerns and discrimination patterns were not country-specific. It requested that governments submit reports, receiving materials from a number of them as well as from regional organizations, UN bodies and NGOs. This thematic discussion was to be one of the CERD's contributions to WCAR (UN Doc. CERD/C/SR.1399). The thematic discussion was held on 15 and 16 August 2000. It was preceded by an informal hearing during which representatives of NGOs decried conditions of Roma to CERD members (see pp. 134–137).

During the first session on the afternoon of 15 August, CERD was addressed by Subcommission experts and by a representative of the UN High Commissioner for Refugees (UNHCR). In his opening statement, CERD Chairman Michael Sherifis stressed that the racial discrimination faced by Roma in many ways symbolized some of the most common contemporary forms of racial discrimination experienced by other ethnic and national minority groups in the world. Therefore, a successful attempt to address the issue of discrimination against Roma might benefit other groups. The President of the Subcommission expressed the hope that this debate would contribute to better coordination between UN bodies in relation to human rights in general and Romani issues in particular. A UNHCR representative briefly detailed the main areas of UNHCR involvement in Romani issues (see pp. 47–9). She argued that, although a very few Central European Roma were granted refugee status in other European States, many refugee claims showed a pattern of discrimination and abuse which, combined with a lack of effective remedy, might justify a fear of persecution in the sense of article 1 of the 1951 Geneva Convention on Refugees. In addition, she thought it a worrying reality that the reception of Romani asylum seekers and refugees in the rest of Europe was often tainted by serious prejudice. She urged CERD to encourage governments to adopt a generous approach when determining the refugee status of Roma, irrespective of whether their cases are covered by the Geneva Convention (Recalled by Mr. Nobel in UN Doc. CERD/C/SR.1423: 2). She also pointed out that, together with CERD, the UNHCR was committed to using the WCAR as a platform to highlight the problems of Romani communities and asylum seekers (UNHCR 2000). The rest of the session was dedicated to the general discussion of racial discrimination against Roma and possible remedies and prevention measures (UN Press Release 2000d).

The following day's discussion concentrated, among other things, on the need for equality and preservation of Romani identity, and recommendations in general. One CERD expert suggested that a Roma-controlled mechanism should be set up to bring cases to courts and Ombudsmen. The deputy of the UNHCHR said that it was the UNHCHR's desire that the voices of the victims be heard over the course of the forthcoming WCAR (UN Press Release 2000e). As with Recommendation XVII, this thematic discussion showed CERD's special interest in Romani issues because it was the first time that the Committee had held a debate on a thematic issue since its inception (some thirty years previously, UN Press Release 2000c). In the opinion of one of the CERD experts, the decision to hold the thematic discussion was one of the most important initiatives ever taken by the Committee (UN Doc. CERD/C/SR.1423: 2).

Office of the UN High Commissioner for Human Rights (OHCHR)[5]

On its own the OHCHR has not taken any specific decisions or actions regarding Roma, with the exception of promoting Romani issues within the framework of the WCAR (see Klimova 2003: Chapter 7). In 1998, the Focal Point on Roma, Sinti and Travellers was established within the (then called OSCE) Europe and North America Unit of the OHCHR 'because of the difficult human rights situation faced by Roma in many countries' of the region (Flynn 6 January 2001). The Focal Point does not have a specific legislative basis. Its tasks are to: collect and analyse information on the human rights situation of Roma in the region; forward specific or individual concerns to appropriate treaty bodies or the Commission's special procedures, and recommend courses of further action. It coordinates and co-operates closely with all other relevant branches and units within the OHCHR (in particular with the Anti-Discrimination Unit – ADU – and OHCHR staff assisting the WGPM), and with relevant regional IGOs (CoE, EU, and OSCE, Day 20 January 2003). A more central focal point, as envisioned in the CERD Recommendation XVII, has however not been established.

Romani Issues and UN Programmes and Funds

UN Children's Fund (UNICEF)

Since the 1990s UNICEF has regularly been including Romani children in its projects and publications, especially regarding the Balkans (for more information search the UNICEF website www.unicef.org and see Save the Children 2001a). There are a number of projects that benefit or target the Romani community in Macedonia (e.g. UNICEF supports literacy programmes for women, nation-state programmes aiming to provide pre-school opportunities for all children, and the nation-state programme to promote breastfeeding), Romania and Former Republic of Yugoslavia (educational programmes, health promotion, and early childhood learning programmes), Slovakia (Study on Children and Women in Low Income Communities, with the majority of interviewees being Romani, and support for a Save the Children country study on the educational rights of Roma), and Bulgaria (information programmes on HIV/AIDS and healthy life-styles, including incorporating specific messages on children/adolescent health in a special Romani TV programme), as well as regional projects (HIV/AIDS prevention programme; prevention of institutionalisation of children under the WB/UNICEF programme: Changing minds, policies and lives; prevention of Iodine deficiency, disorders and promotion of breastfeeding) (Rajandran 9 December 2002). The UNICEF regional office for CEE, the Commonwealth of Independent States (CIS) and the Baltic States has also reportedly been actively promoting the implementation and public awareness of the ICRC, as it relates to Roma, through legislation and specific programmes and awareness campaigns. They have concentrated on activities to assess and improve the situation of Romani children in public care, promoting early childhood development through parent education, and 'ensuring that the juvenile justice system affecting Roma children in particular conformed' to the ICRC (UN Doc. E/CN.4/Sub.2/1999/21). In November 2001, UNICEF participated in an assembly meeting of Romani NGOs of Bosnia-Herzegovina (BiH), followed by a meeting between Romani representatives and authorities on establishing a Romani Advisory Board, taking place within the CoE/OSCE project 'Roma under the Stability Pact'. As a result it has appointed two Romani representatives (Alexandra Raykova from Bulgaria and Indira Bajramovic from BiH) to make an assessment of the situation of Roma in the fields of education and health care in the Tuzla region (CoE 2002a). UNICEF has also prepared or sponsored a number of publications concerning Roma.[6] Moreover, the head of the UNICEF regional office for CEE/CIS and the Baltic States also currently acts as the UNICEF Focal Point on Roma (Black 13 January 2003).

UN High Commissioner for Refugees (UNHCR)

The UNHCR showed no significant interest in Roma until the 1990s, when CEE Roma started asking for asylum in Western Europe and North America. Following the attack on a hostel housing Romani asylum-seekers in Rostock, Germany (August 1992), in March 1993 the UNHCR commissioned a study on Roma in CEE. The survey covered the background and the contemporary conditions of the Roma in five CEE countries and Romani asylum-seekers in Germany. Its purpose was mainly informative (UN Doc. E/CN.4/Sub.2/2000/28), but recommendations for action were included. The study's author also warned that '[t]he Roma, perhaps more than any other identifiable transnational group of people, are subject to … increasing economic deprivation, increasing social instability, and the surfacing of long-suppressed ethnic hostilities, now fuelled by the "skinhead" syndrome' (Braham 1993: Preface).

Except for this the UNHCR has not paid significant attention to Romani asylum-seekers from CEE in its documents, publications or projects, with the exception of issuing UNHCR guidelines relating to the eligibility of Slovak, Czech and Romanian Roma asylum seekers (Gheorghe 2001) and campaigning against Czech Roma becoming stateless as a result of the 1993 Citizenship law. Instead, its main concern with Romani asylum seekers and refugees has related to those escaping wars in former Yugoslavia, especially Kosovo. These concerns are regularly addressed in reports of the Executive Committee of the UNHCR Programme and UNHCR briefing notes, UNHCR emergency updates, progress and global reports on former Yugoslavia, lectures given by UNHCR staff, UNHCR statements to the Third Committee of the UN GA, to sessions of the Commission, to meetings of the Humanitarian Issues Working Group at the Peace Implementation Council, and to the UN Security Council (all available from the UNHCR website, http://www.unhcr.ch). Since 1999, the UNHCR has regularly surveyed the situation of minorities, including the Roma, in Kosovo, in co-operation with the OSCE, producing ten reports to date (see OSCE and UNHCR 1999–2003). One of the aims of these reports is to 'offer useful guidance in determining the refugee claims of Kosovo Roma' (UNHCR 2000). It has also been involved in a number of reconciliation, reintegration and other projects for Romani refugees and returnees from former Yugoslavia, in close co-operation with OSCE and CoE. It has tried to ensure that Roma in ex-Yugoslavia receive suitable housing in the post-conflict relocation. In co-operation with other institutions, it has, for example, initiated a round-table dialogue between Romani and Albanian communities in Kosovo, which resulted in the adoption of a common declaration in April 2000 providing for the safe return of Roma into Kosovo (for details about this document, entitled the *Platform for Joint Action Regarding Kosovar Roma, Ashkalija and Egyptian Communities*, see Save the Children 2001a: 222–224, 239 and 242–244; for general details of these UNHCR initiatives see UNHCR 2000: 5–7). The UNHCR was also involved with regulating problems ex-Yugoslav Roma had with obtaining citizenship (Recalled by Mr. Nobel in UN Doc. CERD/C/SR.1423: 2). It also advocated for the recognition of Kosovo Roma as refugees or persons in need of international protection and, in August 2000, it tried to stop Germany's deportations of Kosovo Roma by writing to the Lower Saxony Interior Minister (UNHCR Briefing Notes 2000 and recalled by Mr. Nobel in UN Doc. CERD/C/SR.1423, 2). Then, in November 2000, it called for an international probe into the massacre of four Ashkalija[7] in an Albanian dominated region of Kosovo (Agence France Presse 2000; see also p. 95). It has also co-operated with the CoE and OSCE on a number of projects within the Stability Pact (for details see Klimova 2003: 115, footnote 105).

In 1999, concerns with Roma in CEE finally came further to the forefront of UNHCR work with the establishment of the Focal Point on Romani Issues within the Prague UNHCR office. This Focal Point was, however, created with no clear mandate. The Prague representative, Jean Claude Concolato, therefore had to decide what its priorities should be. Traditionally, focal points collect and distribute information; the Prague Focal Point is no exception (Concolato 16 December 2002), taking part in European conferences on Romani migrations (organized e.g. by the OSCE and International Centre for Policy Migration Development) and contributing papers and statistics, as well as holding meetings with relevant international and nation-state actors (UNHCR 2002a). Nevertheless, Concolato also decided that an innovative approach was needed, explaining that:

> The goal of UNHCR Prague as the Focal Point on Roma is prevention of irregular migration of Roma population. While the Office is following the Roma issue in other countries of the region, we have put our focus on assisting the Roma in the Czech Republic, through the implementation of a pilot Roma programme that started in 2001. This is mainly because it is practically difficult and ineffective to monitor and respond to varied needs of Roma communities in different countries. Through the implementation of this pilot Roma programme, the Office ultimately aims to help create conditions that enable the Roma to enjoy their rights as citizens and help them integrate in the society; thus, stabilizing the Roma in the Czech Republic (UNHCR 2002a).

The need for a policy of prevention (which this approach emphasises) is based on the following arguments. The UNHCR is interested in the Romani question because of the continuing trend of Romani migration and asylum seeking in CEE. It believes that the majority of the Roma in Central Europe do not face persecution, but discrimination (Kashiwa 10 January 2003). Discrimination against Roma is the main expression of communal tension between them and the non-Roma (Concolato 2000). For this reason, it is important to support the integration of Roma and help improve their conditions, so contributing to building their confidence in their own communities and countries. At the same time, discrimination needs to be addressed so it does not turn into open persecution later (as it did, for example, in the Balkans). However, there are exceptions and that is why the UNHCR advocates that each asylum application must be examined individually (Kashiwa 10 January 2003). Most importantly, the UNHCR believes that, 'in some specific cases, there may be situations in which an accumulation of acts of discrimination may result in an individual situation of persecution' (Concolato 2000).

Further objectives of the UNHCR pilot Romani programme are: to have a positive impact on improving socio-economic conditions of the Roma by assisting the activities of so called bridge people (individuals who have been working on Romani issues and are accepted by both Roma and non-Roma as a type of natural mediator) in order to build their capacities (and the capacities of other relevant actors), and to identify and address the needs/problems which have not yet been recognized or adequately supported; to sensitize the government to the need for accelerating the implementation of the 'Plan of Action for the Roma' and to 'address the Roma issue both domestically and internationally in order to mobilize non-UNHCR support to finance activities for the integration of the Roma' (UNHCR 2002a).

The UNHCR project prioritizes two problems – usury and housing/evictions – as these two are the main factors (though, in many cases, in connection with other factors such as unemployment and *de-facto* discrimination) urging Czech Roma to leave their country and seek asylum abroad (UNHCR 2002a). Since the majority of Roma do not have access to the official banking sector, they often become victims of usury (UNHCR 2002b). Usury leads to asylum-seeking in two ways: some Roma are encouraged by usurers to seek asylum in countries where they can receive social benefits, which are then taken from them by the usurers upon their return (as their asylum applications are usually rejected), others seek asylum in order to escape from the violent acts of the usurers (UNHCR 2002a). In cooperation with partners, the Prague Office adopted a double approach to address the issue of usury – a) repression of usurers, through, for instance, assisting a symbolic court case against usurers in Usti nad Labem (with NGO People in Need) and b) providing social assistance for victims through creating the Emergency Social Fund (interest-free loan arrangement) for the most destitute families in Usti nad Labem and Ostrava (for details about this fund see UNHCR 2002b). At the same time, the UNHCR also has been raising the issue of usury with relevant local and state authorities at various meetings and conferences, including two special sessions of the Czech Governmental Council of Romani Community Affairs. As a result of the UNHCR's actions, some local governments have decided to start an interest-free loan arrangement for socially-disadvantaged people including the Roma, and in August 2002 the Czech Government announced that it was considering the application of the UNHCR project of Emergency Social Fund at the local, and possibly even nation-state, level and creating a special police unit for dealing with the problem of usury (UNHCR 2002a). Similarly, housing problems lead to asylum seeking when Roma are faced with eviction (due to rent arrears and the lack of tenancy right) but cannot find a sufficient alternative (emergency) accommodation (UNHCR 2002a). The UNHCR has also prioritized this issue because the housing project can bring about positive and visible changes in the Roma's daily life in a relatively short time, unlike the majority of long-term governmental projects, and so can act as a confidence-building measure (Concolato 2002; Concolato 16 December 2002; UNHCR 2001a). Due to the limitations of its capacity, the UNHCR has to address this problem with advocacy, rather than direct assistance for housing projects. The Prague Office 'has tried to encourage international institutions, such as the European Union (EU), to consider creating a special international fund for rehabilitation of accommodation for the Roma and other socially-excluded population in Central Europe' (UNHCR 2001a).

UNHCR Prague has also been co-organising, with a Romani NGO Drom, seminars on different issues such as usury, housing, poverty and micro-credit activity, bringing together NGO workers, Romani advisors and government officials to exchange the positive and negative experiences gained through their activities with Roma. Lastly, UNHCR Prague has supported miscellaneous activities aimed at the integration of Roma into the Czech society, such as co-sponsoring the International Romani Festival Khamoro in Prague and assisting the activities of the Open Club/Community Centre for Romani Children in Ostrava and Pardubice, which are operated by NGOs (UNHCR 2002a).

UN Development Programme (UNDP)

The UNDP only started to show an interest in Roma very recently, with the Bulgarian and Romanian country offices carrying out Roma-oriented projects on education and job creation and the Country Support Team in Bratislava overseeing a joint project with the Hungarian Autonomia foundation and the ILO on Roma in the Hungarian labour market (Ivanov 21 February 2003). At the beginning of 2001, the UNDP decided to produce a Roma Regional Human Development Report. This report is to be a part of a broader project whose objective is 'to encourage the debate and exchange of information on the issue, to merge different organizations' efforts where possible and to bring about real change in human development opportunities for marginalized communities of which Roma are the most numerous' (UNDP 2003a). The report, entitled 'Avoiding the Dependency Trap', was released on 16 January 2003 and is presented as the first cross-border (covering Bulgaria, the Czech Republic, Hungary, Romania and Slovakia) comprehensive survey (carried out by the UNDP and ILO) of the Romani community, expanding the analysis 'from the focus on human rights alone to the broader challenge of human development' (UNDP 2003b). Perhaps its most shocking conclusion is that 'by such measures as literacy, infant mortality and basic nutrition, most of those country's [sic] four to five million Roma endure conditions closer to those of sub-Saharan Africa than Europe' (UNDP 2003b). It is, however, very optimistic about remedying the situation. The UNDP believes that the 'report explains why and how the dependency trap into which many Roma have fallen can be avoided. It [...] show[s] that the Roma want to integrate productively into the countries in which they live without losing their distinctive cultural identities, and outlines a number of concrete proposals on how this can be better achieved' (Brown 2003). These proposals relate mostly to positive discrimination in order to 'promote active participation and opportunities for Roma to solve their problems regarding education, employment and political participation' (RFE

2003). They were, though, the subject of strong criticism from academics (see pp. 113–4).

In any case, it remains to be seen whether these recommendations, if implemented, really will make a difference. 'If implemented' is a crucial phrase here as Pal Csaky, the spokesman for the Slovak Deputy Prime Minister, has already complained that the 'report lacks objectivity and is exaggerated' (RFE 2003). The UNDP has attempted to kick start implementation of the report by publicising it among Romani leaders and running a pilot project in the Slovak region of Spis (see p. 113). According to Andrey Ivanov, the author of the Roma Regional Human Development Report, the Spis project

> is very successful because it not just provides support for Roma communities but is very sensitive to interethnic relationships and involves both minorities and majority. It has also strong community mobilization component (encouraging and helping people to solve problems and not solving them on their behalf) and is economically sustainable (not increasing dependency) (Ivanov 21 February 2003).

However, the evaluation reports of this particular project suggest that, so far, these claims are the potential or the goals of the project, rather than the reality, although limited progress has been made (see Musisi and Cristellotti 2002; Musisi 2002). UNDP is also currently preparing both a pilot project on vocational and business education for minority populations (targeting the Roma) in Bulgaria and a feasibility study for projects in Slovakia, Romania, Hungary and the Czech Republic. These projects will seek to implement some of the recommendations of the UNDP report such as an integrated approach to education, qualifications, community development and income generation (UNDP 2003c).

Romani Issues and UN Specialized Bodies

UN Educational, Scientific and Cultural Organisation (UNESCO)

The interest of the UNESCO in Roma started with an article about them in the *UNESCO Courier* in April 1958 (see Barry 1958). However, the next article only came in 1974 (see Ivatts 1974). Two UNESCO-related publications, *UNESCO Features* and *Diogenes*, have also occasionally featured articles on Roma since the 1960s (see e.g. Megret, Undated). In 1984, an entire issue of the *Courier* was dedicated to Roma. Its introductory article was written by Amadou-Mahtar M'Bow, UNESCO Secretary-General, who argued that the Romani historic trajectory 'strikingly illustrates some of the great principles on which Unesco's action is based,' such as universality combined with cultural specificity, and that Romani values and culture' offer 'an outstanding original contribution to the rest of humanity' (M'Bow 1984: 4). Such recognition was, however, never given in an official UNESCO document.[8] In 1998, UNESCO published a book on Romani culture, arts, language and living conditions of Roma in Europe, accompanied by a video and CD-ROM (see Reyniers 1998). It also sponsored a number of publications and projects on Roma, through both its headquarters and National Commissions. I have repeatedly inquired with various officials about UNESCO programmes for Roma and the UNESCO's co-operation with Romani NGOs, but the answer was always the same. They say no Romani NGO has official relations with us and we have no information on UNESCO programmes for Roma (Abtahi 21 January 2003; Ferrier 11 October 2002; Maguire 28 October 2002 and 21 January 2003). (See also pp. 103–109.)

International Labour Organisation (ILO)

The ILO has taken some interest in Roma as subjects of employment discrimination since 1989, starting to pay attention to Roma in some of its projects – work which has intensified since the beginning of the new millennium (see e.g. Molina 1998, ILO 1999). Today, the ILO is well aware of Romani problems, but this concern has not yet been adequately translated into its projects. The Budapest ILO Office is, however, currently preparing a project on education and employment which should, in general, target the Romani community. As of now, there has not been a significant discussion of Romani issues within the annual ILO conference (Thomas 29 October 2002).

Most monitoring of the rights of Roma is carried out within the supervisory system of the ILO 111 Discrimination (Employment and Occupation) Convention of 1958 (111 ILO Convention). As with other conventions, this system consists of annual state reports on compliance with the convention which are examined by the Committee of Experts on the Application of Conventions and Recommendations.[9] Since the late 1990s (and occasionally since the early 1990s), many, although not all, countries with significant Romani populations regularly report on employment and training-related issues in relation to the Roma.[10] Since 1999, the Committee reacts to the requested information concerning Roma and the 111 ILO Convention, requests more information when deemed appropriate and demands submission of information where Roma are omitted.[11] In 2002, for example, it dealt with the situation of the Roma in thirteen countries (Austria, Bulgaria, Czech Republic, Finland, Germany, Hungary, Italy, Poland, Romania, Slovakia, Slovenia, Sweden, and Switzerland), and drew attention to them as a group particularly affected by employment-related discrimination (ILO 2003). Occasionally, Roma are also addressed within the frame-work of the supervisory system of the ILO 122 Employment Policy Convention (ILO 2002a and 2002b). Trade unions, who are, along with employers associations, the ILO's social partners, are also slowly starting to take an interest in the conditions of Roma in some countries. For example, in 1999 the National Confederation of Hungarian Trade Unions, the National Federation of Autonomous Trade Unions and the National Federation of Workers' Councils all reported their concerns about employment discrimination against members of the Romani minority (ILO 2002c). Recently, one of the main ILO social partners, the International Confederation of Free Trade Unions, has also started to call for attention to the problematic situation of Roma (Thomas 29 October 2002).

However, the most significant intervention the ILO has made on behalf of the rights of Roma remains its early (1990) Commission of Inquiry,[12] appointed under article 26 of the ILO Constitution to examine the observance by Romania of the 111 ILO Convention. This Commission of Inquiry, consisting of the Honourable Jules Deschenes and Professors Francesco Capotorti and Budislav Vukas, was constituted following a complaint submitted by thirteen worker's delegates from various coun-tries (for the complete list of names and countries see ILO 1991) that called attention to employment discrimination in Romania, especially in relation to the Hungarian minority. The Commission, however, inquired into discrimination against all of Romania's minorities, including the Roma. It solicited background material from various UN bodies, including reports by Joseph Voyame and a number of NGOs. In the summer of 1990 the Commission heard thirteen witnesses presented by the complainants and five[13] witnesses of its choice. The Commission members also conducted a number of on-site visits and interviews with minority leaders in Romania (see p. 110). Based on the information gathered, on 28 March 1991 the Commission of Inquiry recommended that the Government of Romania adopt, as soon as possible, a number of measures which would help it fully conform to the 111 ILO Convention. Among the recommendations, five paragraphs were devoted to measures related to Roma. These measures were to be aimed at:

> Undertaking a vast campaign, in collaboration with the political authorities, employers' and workers' organisations and other appropriate bodies, with a view to eradicating the traditionally negative attitude towards the Roma (Gypsies) [paragraph 13]. Improving the social situation of the Roma by means of an integrated programme drawn up in collaboration with their representatives, covering education, employment, housing and the other elements necessary to their progress [paragraph 14]. Stepping up existing efforts to train teachers of Rom origin and to ensure that children of Rom origin attend school [paragraph 15]. Allocating the maximum available resources to enable Rom families to improve the utterly deplorable housing conditions under which many of them live [paragraph 16]. Drawing up programmes of special measures as provided in Article 5 of Convention No. 111 to improve the socio-economic status of the Roma; in particular, creating a programme for the recognition of occupational skills which are not formalised by a diploma [paragraph 17] (ILO 1991).

Romania was required to address its progress with implementing these measures in its future reports. As a consequence, since 1991, Romania's reports on the 111 ILO Convention have devoted significant space to the situation of the Roma, and the Committee responds to this information (see also pp. 110–111).[14]

Another ILO Convention – 169 Indigenous and Tribal Peoples Convention of 1989 (169 ILO Convention) – might, in the future, be used to promote the rights of Roma. In a letter dated 20 December 2000, Switzerland's Director of the Federal Department of Economic Affairs requested an official and formal opinion from the International Labour Office (ILO's permanent secretariat) on, (among other things), whether 'travellers, such as those of Jenish, Roma and Gypsy origin' should be covered by the 169 ILO Convention (see Table 2.2). The Office's opinion was issued in 2001 and basically declared that such people should be covered by 169 ILO Convention if they declare themselves to be tribal (see ILO 2001). A similar request was recently raised by Germany but no formal opinion has yet been published. As of October 2002, the 169 ILO Convention has not been used to pursue the rights of Roma (Thomas 29 October 2002). A number of factors make such use in the future questionable. Firstly, the majority of countries with significant Romani populations have not yet ratified the convention (for current ratification information see the ILO website, http://www.ilo.org/ilolex/english/convdisp1.htm). In addition, most Romani leaders do not see their populations as tribal or indigenous (see p. 111 and Klimova 2003: §8.5). It remains to be seen whether Romani leaders from Argentina, Brazil, Colombia, and Ecuador (all of whom ratified the Convention), who are actually in favour of application of this Convention to their people, will push for this to happen.

The biggest progress so far has been achieved by the Colombian Romani NGO Proceso Organizativo del Pueblo Rom de Colombia (PROROM), whose lobbying resulted in the Colombian Ministry of Interior recognising in its resolution no. 022 of 2 September 1999 that the 169 ILO Convention applies to Roma. However, translating this recognition into implementing the rights of Roma under this Convention has been slow (PROROM 2000).

World Bank (WB)

Since the late 1990s, the WB has started to support policy development related to Roma at the country level. For example, in Hungary and Slovakia it is working with governmental and NGO partners on strategies for implementing the governmental policies on Roma. It also supports capacity building activities for monitoring bodies and new offices on Romani issues. It helps with evaluation of past programmes and disseminating the experience/lessons learned to other countries (WB 2002a). WB funded the first stage (2000–2003) of the Pakiv – the European Roma Fund programme for training Roma social managers from Slovakia, Hungary, Romania and Bulgaria (Gheorghe 2001). It also finances and/or carries out research on Romani issues.[15] Additionally, Roma are beneficiaries of many general WB programmes for CEE (for more details see WB 2002a and 2002b). For example, the Child welfare project for Bulgaria targets Romani children using educational initiatives (WB 2002a). (See also pp. 111–2.)

Conclusion

This chapter has demonstrated that, since the 1970s, there has been some interest in Romani issues from a number of UN ECOSOC bodies, namely the Commission, Subcommission, WGPM, several treaty bodies, UNICEF, UNHCR, UNDP, UNESCO, ILO and WB. This interest intensified significantly from the early 1990s, probably because of both the renewed salience of minority rights after the collapse of Communism in CEE, and the westward exodus of Roma resulting from ethnic conflict and hardships caused by (among other factors) economic transition in the region.[16] Three UN resolutions have been devoted, either in large part or completely, to Roma. In addition, one UN resolution has specifically named them among groups with the right to development. Several UN Special Rapporteurs have paid attention to Romani issues in their work. An initiative to establish a UN Special Rapporteur on rights of Roma has, however, so far been unsuccessful. One Roma-specific treaty body recommendation has been issued by CERD, which also organized a thematic discussion on Roma. The interest of UN funds, programmes and specialized bodies has mostly been realized by preparing and/or supporting publications and projects on Romani issues. In addition, UNICEF's work contributes to the application of the ICRC to Romani children, and the ILO monitors discrimination against Roma in employment and training through its own instruments.

This chapter identified the agenda-setting and discursive developments in relation to Roma and many of the key events/actions that led to them, as summarized in Table 3.1. It also identified a number of procedural/institutional developments, but these cannot be *clearly* linked to the key events/actions (see Table 3.2). As Table 3.1 shows, all events/actions can be linked to either agenda or discursive developments or both. However, four agenda developments (including Roma being a more regular item on the agenda of treaty bodies, UNICEF, UNESCO, ILO and WB projects) show no clear link to any of the identified events/actions. On the other hand, all discursive developments were linked with events/actions. The tables also reveal that most developments were discursive or agenda-setting, with a lesser amount of procedural/institutional developments. However, none of these developments were very revolutionary. In terms of agenda-setting, they relate to inclusion in projects (UNICEF, UNESCO, ILO, UNDP, UNHCR, WB), and inclusion in the considera-tions of 1) minority issues by the Subcommission, 2) discrimination in employment by the ILO, 3) treaty commitments by treaty bodies, 4) country and thematic mandates by *some* Special Rapporteurs, and 5) the right to development by the Commission. Roma, unlike (for example) the indigenous peoples, have neither become a global issue on the UN agenda nor an official focus minority group or issue under the global agenda issue of human rights.[17]

In terms of discursive developments, UN member states have made no commit-ments in relation to Roma. The discursive developments identified are limited to acknowledging the problems Roma face and generally vague recommendations for addressing these problems by the Commission, Subcommission, Special Rapporteurs or specialized bodies. Yet, the procedural/institutional changes are the most disap-pointing. While indigenous peoples now have their own advisory body – the Permanent Forum – all the Roma have is a couple of UN agencies' websites dedicated to them (see WB 2002a and UNDP 2003a), three focal points within the UN, and some attention by several Special Rapporteurs, treaty bodies, the Subcommission and within the ILO 111 Convention. This is in stark contrast to the growing number of Roma-specific bodies established by European IGOs, such as the Contact Point for Roma and Sinti Issues at the OSCE Office for Democratic Institutions and Human Rights, the Specialist Group on Roma/Gypsies (see Rooker 2002: 274–278; Barany 2002: 269) and the proposed European Roma Forum within CoE (see Klimova 2002b, CoE 2002b), as well as to the UN procedural/institutional changes related to the indigenous people. The reasons for the differences in the degree of success between the Romani and the indigenous activism are briefly reflected on in Chapter 7. The reasons for the growth of Roma-specific institutions at the European level are not explored in this book. They probably relate to the greater salience of Romani issues in Europe (e.g. the need to improve the treatment and living conditions of Roma in the former Eastern Bloc in order to prevent East-West Romani migrations and asylum seeking) as well as to the goals of the European project of a supranational state in which the power of nation-states is eroded in favour of legitimacy of other (higher as well as lower) levels of power and authority (whose promotion is an inher-ent interest of the European IGOs).

What accounts for this lack of significant Roma-related UN developments? Is it, and the minor developments that have occurred, linked to the actions of Romani and pro-Romani activists at the UN? In order to answer these questions, Part Two analy-ses the role of the Romani and pro-Romani activists in relation to the identified events/actions and agenda, discursive and procedural/institutional developments, as well as their general interaction with the above named UN funds, programmes, and specialized and treaty bodies.

Table 3.1 Main Events/Actions Leading to Agenda-setting and Discursive Developments

Year	Event/action[18] [C[19]]	Agenda setting	Discursive commitment (C)/ acknowledgement (A)/ recommendation (R)[20]
1977	Capotorti's report[21] [SR] Resolution 6 (XXX) [S]	Roma put on the agenda for dealing with minority issues[22] [S]	Presence of Roma in many countries (A), States to accord Roma the same rights as the rest of the population (R) [S]
1989/ 1990	Commission of Inquiry [ILO]	Roma put on the agenda for addressing discrimination in employment [ILO]	Romania to address discrimination against Roma (R) [ILO]
Since the 1990s		Roma as a more regular agenda item [TB/UNICEF/ UNESCO[23]]	
1990-91	Voyame reports[24] [SR]	Roma as a human rights special concern group in Romania [SR]	Roma in Romania subject to human rights abuses, discrimination, racism (including violent acts) and marginalisation with the tacit or even open consent of the authorities; an important minority problem (A) to which Romanian authorities should devote attention (R) [SR]
1991/ 1992	Resolution 1991/21 [S]	Romani issues on the agenda within the framework of prevention of racial discrimination and protection of national minorities [S]	Existing obstacles to human rights of the Roma, their particular vulnerability, manifestations of racism, prejudice, discrimination, intolerance and xenophobia against them; the need for the UN to provide states with advisory services on the topic (A), All Special Rapporteurs to pay attention to Roma (R), States to take measures, in consultation with Romani communities, to ensure equality, protection and security of Roma (R) [S]
1992	Resolution 1992/65 [C]	Roma on the agenda of the 'Minorities' Special Rapporteur[25] [SR]	States to eliminate any form of discrimination against Roma by adopting measures and to use UN advisory services (R) [C]
1993	Eide's[26] report [SR]		Deterioration in the situation of Roma (A) The OSCE and CoE to undertake Europe-wide measures to prevent discrimination and promote equality for Roma (R) [SR]
1993	Braham's UNHCR Report on Roma [E]	Roma on the agenda [UNHCR]	Roma as a transnational group subject to increasing economic deprivation, social instability, and racially-motivated violence (A) Number of specific recommendations for the work of the UNHCR and for establishing various Roma-specific institutions at the European level (R) [E]

Table 3.1 Continued

Year	Event/action[18] [C[19]]	Agenda setting	Discursive commitment (C)/acknowledgement (A)/ recommendation (R)[20]
1997– 2001	Ahanhanzo's reports[27] [SR]	Roma on the agenda for addressing contemporary forms of racism, racial discrimination, xenophobia and related intolerance [C]	The Czech Republic, Romania and Hungary Roma and community building measures, segregation in education, improvements in anti-discrimination law, tolerance and information campaigns, police attitudes and involving Romani organisations in decision-making (R) [SR]
1999– 2000	Initiative for appointing a Special Rapporteur on Roma/ Yuen's working paper on Roma [S/E]	Roma suggested as focus minority/human rights group on the Subcommision's agenda and as an agenda item for the WCAR [E]	Reiteration of the acknowledgement of discrimination against Roma (A), tougher anti-racism laws, state responsibility for protection of the Roma, and an in-depth study of successful adaptation of Roma in South America (R) [E]
End 1990s[28]		Roma on the agenda [UNDP/WR/SR[29]]	
1999– 2002	Weissbrodt's reports[30] [SR]	Roma (temporarily) on the agenda for addressing citizenship problems [S]	The lack of systematic UN effort to understand and address the situation of Roma and their problems of racism, discrimination and citizenship rights (A) [SR]
2000	General Recommendation XVII and thematic discussion [CERD]	Roma reiterated as an item on the agenda for elimination of racial discrimination and as an agenda item for the WCAR[31] [CERD/C]	A number of recommendations for states to adopt specific measures to protect Roma against violence and to improve their living conditions (see pp. 43–4) (R) UNHCHR urged to consider establishing a Focal Point for Romani issues and to take account of Roma as some of the most disadvantaged and discriminated against (A) in the world for the forthcoming WCAR (R) [CEDR]
Since 2000s		Roma on the projects agenda [ILO]	
2001	Resolution 2001/9 [C]	Roma on the agenda for the realisation of the right to development as a vulnerable group [C]	Attention to be paid to Roma in the process of the realisation of the right to development (A/R) [C]
	Recommendation no. 7 and 10 [WGPM]		OSCE and CoE to intensify their work to ensure non-discrimination and minority rights of Roma, and UN treaty bodies to pay attention to Roma [WGPM]
	International Labour Office formal opinion on the applicability of ILO 169 Convention to Roma [ILO]		Roma as tribal people for the purposes of the ILO 169 Convention (A/R) [ILO]

Table 3.1 Continued

Year	Event/action[18] [C[19]]	Agenda setting	Discursive commitment (C)/acknowledgement (A)/ recommendation (R)[20]
2003	Roma Regional Human Development Report [UNDP]	Roma reiterated as a project agenda item [UNDP]	Roma as a development issue and in need of positive discrimination (A) Recommendations to five CEE states giving measures for positive discrimination (R) [UNDP]
2003	Kothari's report [SR][32]	Roma in Romania as a vulnerable group in relation to housing and living conditions [SR]	Roma in Romania as a vulnerable group in relation to housing and living conditions (A) Government to continue monitoring and to enforce anti-discrimination and facilitate obtaining proper identity documents by Roma, Romani needs to be integrated into national housing sector policies in meaningful consultation with them (R) [SR]

Table 3.2 Procedural/Institutional Changes

Year	The specific change [C]
1992	Romani issues delegated to the Subcommission by the Commission [C/S]
Since the end of 1990s	Several Special Rapporteurs start to briefly mention Roma in their reports[33] [SR]
1998	Establishment of a Focal Point [OHCHR]
End of 1990s	Establishment of a Focal Point [UNICEF]
As of late 1990s	Many countries with significant Romani populations regularly report on employment and training-related issues in relation to the Roma within the ILO 111 Convention [ILO]
Since 1999	The ILO Committee pays attention to Roma when monitoring ILO 111 Convention [ILO]
1999	Establishment of a Focal Point [UNHCR]
Beginning of 2000s	Dedicating a specific website [WB]
2003	Dedicating a specific website [UNDP]

Notes

1 e.g. Jose Cutileiro, Special Rapporteur on the situation of human rights in Bosnia and Herzegovina and the Federal Republic of Yugoslavia and Katarina Tomasevski, Special Rapporteur on the right to education (see UN Doc. A/56/460; UN Doc. E/CN.4/2000/6/Add.2; UN Doc. E/CN.4/2001/52; UN Doc. E/CN.4/2002/60; UN Doc. E/CN.4/2002/60/Add.2).

2 The name of this body was the Subcommission on the Prevention of Discrimination and Protection of Minorities until it was changed by an ECOSOC decision on 27 July 1999 (UNIHP, Undated).

3 I was not able to verify whether a debate over the decision to not appoint the Rapporteur took place, as the relevant summary records had not been issued before this manuscript was completed.

4 The full version can be found e.g. in Rishi 1990: 5–6 and Danbakli 2001: 268.

5 Early on, this office was known as the Division of Human Rights. It was renamed to Centre for Human Rights in 1982 and then to OHCHR after it became headed by a High Commissioner in 1994 (UNIHP, Undated).

6 Among those are a book based on the workshop 'Growing Up as a Gypsy' held in 1992 in Florence, Italy (Costarelli 1993); two further series from the UNICEF International Child Development Centre (Stavenhagen 1994; UNICEF 1995); and two 2000 studies, in co-operation with the World Bank (WB) on Vulnerability of Roma children in the Municipality Shuto Orizari and Vulnerability of Roma children in the Dispersed Roma Communities in Skopje (for a complete list of publications see WB 2002b).

7 Groups traditionally considered Gypsy/Romani, but recently claiming a separate Ashkali or Albanian identity (see Table 1.2).

8 Nor any other, for that matter. However, the EU (then EC) at least recognized in 1989 that Romani 'culture and language have formed a part of the Community's cultural and linguistic heritage for over 500 years' (Liegeois 1994: 275).

9 This committee is composed of twenty independent persons renowned in legal and social fields, appointed in personal capacity, and submits an annual report to the International Labour Conference, which is examined by the tripartite committee composed of government, employer and worker members (ILO 1998: 15).

10 To retrieve the individual documents search the ILOLEX database for the phrase 'CEACR: Individual Observations concerning Convention No. 111, Discrimination (Employment and Occupation)'.

11 To retrieve the individual documents search the ILOLEX database for the phrase 'CEACR: Individual Direct Request concerning Convention No. 111, Discrimination (Employment and Occupation)'.

12 Complementary but rare supplement to the regular supervisory mechanism.

13 The sixth invited witness, Karoly Kiraly, did not appear.

14 See documents on Romania in the ILOLEX database under ILCCR (examination of individual cases) and CEACR (individual observation) concerning Convention no. 111.

15 The three most important publications to date are 'Roma and the Transition in Central and Eastern Europe: Trends and Challenges' by Dena Ringold, 'Poverty and Welfare of Roma in the Slovak Republic' by The World Bank, Foundation S.P.A.C.E., Ineko, and the OSI, and 'The Health Status of Romas in Hungary' by Lajos Puporka and Zsolt Zadori from the Roma Press Center (WB Regional Office Hungary, NGO Studies No. 2). For a complete list of publications see WB 2002b.

16 These reasons for the intensified interests are however not analysed in this book.

17 For the list of the UN agenda items see http://www.un.org/partners/civil_society/agenda.htm and follow links to 'issue subheadings' and 'groups in focus'.

18 The table excludes events in the framework of WCAR. For those see Klimova 2003: 388.

19 Code for the UN body to which the discursive development applies: [S] – the Subcommission, [C] – the Commission, [SR] – individual UN Special Rapporteur, [E] – individual expert commissioned to do a study, [TB] – treaty bodies. For others, regular abbreviations are used.

20 Does not include state-specific treaty bodies' recommendations.

21 The Special Rapporteur to carry out a study on the rights of persons belonging to ethnic, religious and linguistic minorities.

22 Yet their situation did not start being systematically addressed until the late 1990s.

23 Given the limited amount of information available on UNESCO's projects on Roma, this is a tentative placement.

24 The Special Rapporteur on the situation of human rights in Romania.

25 The Special Rappporteur charged with preparing a study on possible means and ways of facilitating the peaceful and constructive solution of problems involving minorities. Yet he paid only very limited attention to the Roma.

26 The 'Minorities' Special Rapporteur.
27 The Special Rapporteur on Contemporary Forms of Racism, Racial Discrimination, Xenophobia and Related Intolerance.
28 Meaning since the end of 1990s.
29 Only a number of SR, not all. In addition, they often only refer to them in passing.
30 The Special Rapporteur carrying out a study of the rights of non-citizens.
31 This was further reiterated by the actions of e.g. the OHCHR and UNHCR.
32 The Special Rapporteur on adequate housing.
33 This is the only development that can vaguely be linked to an action or event (see Table 3.1, column 1991–1992).

PART TWO:
INTERACTION BETWEEN
ROMANI ACTIVISTS AND
THE UN SYSTEM

Chapter 4

Using the Formal Access Provided by the UN Institutional Structure

The UN political structure has offered formal access to NGOs since its very beginning. The right to such access is enshrined in the Preamble and Article 71 of the UN Charter. In recent years NGO involvement has risen to unprecedented levels. According to the 1998 Report of Secretary-General:

> NGOs have introduced additional knowledge and information into the decision-making process; they have raised new issues and concerns which were subsequently addressed by the United Nations; they have provided expert advice in areas where they were the main actors; and they have contributed greatly to a broad consensus-building process in many areas which ensured commitment by all actors to a global agenda. This participation has proven to be a very useful addition to the regular intergovernmental work of the Organization (UN Doc. A/53/170).

Their formal access is however limited to the ECOSOC, the Secretariat[1] and treaty bodies, as now explored in greater detail. The four remaining major UN structures – the International Court of Justice, the Trusteeship Council, the Security Council, and GA – provide no formal access (Passy 1999: 153), with the exception of the permanent observer status at the GA (Riggs and Plano 1994: 47). The formal access of NGOs to both the ECOSOC and the Secretariat is limited to consultative status, directly with the ECOSOC and with the Department of Public Information (DPI) of the Secretariat (Passy 1999: 154). The bulk of this chapter describes the formal access offered to NGOs by these two bodies, and the ways in which the Romani and pro-Romani activists used such access. In addition, the majority of UN funds, agencies and programmes have their own procedures and arrangements for consultations with NGOs (Jaeger 1982: 172). However, the IRU only managed to establish formal relations with the UNICEF and therefore this chapter does not deal with the other UN funds, agencies and programmes (see pp. 99–114). The chapter also illustrates the mutual influence between the UN and the Romani activists in terms of agenda, discourse and organization.

The Permanent Observer Status at the GA

This status allows non-member states, IGOs, regional organizations, groups of states, UN specialized agencies, national liberation movements and a limited number of NGOs to participate in the work of the UN on a permanent basis. This participation is limited to the work of the GA, its main committees and conferences; it does not include the right to vote or introduce motions. The participation of some observers is further limited only to discussions on subjects of particular concern to them (see Simma 2002: 189). The major advantage of this status is that it allows unlimited, permanent access to virtually all UN fora and communications facilities.[2] It thus facilitates significant influence in the decision-making processes, even without the right to vote (Koenig 1991).

Achieving this status or, even better, a full membership in the UN, has always been the IRU's goal. The best window of opportunity occurred in the early 1990s when the UN extended the permanent observer status to three non-governmental entities – the International Committee of the Red Cross (in 1990), and the Sovereign Military Order of Malta and the World Federation of Red Cross and Red Crescent Societies (both in 1994) (Simma 2002: 405). Yet, by the end of 1994, the GA had decided to abandon this generous practice and continue granting observer status only to non-member states and IGOs with activities of interest to the GA (Simma 2002: 248). Nevertheless, the precedent was established and the GA might return to the practice, at least in some exceptional cases. The IRU should, however, bear in mind that all the three NGOs were granted the status due to their special role in international humanitarian relations (Simma 2002: 405). If the IRU is to follow this precedent, it must be able to offer the UN some concrete beneficial assistance.

The precedent of liberation movements (e.g. the Palestine Liberation Organization (PLO) and the South West Africa People's Organization (SWAPO)) has also been inspiring for the IRU, but is not directly applicable. The IRU cannot be viewed as a potential government of a territory it seeks to liberate, as there is none. The lack of defined territory is also the criterion that disqualifies the IRU from meeting the conditions for recognition as a state under international law, even if it achieved the other two – a permanent population and an independent government. Such recognition is also a precondition for applying for full UN membership. The IRU has been making an emotional claim to a seat in the GA,[3] arguing that the Romani nation and the IRU (as its organ) fulfill what it believes are all the criteria essential to a nation (e.g. common language, history, flag, anthem, etc.) except that of having territory. They believe that the absence of territory should not preclude them from receiving such status (see e.g. Declaration of Nation in Acton and Klimova 2001: Appendix 1; Hancock 1992). However, the UN does not grant membership to nations, it grants it to states and the above named criteria are not those considered essential under international law; territory is. For the time being, pursuing the NGO precedent might be a more viable strategy. In any case, the procedure for granting the observer status is no different for NGOs and liberation movements. They just have to convince a number of member states to propose that an invitation for them to participate as observers is put on the GA agenda and then convince the GA to adopt it (Suy 1978: 156). In this sense, Scuka's strategy of presenting the Declaration of Nation to various heads of governments to obtain support is not misplaced (see pp. 22–7). He believes that the time is not yet right to make an official request for recognition as a non-territorial nation/state with a full UN membership (Scuka 25 May 2001), which is a sound judgment.

ECOSOC Consultative Status

Although some analysts see the distinction between those NGOs with and without the ECOSOC consultative status as becoming largely academic because 'NGOs have found various means for influencing global policymaking and implementation' (Mingst and Karns 2000: 65), the ECOSOC consultative status remains at the core of formal NGO access to the UN system. The ECOSOC is an important structure within the UN because it is the principal authority for the discussion and elaboration of norms with regard to economic and social questions of international character. The ECOSOC produces studies and makes formal recommendations in its areas of concern, coordinates the work of UN special agencies, organizes world conferences on specific topics, and elaborates norms and universal declarations. Participation in the ECOSOC enables NGOs to challenge directly the elaboration of norms by the international regimes, and to take part in deliberations on almost all UN matters (except security). It also provides access to all UN special agencies and the world conferences organized by ECOSOC (Passy 1999: 154–155). (See pp. 99–114 and Klimova 2003: Chapter 7.)

The Rules Governing the Status[4]

In order to gain consultative status, the UN requires the NGOs to work in the economic and social field (education, health, human rights, culture, science, technology, and related areas) and to conform to the spirit, purposes and principles of the UN Charter (Passy 1999: 153–154). They should support the UN's work (see UN Doc. E/RES/1296 (XLIV), §3) and be able to 'make a significant contribution to the UN through their expertise' (UN Doc. INF1296/7/92). They must be 'of representative character and of recognised international standing' (UN Doc. E/RES/1296 (XLIV), §4), meaning that they need to have existed for three years, must provide evidence of co-operation with the UN on economic and social issues, and must have held at least two general meetings open to members before tendering the file (UN Doc. INF1296/7/9). The NGOs also need to have: 1) an established headquarters with an executive officer; 2) a democratically adopted constitution, providing for the determination of policy by a conference, congress or other representative body, and for an executive organ responsible to the policy-making body; 3) authority to speak for their members through their authorized representatives; and 4) a representative structure and appropriate mechanisms of accountability to members (see UN Doc. E/RES/1296 (XLIV), §4, 5 and 6; UN Doc. E/RES/1996/31, §9–12).[5]

Forming an Umbrella Organization Eligible for the Consultative Status

After several unsuccessful attempts of the early embryonic organizations such as the IRC and the International Gypsy Rights Mission (IGRM) to start formal co-operation with the UN (for details about these organizations see Klimova 2003: §2.3.1.3, §2.3.1.4), Romani activists realized that if they wanted a formal status, they would have to follow the rules of the game.[6] Therefore the IRU, the first durable umbrella organization, was carefully modelled to follow the ECOSOC requirements of eligibility for consultative status. In order to demonstrate that it conformed to the spirit, purposes and principles of the UN Charter, the IRU made a clear reference to the principles and aims of the UN in the preamble of its statutes and quoted UN Resolution 6(XXX) of 31 August 1977 (Rishi 1980: 13). (See pp. 40–41.) Its statutes explicitly stated that they 'have been designed in a way that renders the Romani Union capable of receiving status as a Non-Governmental Organization with the

United Nations, and for this purpose consultation has taken place with the NGO Section of ECOSOC' (Statutes of the Romani Union 1991: §3). Yet the IRU had to distort facts slightly to fulfill the criteria of having existed for three years and having held at least two general meetings open to members at the time of application. While it was officially created just before the 1978 Congress,[7] its application put its founding date as April 1971 – the date of the first Congress – and claimed it was previously called the IRC (see UN Doc. E/C.2/1993/R.4/Add.2, 23).[8] While it is true that the IRC was the secretariat of the 1971 Congress, it is neither true that the IRC was founded at the Congress, nor that the IRC changed its name and became the IRU (see Klimova 2003: §2.3.1.4). Some of the leading officials of the IRC had not accepted the decisions and elections of the 1978 Congress, and had decided to continue the IRC separately from the IRU. Nevertheless, since the majority of IRC officials and members did switch their allegiance to the IRU, the IRU's claim of continuity with IRC was not completely unfounded. Puxon, one of the leading IRC and then IRU officials, explains this as follows: 'I called the RU the successor to the CIR [the French acronym for IRC], which is pretty fair. The RU grew out of the CIR and if Vanko [Rouda, the IRC President] had accepted the democratic decisions of the Geneva Congress, it would have been a matter of re-naming the CIR Romano Jekhethanibe [Romani name for RU]' (Puxon, Undated). In addition, as the application was made in close co-operation with the NGO offices in Geneva and New York,[9] we could consider this 'creative accounting' being sanctioned, or at least accepted, by them. Furthermore, in order to prove the IRU's eligibility, Jan Cibula, the first IRU President, emphasized in many of his speeches that the goals of the IRU were 'in total harmony with the UN Charter' (IRU 1979). His letters to the NGO office prior to obtaining the status also emphasized that IRU wanted to develop its future activities and organizational structure to be in even greater harmony with the UN goals (Cibula 1978b), and pointed out the IRU's activities relating to the UN, such as organizing a UN Day and a Human Rights Day in preparation for the 1979 International Year of Child (Cibula 1978a).

Status Categories

ECOSOC status is divided into three categories: general, special and roster (until 1996 also known as categories I, II and III). General status is the most privileged and is given to very large international NGOs, allowing them to make substantive and sustained contributions to most of the activities of the ECOSOC and its subsidiary bodies. Special status follows, and is for NGOs that are known to have a special competence in only a few of the fields of ECOSOC. Roster status is reserved for NGOs that occasionally make useful contributions to the ECOSOC's work (see UN Doc. E/RES/1296 (XLIV): §16 and 19; UN Doc. E/RES/1996/31: §22–24).

Achieving Roster and then Special Status by the IRU

The criteria for NGOs to obtain consultative status with the ECOSOC were set in 1968. The plan to apply for such status had existed among Romani activists since the 1971 Congress, whose Statutes Commission was allegedly working towards fulfilling this. However, it was not until the 1978 Congress that significant progress was made. Reportedly, the main reason why the IRU wanted to gain consultative status was to be able to address Romani problems within the UN fora and to 'gain authority for action in Europe and elsewhere' (Main 27 February 2003).[10] The IRU's action via-a-vis the UN was not to be of a political character, but rather social, moral and economic, and based on human rights instruments (Main 27 February 2003). However, the findings presented in this chapter suggest the opposite. The IRU's main activities within the UN fora have been related more to promoting its status than to utilising human rights instruments for improving the situation of Romani communities (see pp. 77–78).

In June 1978, the IRU submitted the application for consultative status at the ECOSOC. A Romani delegation was put together to deliver the application to the UN offices in New York, whilst carrying the Romani flag. It was led by Yul Brynner,[11] the famous Hollywood actor and Honorary President of the 1971 Congress, and was also comprised of John Tene, the Vice-President of the IRU's Presidium, and Ian Hancock and Ronald Lee, the North American IRU officials (Rishi 1978/9: 1–2). The delegation also carried a letter from Cibula, explaining the significance of accepting the IRU to the ECOSOC, and reportedly handed this letter, together with the application, directly to the Secretariat of Kurt Waldheim, UN Secretary-General. On 5 July 1978 Jan Cibula met with Waldheim's delegation for two hours, handing them further materials related to the application and a personal letter for Waldheim (Cibula 1978c: 4).[12] This letter detailed the progress the IRU had made with both the submission of its application and the enlisting of support for the 1978 Congress (Cibula 1978f). Cibula also tried to enlist the support of the Swiss government for the IRU application. On 13 June 1978 his delegation reportedly met 'the highest Swiss authorities,' which were ready to support their aspirations (Cibula 1978c: 4). On 15 June 1978 Cibula wrote to Virginia Sauerwein, the head of the NGO Section of ECOSOC, informing her about the 1978 Congress, the IRU's contact with UN officials, and their supposed recent successes in negotiating with a number of countries. He also explained that some of the IRU's rivals, such as the IRC, might try to discredit the IRU because of an ideological split.[13] At the end of the letter, Cibula expressed the hope that the IRU would soon obtain the consultative status (Cibula and Gilles 1978). Cibula also requested (and received) the names of the members of the UN Committee on NGOs for lobbying purposes (Gelbe-Haussen 1978; NGO DIESA 1979).

The UN Committee on NGOs decided upon the application of the IRU in their New York meeting in March 1979. A twelve-member IRU delegation[14] attended this meeting, reportedly upon the invitation from Waldheim (Cibula 1981a).[15] The Indian Ambassador to the UN, Rikhi Japal, gave his full support to the application and also said that he would support upgrading to special status (Romani Union (Romani Ekhipe) Granted Consultative Status by UN 1979: 1).[16] The application was further supported by the Soviet Union, the UK and others, and was therefore accepted (World Romani Congress Activities of its Presidium 1980: 34). IRU officials later stated that one of the bases for the granting of this status were numerous letters from people in many countries who testified to the international standing and seriousness of the IRU (Cibula et al. 1981). Despite its request for special category, it was initially placed in roster status. This took a while to sink in. In May 1979, the Geneva NGO Liaison had to remind Cibula that the IRU was granted roster not special status as he indicates on letters to the European Community (Martineau 1979a). In fact, Puxon had considered applying straight for general instead of special status but after discussing this matter with the NGO office in Geneva decided that special status was more justified at the time (see Webb 1978; Puxon 1978a and 1978d). Obviously, according to the UN Committee on NGOs even the request for special category was over-ambitious. The application was filed and approved under the name Romani Union, even though the letterheads and press releases of the IRU have used the name Romani Internationalno Jekhethanibe (meaning the IRU in the Romani language) since its inception in 1978 (see e.g. IRU 1979). Within ECOSOC, the name was only officially changed to IRU in 1993 (during the reclassification to the special status). However, this book refers to this organization as the IRU throughout in order to avoid confusion, for example with nation-state chapters called Romani Union.

In 1981 there were high hopes for upgrading to the special status because N. Krishnan, who had been in touch with IRU leaders such as Saip Jusuf when acting as India's Ambassador to Yugoslavia, was appointed India's Ambassador to the UN in New York, yet nothing materialized (Rishi 1981a: 5–6). On 12 September 1985, IRU officials met Virginia Sauerwein from the NGO Office to inquire about re-classification, and in 1986 asked for the reclassification application form – yet never submitted it (Cibula 1985). They finally applied for upgrade in 1993, and were successful. Although the Indian contingent of the IRU claims that this was again due to India's help (News and Reviews 1994), this time India did not actually help much because, unlike in 1979, it was not a member of the Committee on NGOs (Ayoub 1992). However, according to Hopson and Hancock, the IRU upgrade was helped by the support of states which had contacts with Roma in their own countries (Main 1994: Chapter 3, Part I, B1a). The Irish representative of the Committee on Non-Governmental Organizations (CONGO) even passed on his right to speak to Hancock, so that Hancock could deliver a plea for the upgrade, explaining that this upgrade was very important to Roma because it would give them the right to deliver written and oral interventions upon their own initiative (Main 1994: Chapter 3, Part I, A2b). In this way, Romani leaders would be consulted on decisions pertaining to the Roma, thus preventing wrong decisions being taken due to lack of understanding of the Romani culture and the situations in which Roma live. He illustrated his point using an example of a governmental decision in the Czech Republic to forcefully move Roma into housing unsuitable to their needs and lifestyle, resulting in vandalising of the housing that could have been avoided were Romani representatives consulted (Hancock 13 February 2003). Obtaining the special consultative status signified the favourable attitude of the UN towards the IRU, as it is only granted to NGOs who are particularly competent in their field and are known at the international level. Some IRU representatives believe that the main value of this status is that it helps to keep governments in check. For example, Marco Kappenberger stated in his letter to Eliane Lacroix-Hopson that getting the consultative status 'is the achievement that reminds constantly Governments not to do anything against the Roma (because nobody likes to latter hear the truth in the Human Rights sessions of the UN)' (Kappenberger 1985). As of 2003, the IRU remains the only umbrella Romani organization with UN consultative status, although the pro-Romani ERRC and a national Romani NGO Dzeno Association from the Czech Republic gained special and roster statuses in 2001 and 2003 respectively (see UN Doc. E/2001/INF/2/Add.2: 143 and UN Doc. E/2003/INF/2/Add.4: 194).

General Rights and Duties Associated with the ECOSOC Status

The three main rights associated with the consultative status are: 1) participation in meetings of ECOSOC-related bodies (e.g. commissions, subcommissions, and working groups),[17] 2) delivering written and oral interventions during these meetings,[18] and 3) designating permanent representatives to the UN headquarters in New York, Geneva and Vienna (UN Doc. INF1296/7/92: 1). Certain subsidiary organs do extend similar rights to NGOs without ECOSOC status. In particular, procedures established by the ECOSOC and the Commission allow NGOs to submit information regarding allegations of human rights violations even if they do not have consultative status (UN Doc. A/53/170). The Working Group on Indigenous Populations and the WGPM of the Subcommission both allow the participation of all NGOs in their deliberations, regardless of whether they have status, in order to 'encourage the exchange of observations and the submission of useful information, in particular in respect of some of the situations of ethnic minorities at the local level' (UN Doc. E/CN.4/Sub.2/1996/2: §14 and 15).

Two additional opportunities arising from the consultative status are providing technical aid to the Special Rapporteurs of the Commission and Subcommission[19] and participation in NGO ECOSOC activities. In addition, NGOs in general status can propose agenda items for the ECOSOC and subsidiary bodies (see UN Doc. E/RES/1296 (XLIV): §21 and 27 and UN Doc. E/RES/1996/31: §28 and 34). As of 1996, NGOs with any ECOSOC status that express a wish to attend relevant international conferences (including the preparatory meetings) convened by the UN shall receive accreditation (see UN Doc. E/RES/1996/31: §42).[20] However, no ECOSOC status gives NGOs the right to participate in decision-making through a vote. The main duty of NGOs (but only those with general and special status) is to submit quadrennial reports on their activities within the UN framework for examination by CONGO (UN Doc. E/RES/1996/31: §61c).

The IRU's Utilization of the Rights, Opportunities and Duties Associated with the ECOSOC Consultative Status

As stated earlier, consultative status provides NGOs with three main rights, two related opportunities and one duty. The utilization of each by the IRU (with reference to other organizations where appropriate) is now considered in turn, with the exception of the right to deliver written and oral interventions. Since this right is related to using the configuration of power and is crucially important to answering one of the main questions of this book, a large part of Chapter 6 is devoted to it.

Participation in Meetings of ECOSOC-related Bodies   This right (together with the right to deliver interventions) allows the IRU's representatives to sensitize more powerful UN actors who are able to propose concrete resolutions or actions. Together with the right to designate permanent representatives to the UN, it also allows the IRU (and in the future the ERRC) to gain publicity as the representative of the world's Roma (Main 1994: Chapter 2, Part IV, A1).

However, participation of the IRU in meetings of ECOSOC-related bodies has been very sporadic and usually only took place when written or oral interventions were being made (see Chapter 6). It has primarily targeted the Subcommission and the Commission although, on a number of occasions, the IRU representative Nicolae Gheorghe reportedly participated in CERD meetings (e.g. in 1990, 1991 and 1995) (Gheorghe 4 December 2002; UN Doc. E/C.2/1993/R.4/Add.2: 33).[21] Besides the meetings at which interventions were submitted or presented, UN records revealed participation in just two meetings – the 14th general assembly of the conference of NGOs in consultative status with UN ECOSOC (2–5 July 1979, Geneva) (see Conference of Non-Governmental Organizations 1979) and the thirty-second Subcommission session (20 August – 7 September 1979) (see UN Doc. E/CN.4/Sub.2/435: 3 (Annex I)). The IRU records claim that its representatives also attended the thirty-third Subcommission session (18 August – 12 September 1980) (UN Doc. E/C.2/1993/R.4/Add.2: 33), yet the UN records do not list the IRU among participating NGOs (UN Doc. E/CN.4/Sub.2/459: Annex I)). It is possible that the IRU registered too late to be put on the participants list, or that Marco Kappenberger registered as representing the Baha'i International Community, yet also attended on behalf of the IRU (see the next paragraph) (see UN Doc. E/CN.4/Sub.2/459: 2, Annex I).

Given the limited human and financial resources of the IRU, it is not surprising that it restricted its participation to those meetings in which it had decided to deliver interventions. However, it disregarded the opportunity that the other meetings provided for individual lobbying in order to sensitize relevant governmental, inter-governmental and non-governmental actors to the Romani cause. This was a strategic mistake because such lobbying can be a more efficient tool than delivering interventions (Sankey 1996: 271).

Apart from the IRU's actions, representatives of nation-state Romani NGOs and of the pro-Romani ERRC participated in sessions of the WGPM as observers, occasionally delivering oral statements despite not having ECOSOC consultative status (see pp. 133–4). Together they have attended six of the eight sessions of the WGPM that took place so far. The second session (May 1996) was only attended by the ERRC (ERRC 1996d). The third session was attended by the Romani CRISS from Romania and the Central Council of Roma and Sinti (the Zentralrat) from Germany (UN Doc. E/CN.4/Sub.2/1997/18), the fifth was attended by the Delhi Forum-Banjara People from India (at times associated with the IRU through the Congresses), Romani CRISS and Zentralrat (UN Doc. E/CN.4/Sub.2/1999/21), the sixth by Romani CRISS (UN Doc. E/CN.4/Sub.2/2000/27), the seventh by the Consejo Gitano from Spain, Rom-Star Organization, Rroma Centre of Public Policies 'Aven Amentza' (Aven Amentza), Rroma Students and Youth Against Racism Alliance (SATRA/ASTRA) (all three from Romania) and Roma Association of Izmail and Region from Ukraine (UN Doc. E/CN.4/Sub.2/2001/22), and the eighth by the Anglunipe Youth Organization (Former Yugoslav Republic of Macedonia (UN Doc. E/CN.4/Sub.2/2002/19). The ERRC also attended an OHCHR expert seminar on 'The Interdependence between Democracy and Human Rights' in Geneva (24–26 November 2002) (ERRC 2002a: 169).

Designating Permanent Representatives to the UN Headquarters   The right to maintain permanent representatives in the UN headquarters offices offers NGOs the possibility of regular, active participation and increased visibility. It is an important tool for conducting public relations within the UN system and staying up-to-date on all UN developments (Main 1994: Chapter 2, Part IV, A1). However, this right has not been *fully* utilized by the IRU and has been marred by personal fights over using this 'privilege,' as now detailed.

Since gaining consultative status, the IRU has been appointing permanent representatives to the UN in New York, Geneva and Vienna, but these representatives have never regularly taken part in the work of the UN, for a number of reasons. Firstly, they usually have not resided in the vicinity of these places and were therefore unable to attend meetings often. Secondly, they have had to maintain regular jobs in addition to their IRU UN appointments. Thirdly, the IRU often did not have the financial means to reimburse the travel expenses of its representatives, let alone the time spent in meetings. Therefore meeting attendance was very sporadic.

The main UN representatives in New York were Ian Hancock (1986–1999)[22] and Emil Scuka (2000-present). In Geneva it was Jan Cibula until 1990. Various other people were also accredited as alternatives to Geneva such as Vincenz Rose and Stefan Kwiek for 1980 and Sait Balic, Rajko Djuric, Romani Rose and Adolf Anton Franz for 1981 (See Cibula 1979c; Martineau 1981a). Since 1990 the position in Geneva has alternated among various Presidium members, but none of them have made use of this position. The IRU has also been appointing various representatives to Vienna (such as Tomas Holomek in 1979, see Cibula 1979d and 1979e), yet rather symbolically, as none have been able to actively use their positions. The NGO Information Officer in Vienna, Mr. Reidbauer, informed me that the file on the IRU contains appointment forms for all years but no other information (as the IRU had not submitted any). As far as he was aware, the IRU had not been active within the Vienna offices. Interestingly, until today it is the former IRU President Rajko Djuric who appoints representatives to Vienna (Reidbauer 21 November 2002) although since 2000 he has no legal authority to do so as he no longer holds any executive position. The UN, however, does not seem to notice or mind. The presence in New York and Geneva has been more real than in Vienna but, as all of the main representatives could attend just one UN meeting a year at best, some of them delegated their powers to non-IRU non-Romani members. Such delegated representatives were Eliane Lacroix-Hopson in New York (1985–2000) and Marco Kappenberger in Geneva (1979–1990),[23] both members of the Baha'i International Community. Kappenberger gained this position through friendship with Cibula, and subsequently suggested Hopson for the New York post (Lacroix-Hopson 1992b and 3 April 2001). Hopson recalls that Robert Muller, Assistant to the Secretary-General, and Virginia Sauerwein, Chief of the NGO Unit, expressed relief at her 'sorely needed' appointment (Lacroix-Hopson 1992b). However, the representation by Hopson and Kappenberger was of limited use. Although they attended UN meetings regularly and could therefore pass on relevant information to the IRU, they took virtually no direct action to promote the IRU's goals. Kappenberger did assist Cibula with drafting some documents, yet made no interventions on behalf of the IRU. He continued to be the Baha'i UN representative and only delivered statements on their behalf, on issues unrelated to Roma (UN Doc. E/CN.4/Sub.2/SR.881). He also drafted some letters to the UN NGO office in Geneva on behalf of the IRU, but they were mostly emotional statements and were not constructive (Gheorghe 4 December 2002).

Hopson partly used her IRU post to promote interests of yet another group she was affiliated with – the Hopi. Her activities nevertheless helped gain the IRU some publicity within the UN system. She was very active in several NGO Committees (e.g. the NGO Committee for Human Rights as of 1986 and the NGO Committee for the International Year of Indigenous Peoples since 1991) and in co-operation with the DPI (see pp. 81–2). In her thesis, Lynnaia Main concludes that all these activities helped to increase the visibility of the IRU, to establish its legitimacy as a representative of the Roma, and to create networks with various UN actors, including NGOs, members states or the UN administration (1994: Chapter 2, Part IV, A1c). While some visibility and publicity were achieved, these seem to have been personal to Hopson. Her networking achievements and her credentials to promote the goals of IRU are questionable. In an interview with the author she claimed to have good relations with the NGO officers in New York, especially Michele Fedoroff (3 April 2001). This was however not confirmed in my interview at the NGO office in New York (Fedoroff 4 April 2001). Not knowing much about Roma (Hancock 11 April 2001),[24] she could hardly contribute to raising awareness about their culture and activism. By holding prejudices against Roma,[25] she could hardly dispel them within the UN. In fact she contributed (perhaps unwittingly) to spreading prejudiced views against the Roma when unjustly criticising the activities of Latin American Roma (see endnote 25), and undermined the IRU's standing at the UN by claiming that it disintegrated in 1999 after Hancock, whom she considered her boss, had resigned. Besides spreading this rumour through the letter mentioned in endnote 24, she also told it to the UN NGO office in New York (Lacroix-Hopson 3 April 2001). She might have done so with the best intentions, believing that she was doing a service to the Roma by criticising their corrupt leaders, but her actions were potentially very damaging to both the IRU's image and the image of Roma in general, and must therefore be taken into account in a book that evaluates the success and failure of the IRU's interaction with the UN. Although Hopson regularly consulted with Hancock about her work, she was otherwise out of touch with the IRU. Only once did she meet with Gheorghe, when giving input for the reclassification application (Lacroix-Hopson 24 February 2001). According to Jud Nirnberg, assistant to then General Secretary of IRU Emil Scuka, when he asked her to provide a report on her activities for the IRU secretariat, she appeared offended and did not fulfill the request (22 October 2000).

Although the permanent representatives did not use their right to appear at the UN often, they jealously guarded their positions. The right to be the main representative of the IRU at the UN in New York was especially contested. In one episode in 1997, 'Gypsy King from Brooklyn' Vitold Lakatosz[26] claimed to be the 'world representative of Roma at the UN'. To this end he printed a business card carrying this title and convinced the NGO office to give him a visitor's pass (see e.g. Nolan 1997).[27] This act was condemned by Hancock, the 'lawful' IRU representative to the UN (Hancock 11 April 2001), yet Lakatosz's claim was not completely unfounded. A document from a meeting of five[28] Presidium members (Lakatosz, Balic, Djuric, Cioaba, and Hancock), circulated amongst IRU members, lists Lakatosz as one of eighteen presidium members of the Romani congress who were elected at the Romani Presidium meeting held in Warsaw on 17 October 1989 and approved at the meeting in New York on 20 November 1989. The document says that all of these people are authorized by the International Romani Congress [sic] to ECOSOC UN and to other organizations such as UNESCO and UNICEF. The same document identifies Cioaba (as opposed to Hancock), as the representative of the [International] Romani Union at the UN ECOSOC (Presidium of the Romani Congress, Undated). In addition, according to Hancock's testimony, Lakatosz 'is in possession of documentation indicating that in 1991 he was sold the IRU presidency for several thousand dollars' (Hancock 1999b).

A more serious contention occurred because of the then IRU President Djuric acting unilaterally. In 1993, at a crucial time when the IRU needed to keep a good image in order to receive the requested status upgrade, he intended to replace the elected Hancock by a non-Rom, Pietrosanti from the TRP, as the main representative in New York. Despite having no authority to do so, he entered Pietrosanti as the main representative in New York on the 1993 form for designation of representatives.[29] According to Hancock, the reason for this was that Pietrosanti promised funding and premises located in New York for an IRU office (Hancock 1993a). Upon the protests from other IRU officials who had learned about this act, and upon Hancock's negotiations with the NGO/DIESA Office in New York, Hancock kept his position. Hancock wrote to Farida Ayoub of the NGO Unit, DIESA explaining that Djuric intended to replace him with Pietrosanti which was unacceptable for the following reasons: according to IRU statutes Djuric had no authority to do so, non-Romani persons are not allowed to hold executive positions in the IRU, Pietrosanti was a member of a political party which planned to sponsor the IRU which violates the ECOSOC status requirements, and Pietrosanti lived in Prague, not New York, could not speak Romani, was unfamiliar with Romani culture and history and did not know any of the members of the IRU presidium he intends to head (Hancock 1993a). Hancock also sent a letter detailing his objections directly to Pietrosanti (Hancock 1993b). In 1999, in his resignation letter to the IRU Hancock states that '[n]egotiations in 1993 between the IRU President and Mr. Paolo Pietrosanti of the Transnational Radical Party for that organization to take over the IRU lasted for nearly that whole year, without any consultation whatsoever with presidium members' (Hancock 1999b). Similar problems occurred in 1997 when Djuric decided to designate himself as the main representative to New York and to appoint Judith Latham, a non-Romani employee of Voice of America, who in Hancock's opinion was familiar with neither Romani values nor the UN (Hancock 1993a) as the alternative representative. Apparently Djuric did not even consult Latham about this beforehand. She was embarrassed by his action and had no desire to take the position (Hancock 13 February 2003). In contrast, Hopson claims that Latham resigned from the position after Hopson had explained the situation to her (Lacroix-Hopson 3 April 2001). Unilateral changes in the appointment of representatives and the address of IRU headquarters had been made since the beginning of Djuric's career as the IRU President. Already in 1991, Ayoub inquired about clarification of the questions of IRU representation, stating that the 1991 accreditation form was signed by Jan Cibula as Head Coordinator and Chief Executive Officer and gave Bern as headquarters. Ms. Hopson who is however listed as an alternative representative in New York tells the office that Hancock is now the sole person authorized to represent IRU at the UN and all correspondence should be sent to his address in Texas. While Emil Scuka is listed as Secretary-General with address in Prague, IRU letter requesting re-classification gives headquarters in Belgrade. In addition a letter from the Prague office requests accreditation of Mr. Davis as a UN representative although he was not listed on the 1991 accreditation form (Ayoub 1991). Djuric in response sent a letter asking that all correspondence be sent to Texas to Hancock as the main IRU representative to ECOSOC (Djuric 1991 and 1992). Yet only few months later, 18 July 1992, Djuric wrote to Ayoub again indicating that the headquarters of IRU are neither in Austin nor in Bern but in Berlin which prompted another query from Ayoub (Hancock 1993a). In 1998 Hancock reacted by circulating a letter entitled 'Unauthorized Appointment of IRU United Nations Representative' to all IRU officials (Hancock 1998). Because of these issues he resigned from the IRU a year later (Hancock 1999b), at which point he signed a letter prepared by the IRU stating that he was no longer authorized to represent them at the UN or in any other negotiations (IRU 1999a).

These squabbles have undermined the credibility of the IRU at the NGO office – credibility that the IRU will clearly need to rebuild before applying for the desired upgrade to general consultative status. They also wasted time and energy which could have instead been used on conducting public relations. However, at the same time, it should be noted that such clashes in NGO leadership are common, as NGOs are often headed by charismatic people who tend to become somewhat authoritarian and possessive of their organizations (Willetts 1982: 188). In addition, international NGOs like the IRU are likely to encounter internal conflicts due to the merging of leaders coming from different national traditions (Reinalda and Verbeek 2001: 150).

Providing Technical Assistance to the Special Rapporteurs of the Commission and Subcommission   This opportunity allows Romani activists to establish themselves as experts on Romani issues in official UN circles (Main 1994: Chapter 2, Part IV, A1) and has been used in the following instances. The IRU's application for consultative status claims that they had provided Francesco Capotorti, Special Rapporteur of the Subcommission, with material for his Study on the Rights of Persons Belonging to Ethnic, Religious and Linguistic Minorities (E/CN.4/Sub.2/384), before obtaining a consultative status (UN Doc. E/C.2/1993/R.4/Add.2: 25). However, this is not entirely correct. Capotorti was presented with Puxon's report on Roma (Puxon 1973) but only after his study was completed and discussed by the Subcommission (see p. 40). After this discussion, Capotorti was willing to incorporate small revisions but declined to produce a further study (UN Doc. E/CN.4/Sub.2/SR.795: 14). In addition, he did not easily read English, the only language in which Puxon's report was available at that time (Whitaker 26 February 2003). His report therefore refers to Roma but not on the basis of Puxon's work (see pp. 38–40). He in fact presents no information on Roma in several countries which were covered by Puxon's report.

Since obtaining the status, the IRU has only made one substantial use of this method, when Gheorghe worked with Voyame, the Commission's Special Rapporteur on the situation of the humans right in Romania, in 1990 (see pp. 36–7). This provided the IRU the opportunity to provide evidence of discrimination against the Roma, and thus to establish its expertise on Romani issues within the UN system. Gheorghe was informed about Voyame's work by his colleagues from the International Federation for Human Rights (IFHR) and requested a meeting. Voyame was already familiar with the work of the IRU through previous contact with Cibula in Switzerland (in Voyame's capacity of Director for the Canton Police and Legal Department in Bern (Cibula 1978g)) and was very open and friendly (Gheorghe 4 December 2002). Gheorghe and Voyame met twice in 1990 and once in 1991, and Voyame incorporated the information provided by Gheorghe in two of his reports (UN Doc. E/CN.4/1991/30: 3; UN Doc. E/C.2/1993/R.4/Add.2: 37; Gheorghe 1991a: 5; UN Doc. E/CN.4/1992/28: 2–3). Gheorghe sees this as an important achievement, because the 1991 report not only recognizes particular discrimination against Roma, but is also the first UN document which presents a specific nation-state agenda for dealing with Roma within the framework of both human and minority rights issues (Gheorghe 1991a: 5).

The IRU also claims to have had regular contact with Asbjorn Eide, the Special Rapporteur of the Subcommission charged with preparing the study on possible ways and means of facilitating the peaceful and constructive solution of problems involving minorities, and provided him with information on Roma in accordance with the Resolution 1992/65 (IRU 1993: §15). (See also p. 35.) This contact was mostly restricted to Gheorghe, who met with Eide on several occasions during the meetings of the Commission and Subcommission and provided him with information. In February 1991, he also participated in a seminar in Oslo upon Eide's invitation (Gheorghe 4 December 2002). However, Eide's report does not refer to any materials submitted by the IRU (UN Doc. E/CN.4/Sub.2/1993/34) and does not list them among the NGOs that submitted written materials (UN Doc. E/CN.4/ Sub.2/1993/34/Add.2).

The ERRC has also assisted a Special Rapporteur, actually before it had received consultative status, both directly and indirectly. Glele-Ahanhanzo, the Commission's Special Rapporteur on Contemporary Forms of Racism, Racial Discrimination, Xenophobia, and Related Intolerance, used information published by the ERRC in his 1998 annual report (UN Doc. E/CN.4/1998/79: 13), and then used information received directly from the ERRC in his 1999 annual report (UN Doc. E/CN.4/1999/15: 21–22). His 2000 annual report also incorporates information from the ERRC and the Zentralrat (UN Doc. E/CN.4/2000/16: 11–13). In September 1999, ERRC staff members (Dimitrina Petrova, Veronika Leila Szente and Markus Pape) met with Glele-Ahanhanzo during his field trip to Hungary, the Czech Republic and Romania (ERRC 1999d: 89). During this field trip many other Romani activists also had the opportunity to meet the Rapporteur (see UN Doc. E/CN.4/2000/16/Add.1: 13–19 for the list) and provide him with information which helped determine his conclusions and recommendations about discrimination against Roma (see p. 37). Furthermore, in January 2002 the ERRC submitted a memorandum concerning the right of Roma in Romania to adequate housing to Miloon Kothari, the Commission's Special Rapporteur on adequate housing, before his mission to Romania (ERRC 2002b). Kothari did in fact pay attention to Roma during his mission and acknowledged that he had done so because of a number of submissions he had received on this topic from the civil society, including the ERRC. His report frequently cited the information provided by the ERRC (UN Doc. E/CN.4/2003/5/Add.2: 7, 14–15). (See pp. 37–38.) Reportedly, Hancock also negotiated with the CHR in Geneva and New York about preparing a formal report on the situation of Roma in Europe and North America (Hancock, Undated), but nothing came out of this.

As this overview shows, Romani activists have not been very proactive in targeting UN Special Rapporteurs. The only instance of direct initiative in contacting a relevant Rapporteur was Gheorghe's interaction with Voyame (upon the impetus from a non-Romani NGO). Romani activists have so far not monitored the appointments of UN Special Rapporteurs in order to target them to promote the Romani cause. Perhaps this should be one of the duties of the permanent IRU representatives to the UN. However, as we established above, the majority of the 'permanent' representatives are permanent only on paper and rarely have any contact with the UN. The IRU thus clearly needs a boost to its human and financial resources in order to be able to take a full advantage of its consultative status. The outcome of targeting of Voyame shows that interaction with UN Special Rapporteurs has a strong potential for putting Romani issues on various agendas and is thus a worthwhile endeavour. The targeting of Kothari by the pro-Romani ERRC shows a sign of a new promising trend towards monitoring the appointments of UN Special Rapporteurs on relevant issues for the purposes of providing them with information. Athough the ERRC is well-suited to filling this gap in the IRU's work, given the uneasy relationship between Romani and pro-Romani organizations in general and the IRU and ERRC in particular (see Klímová 2003: 2.3.2 and 7.3.1.1), it is in the IRU's interest to keep pace with the ERRC's efforts to co-operate with the UN Special Rapporteurs.

Participation in ECOSOC NGO Activities   Consultative status also provides the opportunity for co-operation with other NGOs – an opportunity used almost exclusively by Hopson, who was in a sense the only truly *permanent* (regularly attending) IRU representative at the UN. As regular contact is a pre-condition of successful co-operation, Hopson had much more opportunity to utilize her position for co-operation than Romani representatives who appeared in the UN fora only rarely. She was one of the four co-founders of the NGO committee towards the International Year of World's Indigenous People (1993), which worked under the guidance of the CHR in New York. At the Committee's first official meeting at the UN on 13 January 1992, she made two proposals, one of them being for the World's Indigenous Peoples to unite and apply for Observer Status at the UN GA. This request was taken onboard, resulting in the creation of the alternative Permanent Forum for Indigenous Peoples (A Permanent Forum on Indigenous Issues 2000: 1).

Submission of Quadrennial Reports   The IRU's only duty to the ECOSOC is to submit quadrennial reports, a requirement so far only imposed in 1997 and 2001 because they gained the special status in 1993. The first report was submitted after a delay in 1998 (Fedoroff 4 April 2001), while submission of the second was still pending at the end of 2002. Failure to submit this report could lead to suspension or withdrawal of the status (see UN Doc. E/RES/1996/31: Part VIII). It was not possible to review the 1997 quadrennial report because Hancock, the only IRU person in possession of it, was not able to locate the report in his archives and the NGO/DIESA office refused me access. In any case, the fate of this report is curious because, as of February 2003, the report has not appeared among the compilation of quadrennial reports that have been reviewed by the NGO Committee (UN Library UN/SA Reference Team 13 February 2003).

The reasons behind the failure to deliver quadrennial reports boil down to the non-existence of a proper permanent representative to the UN – one who would co-ordinate *all* the interaction between the IRU and the UN and could then prepare reports about it. Instead, when asked to account for the IRU's activities at the UN (for example for the purposes of upgrading its status as mentioned earlier), the IRU representatives have to frantically try to dig up any small evidence of any interaction between any of its members (organizations or individuals) in order to show some activity. Given the fact that the IRU was largely inactive, and therefore has little to show, for the period between 1997 and 2001, perhaps its leaders hope that they can get away with not submitting a report or delaying it sufficiently long to muster some activity in the meantime. But, with Hancock and Gheorghe (the authors of the upgrade report) having left the IRU, the real problem is probably that no one else is willing or able to compile report of its activities.

Formal Access to Human Rights Treaty Bodies and its Utilization by Romani Activists

Another important part of the formal access to the UN system is participation in the work of UN treaties supervisory bodies (see pp. 42–45). During the 1990s NGOs started playing an increasingly important role in the human rights treaty bodies by scrutinizing reports at the nation-state level, providing information to treaty bodies, assisting in the dissemination of information and contributing to the implementation of recommendations by the treaty bodies. Although CRC is the only treaty monitoring body that specifically envisages NGO cooperation (under article 45), all of the other main bodies (CESCR, HRC, CERD and CAT) have developed 'extensive and fruitful relations with NGOs and place the highest value on NGO contributions' (UN Doc. E/AC.70/1994/5).[30] Since 1992 all the human rights treaty body chairpersons have strongly urged all NGOs in the human rights field to provide information to the treaty bodies on a systematic and timely basis. NGO contributions primarily consist of written information about the implementation of the respective instruments in particular countries. NGO information can also be submitted orally. For example, on the basis of written information that they have submitted, the CRC invites NGOs to present oral contributions during the pre-sessional working group which conducts the preliminary review of state party reports. At the CESCR, 'NGOs intervene at each pre-sessional working group as well as during the first afternoon meeting of each session. In addition, NGOs are important contributors to general discussions organized around specific thematic issues by some of the Committees' (UN Doc. E/AC.70/1994/5). While this access enables NGOs to exercise influence, the treaty bodies also benefit from it. For example, in the case of the CRC, pursuant to article 45(b) of the Convention, NGOs assist in implementation through the provision of technical assistance. NGOs also help to sensitize and mobilize public opinion for the promotion and protection of the rights guaranteed in the main international human rights instruments through awareness campaigns and advocacy (UN Doc. E/AC.70/1994/5).

However, this access has not been used by Romani NGOs. In her book, Rooker finds no evidence of information submitted by a Romani NGO to the following monitoring bodies – HRC, CESCR, and CERD – although, since 1992, all of these bodies regularly mention information submitted by NGOs like Amnesty International and Human Rights Watch (Rooker 2002: 370). Since these are the bodies that have discussed Romani issues the most, it is unlikely that Romani NGOs would submit information to the other monitoring bodies, who dealt with Roma less. Indeed, my preliminary research found no evidence of materials submitted to these other monitoring bodies; detailed research is therefore not warranted for the purposes of this book. In fact, the IRU never seriously discussed submitting materials (Hancock 13 February 2003). The reasons for this are probably similar to those identified above in the section on Special Rapporteurs. The IRU representatives are mostly tied up in activities of their organizations at the local and nation-state level and there is no specific IRU person designated with the task of providing information to the UN monitoring bodies. As gathering such information is rather time-consuming and requires qualified staff, the IRU and its member organizations simply do not have the human and financial resources to systematically engage in such work. Fortunately, as of 1998, the pro-Romani ERRC (which has the necessary human and financial resources), *has* taken up the task of providing materials to the UN treaty monitoring bodies. Between 1998 and 2002, it presented country-specific materials to CERD, CRC, CESCR, CAT and HRC. In particular, they were: written statements for CERD (1998 Czech Republic, 1999 Italy, Romania; 2001 Greece, Italy, Ukraine; 2002 Croatia, Moldova, Hungary); written statements for CRC (2002 Ukraine, Poland); written statements for CESCR (2002 Poland, Slovak and Czech Republics); cases for CAT (1998 Hungary and FRY, 1999 FRY, Italy); and cases for HRC (1999 Romania, 2001 Czech Republic, 2002 Hungary).[31] When presented in the form of written statements, these materials usually include recommendations of state actions to be taken, some of which have been incorporated in the resulting UN documents (e.g. the CERD Concluding Observations). In some materials, the ERRC only used cases to illustrate the violations of treaty rights of Roma in specific countries. To date, one of the biggest successes of the ERRC's work with the treaty bodies was the CAT decision, based upon an application filed by the ERRC and Humanitarian Law Center, that the FRY violated several of CAT provisions in the Hajrizi Dzemajl et al. v. the FRY case (CAT/C/29/D/161/2000), concerning a 1995 incident of total destruction of an entire Romani settlement in the town of Danilovgrad, Montenegro. Gloria Jean Garland, ERRC Legal Director, described this as the most important decision ever made by CAT, not just for the Roma, but also for all other victims of human right abuse. In her words:

> [o]n this occasion, the Committee made clear that torture, inhuman and/or degrading treatment or punishment has to be seen in a positive obligations context. States have a duty not only to refrain from such acts themselves, but also to prevent and suppress human rights violations between private individuals as well as to provide redress to victims of abuse perpetrated by non-state actors (ERRC 2003).

Besides submitting written materials, the ERRC attended the relevant CERD sessions in 1998 and 1999 (making an oral presentation on Italy), and on 15 August 2002 it held a joint briefing with the *Hungarian Helsinki Committee* and the *Roma Press Center* on the situation of Roma in Hungary before the CERD (ERRC 1998: 67; ERRC 2002a: 168; ERRC 1999a: 79). Unlike the IRU, the ERRC has thus started to take an active part in the work of the UN treaty monitoring bodies. Again, as pointed out earlier, the question is whether the IRU should be content with this.

Consultative Status and Relations with the Secretariat

The formal access to the Secretariat is regulated in two ways. The ECOSOC status sanctions interactions between the Secretariat and NGOs, while a consultative status with DPI allows NGOs further scope for interaction.

Co-ordination of NGOs in ECOSOC Consultative Status in Relation to the
Secretariat and the IRU's Interaction with the Secretariat

The ECOSOC status enables NGOs to consult with Secretariat officers on matters of mutual interest or concern, upon a request from the NGO or Secretary-General (UN Doc. E/RES/1296 (XLIV): §44; UN Doc. E/RES/1996/31: §65). The Secretariat should also provide NGOs with information and technical support and arrange infor-mal discussions on matters of special interest to NGOs (UN Doc. E/RES/1296 (XLIV): §46; UN Doc. E/RES/1996/31: §67). In recent years, the Secretary-General's meetings with the heads of prominent NGOs have become more and more frequent (Fagot Aviel 1999: 163). The consultative process with the Secretariat is facilitated by the NGO/DIESA which serves as the substantive secretariat of the ECOSOC CONGO, composed of 24 Member States and administering consultative status for NGOs. In addition, the UN Office at Geneva has an NGO Liaison Office which deals with NGO logistics (UN Doc. A/53/170). Lately, the most substantive departments of the Secretariat have appointed one or more NGO liaison officers to facilitate NGO access and communication.[32]

However, the only evidence of interactions between the IRU and Secretariat that I found were letters to and private meetings with the Secretary-General, as now detailed. Besides the already-mentioned letter Waldheim received before the IRU gained consultative status, he received two more letters once the IRU had a status. Cibula wrote to him immediately after the status was conferred in New York to thank him very much for this, to explain some of the international Romani problems, to complain that the IRU was not allowed to deliver a speech during the meeting at which the decision about its status was taken, and to discuss the future financing of the IRU. In this letter, Cibula interpreted the fact that he was not allowed to deliver his speech as discrimination, although he was previously informed by the NGO/DIESA section that he could not be promised the floor because the agenda does not include time for NGO speeches. NGOs are only asked to speak if any questions arise which is impossible to determine before the meeting (Reece 1979). The letter ended with the hope that Waldheim would pay attention to Romani problems in the future and meet with Cibula to discuss them. The letter was preceded by a phone call to Waldheim's Special Secretary Jenzen, who allegedly recommended that Cibula write to Waldheim (Cibula 1979f). A few months later, one of the IRU's Secretaries, Ivanov Gusti, took the liberty of sending Waldheim an appeal to not forget the rights of the Roma and help them. Unfortunately the letter was written in such bad German that it could hardly be taken seriously by the Secretary-General (see Gusti 1979).[33]

The next Secretary-General, Javier Perez de Cuellar, also received two letters. On 12 March 1985, Balic, then IRU President, reportedly wrote asking the UN to inter-vene to support the IRU's claims of obtaining Holocaust war crimes compensation from Germany (Balic 1985: 6).[34] During the 1990 Congress (on 11 April), the IRU Presidium sent Perez de Cuellar another letter, asking him to raise the question of the legal and political status of Roma at the UN, and to put it on the GA agenda with a view to adopting a Roma-specific resolution based on the UN Charter, UDHR, ICERD and Genocide Convention. It stated the resolution should further recognize Roma as a dispersed nation of Indian origin, condemn the unsatisfactory situation of Roma in many countries, call upon member states to consistently apply international human and minority rights standards to the Roma, encourage Romani efforts to

preserve their national identity and encourage states to support them in this endeavour, and to call on Germany to finally provide Holocaust compensations to Romani
victims. In relation to Holocaust reparations, it suggested that alternatively Germany
could provide funds for an international Romani centre to be located in Germany,
Austria or Switzerland. This letter also stated that the current situation of Roma in
many countries is in violation of the minority rights provisions, ICERD and UDHR,
and that the UN should urge member states to help the Romani population to achieve
living and educational standards similar to the rest of the population. It also informed
the Secretary-General that the 1990 Congress adopted a standardized Romani alpha-
bet (enclosed with the letter) and baptized the first Romani primer, proving that Roma
fulfill one of the crucial criteria of a nation – a common language. The letter asked the
Secretary-General to use the powers granted to him to put this item on the GA or at
least ECOSOC agenda, and to allow Romani representatives to speak before these
bodies. It also asked for the IRU to be acknowledged as the sole spokesperson of the
Romani nation at the UN (Djuric et al. 1991). In response, the IRU only received
thanks for the information about the 1990 Congress and wishes of success for their
initiatives. No comment was made on their demands (Perez de Cuellar 1991).

   I found no evidence of letters to the next Secretary-General, Boutros Boutros-
Ghali (1992–1996), which is unsurprising as the IRU was largely inactive during
his time in office. No evidence was found of letters to Kofi Annan (since 1996),
although Annan did have a personal meeting with the IRU President Scuka and
Pietrosanti, his Commissar for Foreign Policy, in 2001. Scuka and Pietrosanti
wanted to explore the possibility of the Romani nation being represented at the UN,
not merely by the IRU as an NGO, as had been the case since 1979, but on equal
terms with other nations, however without becoming a state (UN 2001a). Two of
the crucial questions they posed to Annan were whether the state is still the most
adequate way for the democratic organization of people, and whether the rule of
state was more important than the rule of law (encompassing democracy, liberty,
freedom). They argued that a transnational nation like Roma needs a transnational
rule of law (CNN 2001) and presented Annan with the Declaration of Nation (see
pp. 22–7). They also informed him about a Memorandum of Understanding and
Cooperation that had recently been signed by the IRU and the Ministry of Foreign
Affairs (MFA) of the Czech Republic, which supports the recognition of Roma as a
nation.[35] During the discussion, these IRU representatives described the Romani
nation 'as a colourful and optimistic people living all around the world, its structure
similar to the structure of the United Nations itself' (UN 2001a). According to
Scuka, Annan was well informed about the high level of discrimination and racism
against Roma in many parts of the world, and was particularly familiar with the
situation of Roma in Hungary, which he had visited last June. They felt that Annan
was prepared 'not only to hear the voice of the Roma people, but also to help them'
(UN 2001a), when the time is right (Scuka 10 September 2001) (see also p. 99).
They were also successful in convincing Annan that Scuka is '*the* leader of the
Romani people', despite this being by no means undisputed among Romani
activists at large. Addressing the NGO Forum at the WCAR on 30 August 2001,
Annan stated that he received 'the leader of the Romani people' at UN headquarters
in New York (UN Off the Cuff 2001).

   The lack of interaction between the IRU and the Secretariat, apart from targeting
the Secretary General, is probably the result of the IRU's need to prioritise due to

insufficient human and financial resources. Its representatives thus targeted the highest level directly but, with the exception of achieving a meeting with Kofi Annan, to no avail. Going through the lower levels of the Secretariat might in fact have been more productive as the administrators themselves can be powerful allies for NGOs (for more on this see Chapter 6). The lack of any constructive response to the IRU's letters from the Secretary Generals might also be due to the political nature of the IRU's demands because, as Willetts suggests, interaction between the Secretariat and NGOs is meant to be non-political in nature (1996: 44). Their one success in obtaining an audience with Annan was a result of the successful exploitation of a favourable configuration of power by the IRU representatives, suggesting that they are now learning to use their allies better (for details see Chapter 6).

DPI Consultative Status and the IRU

The formal consultative status with the DPI was authorized by ECOSOC resolution 1297 (XLIV) of 27 May 1968. Until then the DPI was only encouraged to assist those NGOs interested in spreading information about the UN (GA resolution 13 (I) of 1946). The conditions of eligibility for consultative status are that the NGO shares the ideals of the UN Charter, solely operates on a not-for-profit basis, has demonstrated an interest in UN issues and proven its ability to reach large or specialized audiences (such as educators, media representatives, policy makers and the business community), and has the commitment and means to conduct effective information programmes about UN activities. The purpose of this association for the DPI is really to use NGOs as local distributors of UN publications and other information products to audiences around the world (Thorup-Hayes, Undated). In return, the DPI/NGO Section offers NGOs a number of services (for details see Klimova 2003: 172, footnote 179). Closer collaboration between NGOs and the DPI takes place through the 18-member NGO elected representative body – the DPI/NGO Executive Committee, which acts in an advisory and liaison capacity to channel information and to represent the interests of NGOs associated with the DPI (DPI NGO Section, About Us; DPI NGO Section, NGOs and the United Nations Department of Public Information).

The IRU obtained a consultative status with the DPI shortly after gaining the roster ECOSOC status (Hancock 13 February 2003), but used few of the services and only for a short time. While Hopson was active for the IRU, she was attending weekly NGO briefings, yearly conferences and regularly checking material at the DPI/NGO Section. She also supported, in the IRU's name, the manifestations of the ECOSOC on Peace and the Environment in 1986 and 1987 (Main 1994: Chapter 2, Part IV, A1c). Since 2000, the IRU's consultative status with the DPI has been symbolic, as no permanent representative resides in NY and participates in the work of the DPI. The DPI/NGO directory still lists Hancock as the contact person for the IRU,[36] who claims that this status (as well as the one for UNICEF) was personal to him and thus lapsed when he resigned (Hancock 1998). The DPI still sends him all the correspondence, which he is no longer authorized to answer (Hancock 13 February 2003). Perhaps the DPI will finally realize this when it finishes its recent review process of the NGOs associated with it (see Thorup-Hayes, Undated), and finds it does not have the requested report about the IRU's work. It remains to be seen whether the ERRC's co-operation with the DPI will be more productive. So far the ERRC's main participation was attending the 2002 annual DPI/NGO conference at the UN head-quarters in New York (9–11 September 2002) under the name 'Rebuilding Societies Emerging from Conflict: A Shared Responsibility' (ERRC 2002a: 168).

Consultative Status with UN Children's Fund (UNICEF) and its Utilization by Romani Activists

As of 1950, UNICEF has been granting consultative status to NGOs that engage in child-related activities and hold ECOSOC consultative status. The UNICEF status allows them to be represented as observers at meetings of the Executive Board, and, with the agreement of the Board's Chairperson, to deliver oral and written statements on agenda items. UNICEF has also had rich operational relations with NGOs (see Klimova 2003: 173, footnote 188 or UN Doc. A/53/170).

The IRU gained consultative status with UNICEF in 1987 (Lacroix-Hopson 1993), with Ian Hancock as their representative. Although UNICEF headquarters in New York confirmed that the IRU has had consultative status with them, they maintained that they have no records of any co-operation (Yoshida 10 January 2003). This is probably partly because the IRU has not been taking advantage of its right to participate in the meetings of the Executive Board. This book therefore has to rely on the information provided by Romani activists themselves.

According to their information, before gaining the consultative status, the IRU had prepared a study about Romani children as a contribution to the International Year of the Child, 1979 (UN Doc. E/C.2/1993/R.4/Add.2: 23). In 1987, Hancock's report on the plight of Romani children appeared in *Action for Children*, the UNICEF's main periodical, in both French and English (Hancock 1987a and 1987b). Allegedly he was also on the editorial board of this periodical.[37] The IRU also claims to have regularly provided information packages to UNICEF agencies in the USA and other countries and to have been very active in various UNICEF working groups and other meetings, working for the observance of the ICRC (through the NGO Committee on UNICEF, Working Group on the Rights of the Child) and with the UNICEF special programme (UN Doc. E/C.2/1993/R.4/Add.2: 36). In September 1987 it co-sponsored the UNICEF Conference on ICRC in Lignano Sabbiadoro, Italy (Lacroix-Hopson 1993). This event was attended by both Hopson and Kappenberger (Lacroix-Hopson 1992b). The latter described it as 'a great success and an unforgettable event, […] with the IRU […] acting for the children of the planet,' creating international law (Kappenberger 31 January 2003).

In 1990 the IRU prepared a field-trip-based report on the situation of Romani children in Romania (see p. 133). In the mid-1980s, UNICEF financed an issue of *Chavrikano Lil*, the first children's Romani language publication, which was then suspended in 1985 after just three issues. In 1994 the First World Conference of Romani Editors-in-Chief held in Belgrade from 17–21 December resolved to ask UNICEF to fund the renewed edition. However, the Open Society Fund has instead financed the new edition of this magazine from 1996 (Luksic-Orlandic, Undated). The IRU branches in Romania and the Czech and Slovak Republics have presented projects on the situation of Roma to UNICEF offices in those countries (IRU 1993). For example, in Romania Romani CRISS co-operated with UNICEF on publishing several books for Romani children (Courthiade 18 March 2003). Also, in many countries, the UNICEF National Committees co-operate with local Romani NGOs (see e.g. UNICEF Albania, Undated). The CEE/CIS/Baltic States regional UNICEF office supports the ERRC's publications by providing articles and input relevant to the region, and disseminates the ERRC's publications among country offices and UNICEF partners (Rajandran 9 December 2002).

In general, the pattern of co-operation between UNICEF and Romani NGOs is that at the nation-state level Romani NGOs often approach UNICEF for support at the same time as UNICEF offices actively seek co-operation with Roma. At the regional level, however, recently the initiative for co-operation has mostly come from UNICEF (Cohen 15 January 2003). In preparation for the UN GA Special Session on Children (8–10 May 2002), UNICEF called on Romani NGOs to take a number of steps, such as joining in the preparation of nation-state reports to ensure and facilitate the inclusion of the situation of Romani children, and organizing and attending meetings and cultural events related to the session (for the full list of these suggestions see Rajandran 2000), but none of this happened.

Nevertheless, some co-operation related to the Special Session did occur between the ERRC and UNICEF. The ERRC was already involved in UNICEF activities in 1999 when it presented Romani rights issues at a UNICEF conference on the CRC in Florence. In early 2001 it attended another UNICEF conference on children's rights in Geneva and contributed to the Roma-related section (ERRC 1999b: 66; ERRC 2001a: 106). As a result of this co-operation, in June 2001 UNICEF supported the participation of Refika Mustafic, a Romani delegate of the ERRC, in the third substantive session of the preparatory committee (PrepCom3) for the 2002 UN GA Special Session on Children, taking place in New York (Rajandran 9 December 2002). Upon Mustafic's initiative, the CEE/CIS Regional Caucus of PrepCom3 discussed the importance of education for Romani women and girls, the education of parents, and the involvement of young Roma in programmes for social inclusion, for these were serious regional issues invisible in the Outcome Document (NGO Committee on UNICEF 2001). Mustafic also attended two regional preparatory meetings (9–10 April 2001 in Bucharest and 15–18 May 2001 in Berlin), yet their outcome documents do not mention Roma (Child Rights Information Network 2001; ERRC 2001c: 104).

Mustafic had left the ERRC by the time of the Special Session, so they sent Larry Olomoofe, a non-Romani staff member, instead (see ERRC 2002c: 121). Olomoofe was not very impressed with the arrangements for the Special Session. He recalls that the costs of attending were too high for Romani NGOs, and therefore none attended. Due to post-11 September security issues, many sessions that involved governmental delegates were closed, with only a few selected NGOs invited. The rest of the NGOs (over 3800 in number), were left to attend fringe meetings, none of which had the plight of Romani children on their agenda (Olomoofe 16 January 2003). According to Mary Robinson, 'the voices of Romani and Traveller children were heard' at the special session (Ulster University 2002) yet Olomoofe did not confirm this information (Olomoofe 16 January 2003). Save the Children Scotland however discussed the draft of the Special Session document 'A world fit for children' with over hundred children in Scotland, including Travellers and Gypsies, during April and May 2001. Their ideas were transmitted to the Special Session by a young Scottish delegate attending the session as a part of the UK governmental delegation. In their comments, the Traveller children emphasized the need for adults to listen to them, and having a safe environment without discrimination and bullying, decent living conditions, and friendly yet professional teachers (see Save the Children Scotland 2001). The ERRC's main aim for the session was 'to raise the profile of Roma rights among the wider international community' (Olomoofe 16 January 2003). According to Olomoofe, the awareness of the plight of the Roma amongst the international activists present at the session was rather poor. Many (including UNICEF officials) had never heard of Roma. The ERRC's 'ultimate goal was to have the Roma rights issue become an area of activity that involved the UN and their considerable resources' (Olomoofe 16 January 2003). Olomoofe therefore used his attendance at the session to lobby a number of UN officials (mainly UNDP), human rights lawyers and other NGOs to getthem more involved with Romani issues. He also handed out a document entitled 'Barriers to the education of Roma in Europe' which the ERRC had published specifically for the event. The most significant outcome of his lobbying was that the UN Works Department of DPI recently incorporated the educational segregation of Romani children in the CEE region into a series of UNICEF televisual documentaries on themes affecting children globally.[38] The final document produced by the Special Session made no specific mention of Romani children, although it did, for example, mention indigenous children (UN Doc. A/S-27/19/Rev.1: Annex). Within this document, Romani children were considered to be simply 'children of minorities,' which is consistent with UNICEF's long-term approach to Roma. Nevertheless, regarding nation-state commitments, Romania pledged to offer free meals to stimulate school attendance by Romani children (NGO Committee on UNICEF 2002).

As a result of its involvement in the Special Session campaign, Romani activists were offered membership in the NGO/UNICEF Regional Network for Children in CEE, CIS and Baltic States. This network was initiated with UNICEF's support as a follow-up activity to the Special Session, and was officially inaugurated on 29 June 2002 in Sarajevo (Regional NGO Network for Children 2002a). Its mission is 'to strengthen and facilitate cooperation for children's rights and well-being, in the framework of the [...] [I]CRC' (Regional NGO Network for Children 2002c). Its first campaign 'Leave no Child Out' aims to address the issues of poverty, intolerance and exclusion of children and young people in the region (Regional NGO Network for Children 2002a). Specific country and regional plans were to emerge in 2003 (Rajandran 9 December 2002). In this campaign, the network decided to treat Roma as a specific focus group because they face even more discrimination and social exclusion than other minorities, and are increasingly placed in educational and other institutions on the basis of faulty intelligence testing (Regional NGO Network for Children 2002c). In addition, according to the network's statutes, Romani NGOs are offered a membership with the right to elect a co-ordinator to represents them on the network's executive body – the council, additionally composed of twenty-seven representatives of nation-state NGO networks (one for each country), one UNICEF representative and one representative each for International NGOs (INGOs) working in the region and for sub-regional NGOs respectively (Regional NGO Network for Children 2002b).

During the preparatory meetings of the network, two representatives from the ERRC expressed interest in participating. Their interest continued to the third meeting, where Mustafic attended, but after this neither she nor anyone else from ERRC answered the networks further invitations for co-operation (Nistorescu 24

January 2003).[39] The network therefore invited Hristo Kyuchukov (Nistorescu 24 January 2003), the current General Secretary of the IRU, to the last preparatory meeting in December 2001. Kyuchukov promised to assist the interim Chair of the network in drafting documentary requirements for the inaugural Regional Council of the network, and the IRU was to be the interim focal point for Romani NGOs within the network (Little 2001: 7–8). However, he then ignored most of the network's correspondence and eventually was not able to guarantee his future involvement, declining participation in the network launch in June 2002. The network is therefore still looking for a Romani NGO that would be able and willing to take a leadership role with other Romani NGOs in the region and the seat at the network's council (Nistorescu 24 January 2003).

Conclusion

The chapter described the ways in which Romani activists have been trying to 1) establish themselves as actors in world politics through interaction with the UN system and 2) bring about agenda, discursive and procedural/institutional changes, using formal access provided by the UN. Gaining UN membership, or at least a permanent observer status at the GA, remains the ultimate goal but no official action has yet been taken within the UN fora towards achieving it. Yet, the IRU has already achieved two degrees of ECOSOC NGO consultative status, as well as consultative status with the DPI and UNICEF, which guarantee it the right to have its voice heard by ECOSOC subsidiary organs. Upon receiving the consultative status, the IRU took some advantage of the associated rights, although internal factors (such as lack of human and financial resources and experience) prevented it from taking full advantage. Their permanent presence at the UN headquarters was generally rather symbolic and/or carried out by non-Romani allies whose utility for the Romani cause was limited. Moreover, the IRU's attendance at UN meetings and participation in NGO activities was sporadic and their technical advice to UN Special Rapporteurs was limited to just a few instances. It can be argued that until the IRU's status was upgraded in 1993, it did not have an automatic right to attend all meetings, yet it did not attend even the majority of meetings related to human and minority rights for which it had or could have easily obtained access. Was this due to the IRU's limited resources, as explained earlier (pp. 18–19), or simply due to the lack of interest? While some of the IRU's representatives believe that the inactivity was largely a result of the lack of resources (Hancock 13 February 2003), others admit that attendance of UN meetings was never the IRU's priority (Gheorghe 4 December 2002).

Overall, the IRU did not use all the access opportunities offered by the consultative status. For example, until the WCAR in 2001 (see Klimova 2003: Chapter 7), Romani activists never took the opportunity of participating in any significant UN conferences. Similarly Romani activists took no advantage whatsoever of the access to human rights treaty monitoring bodies. This void was eventually filled by the pro-Romani ERRC in 1998. Since these monitoring bodies could well be those with the most power to improve the situation of the Roma, this suggests that Romani activists have been more interested in promoting the IRU's status within the UN (as the main representative of Roma), than actually fighting for the improvement of the conditions of the people they claim to represent. This quest for status is, however, not so surprising for at least two reasons. Firstly, it comes from the 'new Romani elites' which see it as an opportunity to finally achieve some prestige in a non-Romani world that had previously marginalized them. Secondly, the UN is indeed 'an institution where many people are highly concerned with questions of status' (Willetts 2000: 191). Thus one could argue that achieving a high status needs to be a priority for further action when resources are limited. Yet, equally, one could argue that precisely because the resources of Romani activists are very limited, they should use them towards more practical goals. At the same time, the IRU has not even done enough to promote its status. For example, it did not use the chance of making recommendations to the open-ended working group reviewing the procedures for consultations with NGOs to ask for enhanced co-operation opportunities (see UN Doc. E/AC.70/1994/5/Add.1). In addition, the IRU has been rather lax about fulfilling its only duty to the ECOSOC – submission of quadrennial reports – which could lead to suspension or even withdrawal of the consultative status. Since the IRU's priority seems to be gaining an ever-more prestigious status with the UN, this attitude is counterproductive. A possible explanation for this attitude is that not only does the UN not see Romani activists as important enough to accord them the status they desires, Romani activists also does not see the UN as important enough to follow its rules when that involves too much effort. The conclusion emerging from my understanding of the dynamics of global Romani activism is that the UN status has so far been sought primarily as means of prestige which can then be used during lobbying at other fora – nation-state and European. For this purpose, being seen and heard at the UN is not essential; being associated with it is enough.

The IRU has also not been very successful in co-operating with the Secretariat. It wrote to Secretary-Generals a number of times, but never managed to convince them to take an interest in their demands and discuss them further. Only in 2001 did a Secretary-General (Annan), meet IRU representatives, but he resorted to the format of a ceremonial visit rather than concrete political negotiations. This meeting nevertheless served the functions of encouraging Romani activists to continue their work, seeing that the Secretary-General was sympathetic to the goals of the Romani people, and of increasing publicity. The rights associated with the DPI status were only partially utilized by the IRU, and only for a short time. Similarly, the IRU has not used its right to attend meetings of the UNICEF Executive Board and deliver statements and failed to establish significant operational relations with UNICEF. This suggests that its current status still allows it to pursue a number of avenues which have not been tried. Actions speak louder than words; perhaps Romani activists should devote some more of its energy to concrete co-operation with the UN as opposed to constantly seeking higher recognition. This could actually more successfully facilitate their goal of becoming important actors in world politics, able to influence UN agenda, discourse, and procedures/organization.

When we compare the results of more than two decades of interaction between the IRU and the UN with the few years of interaction between the pro-Romani ERRC and the UN, the ERRC's actions already show much more potential. The ERRC's approach is more systematic, specifically targeting the treaty monitoring bodies and the Special Rapporteurs with concrete complaints and recommendations. While the ERRC clearly has much better human and financial resources, it also has a more focused and practical agenda. Its work could in fact be complementary to the work of the IRU if the IRU could see the ERRC more as a partner, rather than a competitor, for the post of the main organization speaking on behalf of the Roma (for more see Chapter 6).

Based on the findings of this chapter, links can be established only between three actions leading to changes in the UN system (identified in Chapter 3) and the actions of Romani and pro-Romani activists – Voyame's, Glele-Ahanhanzo's and Kothari's reports, which in turn lead to three discursive and three agenda developments (see Table 3.1). The discursive developments relate to acknowledgement of violations of human rights of Roma in Romania (including right to housing), the Czech Republic and Hungary, and recommendations for the governments to address them. The agenda developments are the incorporation of Roma into the agendas for addressing contemporary forms of racism, racial discrimination, xenophobia and related intolerance and for monitoring human rights of Roma in Romania (both in general and in particular regarding to housing). Romani activists tried to instigate a more significant agenda change – putting Roma on the UN GA agenda as a global issue – but in vain. The IRU also claims to have influenced Eide's and Capotorti's reports but the evidence here is weak. In terms of the influence of UN discourse on the discourse of global Romani activism, we can see that the IRU's discourse was initially very influenced by its desire to co-operate with the UN, frequently referring to the spirit of the UN Charter in speeches and documents. The IRU has also been trying to present the Romani nation as a global UN-like entity. The mutual influence of the discourses of the UN and Romani activists will be analysed further in Chapter 6.

The chapter also shows that the organizational structure of the main global Romani organization, the IRU, was strongly influenced by the rules that govern co-operation with the ECOSOC. As co-operation with the UN was one of the main goals for which the IRU was created, when so doing the IRU followed point by point (at least in theory if not always in practice) the UN guidelines for eligibility for NGO ECOSOC consultative status. Also, the most recent transformation of the IRU into a government-like body reflects the desire to gain a seat in the GA either as a fully-fledged member or at least as an observer; a privilege that is reserved only for lawful, or at least embryonic, governments or intergovernmental organizations. On the other hand, the lobbying of Romani and pro-Romani activists at the UN cannot be clearly linked to any of the procedural/institutional changes in the UN system (see Table 3.2). The IRU's main aim of restructuring the UN so that it could receive the status of a non-territorial nation or non-territorial state has not yet been discussed in the UN fora, although the IRU claims that the idea resonated sympathy from the current Secretary-General.

Notes

1 Passy (1999: 153) incorrectly states that no formal NGO access to the Secretariat exists.
2 Note, however, that the degree of access granted varies according to the nature and functions of each observer (see Koenig 1991; Simma 2002: 249).
3 At times, some of the IRU's officers, such as Marcel Courthiade, have claimed that the IRU gained such a seat in 1993 along with the ECOSOC special consultative status (see Cortiade and Duka 1994: 35 and RANELPI 2001). Similarly, Cara Feys states that the IRU has a seat and voting rights in the ECOSOC (1997). Both claims are incorrect and probably result from misunderstandings of the complicated, differentiated and multi-layered structure of UN rights and privileges.

4 For a brief description of the development of these rules see Klimova 2003: 141, footnote 26.
5 Requirement no. 4 was added only in the latter resolution. Until 1996, consultative status was reserved for international NGOs (with occasional exceptions) (see UN Doc. E/RES/1296 (XLIV), §7 and 9), but since 1996 nation-state NGOs, especially from developing countries and countries in transition, have been encouraged to apply for consultative status (see UN Doc. E/RES/1996/31, §5, 7 and 8).
6 Some of the earlier organizations had also tried to play the UN game by using the UN language in order to increase their chances of gaining consultative status. For example, when the IRC prepared a report on the situation of Roma in Europe, it claimed to be doing so as a 'part of its work for Human Rights Year' (IRC, Undated). Some academics argue that the need for 'following the rules of the game' presented a dilemma for Romani leaders who had to adopt to 'modernity' by redefining Romani identity, political organization and practices in order to integrate into the modern political society. As a trade-off, this modern elite became somewhat separated from what are believed to be traditional aspects of Romani culture and political identity (see e.g. Main 1994; Liegeois 1976). The efforts of Romani political mobilization have consequently been hindered by the disputes among the 'traditional' and 'modern' leaders, questioning each other's legitimacy, and by the lack of popular support for the modern elite (see e.g. Mirga and Gheorghe 1997). While this modernity/tradition dialectic is certainly an interesting aspect to explore (drawing parallels with the experiences of indigenous, religious and other groups), it is not the aim of this book.
7 The name Romani Union itself was only approved at the meeting of the 1978 Congress Presidium on 12 April (one day after the Congress) (World Romani Congress Activities of its Presidium 1980: 29).
8 Continuity with the IRC would actually have given it an even earlier founding date than 1971 (see Klimova 2003: §2.3.1.4).
9 IRU (then using the name World Romani Congress) forwarded its statutes to the NGO Liaison in Geneva to get advice on whether they were acceptable (Puxon 1977a). See also Puxon 1977b.
10 This information is based on Main's interview with Eliane Lacroix-Hopson.
11 Claimed to be half-Mongolian, half-Romani (Puxon 1986: 17; Rishi 1992: 115). For obituaries remembering Brynner's life and involvement with Roma see Hancock 1986; Puxon 1986; Sharma 1986.
12 Another source states that Cibula met Waldheim personally to discuss the status of the application (World Romani Congress Activities of its Presidium 1980: 32). The earlier version of the story is however more likely. This was not the first time Cibula wrote to Waldheim. Prior to the 1978 Congress, he wrote to him explaining that the IRU (note that he uses this name although it was only officially approved in April 1978, see endnote 7) hoped to obtain consultative status and planned to hold the Congress. In connection with this, he asked whether the Secretary-General could attend the Congress and whether the UN could help, firstly by providing rooms for this congress or future meetings and secondly by ensuring that Roma in all countries were allowed to attend the congress and establish organizations. The letter also included some details about Roma and their organizational plans (Cibula 1978d). Within a few days an answer was received pointing out which UN offices the IRU needed to contact with these requests. Given other official engagements, the Secretary-General declined the invitation to the Congress. The replying letter nevertheless thanked Cibula for his information about the Congress, wished him the best of luck and informed him that his first two requests had been passed onto the relevant offices in the UN (Myahofer-Gruenbuehel 1978a). Cibula responded with a request for at least a written statement from the Secretary-General that could be read at the Congress (1978e). Again in little time, his Special Assistant replied that unfortunately such greeting messages are only issued for occasions officially connected with the UN (Myahofer-Gruenbuehe 1978b).

13 He also wrote to the NGO Liaison office in Geneva several times, informing them about the possibility of the IRC trying to ruin the IRU's application (see Cibula 1978g; Cibula 1979a; Cibula 1979b).

14 Jan Cibula, Menyhert Lakatos, John Tene, Norbert Herzog, Romani Rose, Stevica Nikolic, Gusti Ivanov and others (World Romani Congress Activities of its Presidium 1980: 34).

15 However, I found no evidence of such invitation. Cibula probably used this wording just to give his delegation more importance. In the same manner, in his correspondence he at times calls the NGO office Waldheim's office.

16 Main incorrectly states that, as a rule, each NGO file has to be presented by a UN member state as a precondition for obtaining status, and therefore the IRU had to enlist India's support (Main 1994: Chapter 2, Part III, B2).

17 NGOs with general or special status can have observers at all meetings, those on roster only at those concerned with matters within their field of competence (see UN Doc. E/RES/1296 (XLIV): §22 and 28 and UN Doc. E/RES/1996/31: §25 and 35).

18 According to both the 1968 and 1996 resolutions rules regarding statements were as follows: NGOs with general and special status can present written statements directly to the ECOSOC and to its subsidiary bodies, while those on roster can do so only upon request. Only those with general and exceptionally with special status can be heard directly by the ECOSOC. Both those with general and special status can be heard by the ECOSOC subsidiary bodies, while roster can do so only upon request from the subsidiary body and recommendation from the Secretary-General (see UN Doc. E/RES/1296 (XLIV): §23, 25, 29 and 31 and UN Doc. E/RES/1996/31: §30–32 and 36–38).

19 Such a task is not reserved for NGOs with a status (UN 2001b), but the status facilitates contact with the Rapporteurs during meetings of the subsidiary bodies.

20 As a rule, until 1996 NGOs could participate only upon UN invitation (see UN Doc. E/RES/1296 (XLIV): §34). Thus, NGO participation in conferences was determined on a case-by-case basis for each conference (UN Doc. A/53/170).

21 It was impossible to verify this participation in UN records because the CERD documents issued in relation to these sessions do not include a list of participating NGOs (see e.g. CERD/C/SR. 863–888, 889–913, and 914–937 and A/45/18 and A/46/18).

22 Before 1986, the IRU did not have a permanent representative in NY (Hancock 13 February 2003).

23 Hopson however claims that Kappenberger was still the IRU's representative in Geneva in 1992 (Lacroix-Hopson 1992b).

24 I also had this impression from personal oral and written communications with Hopson. For example, her letter to Carole Kalafatic of 3 April 2001 (of which she gave me a copy during her interview) states several incorrect facts such as that the 1971 Congress took place in Paris not in London, organized by the RU (instead of the IRC); that Yul Brynner was the IRU President until his death (he was only Honorary President); and that the IRU disintegrated in 1999 and that it no longer has the right to representation in the UN because this was personal to her and Hancock.

25 In her interview with me as well as the letter mentioned in endnote 24, she insisted that the recent meeting of Romani representatives in Quito in the WCAR framework and the documents they produced (see Klimova 2003: §7.2.2 and §8.2.3) are all fabrications because Roma are very good at acting. She claimed that the organizations these leaders claimed to represent do not exist and that they were distorting facts by claiming e.g. that the 1971 Congress took place in London, not Paris. Instead she was the one with the wrong facts.

26 In one IRU document Lakatosz is listed as President of the American Coalition of Lovara Roma and Eastern Regional Director of the U.S. Romani Union and it is claimed that he was elected the President of the US IRU (Bencsi 1989: 1 and 5).

27 Similarly, Jimmy Marks, another 'traditional' American Romani leader, carries similar business cards with his own name (Hancock 13 February 2003).

28 The minimum number needed for the Presidium to be allowed to produce official documents (see Statutes of the Romani Union 1991: §12).

29 I have a copy of this form from personal archives of Nicolae Gheorghe. This form also designates Djuric as an additional representative to Geneva and main representative to Vienna. The main representative to Geneva is Emil Scuka and the alternative representative to Vienna is Alla Savitsh.

30 The NGO access to the various treaty bodies has however differed throughout the time (for details see Klimova 2003: 64, footnote 151).

31 All these submissions can be viewed at the ERRC's website, http://www.errc.org, under the heading 'legal advocacy'.

32 These informal arrangements vary greatly from department to department and from issue to issue (for details see Klimova 2003: 168, footnote 164). However, I found no evidence of this Liaison Service being useful to Romani activists.

33 The copy of this letter says that the original was handed to the Secretary-General's secretary on 20 July 1979.

34 I was unable to obtain a copy of the actual letter to the Secretary-General.

35 It explicitly says that the MFA 'does not see the request for the general recognition of the Roma nation as set by the 5th IRU World Congress as a problem of principal nature' (Memorandum of Understanding 2001).

36 See the IRU entry in DPI NGO Section, *The Directory of NGOs associated with DPI.*

37 It was not possible to verify this information as the periodical does not list members of the editorial board.

38 The Romani series was to be broadcast in spring of 2003 on the Bravo kids channel in Europe (Olomoofe 16 January 2003).

39 The silence from the ERRC was probably due to the fact that Mustafic had left the organization and all her activities were not immediately fully transferred to her successor. As a result of her early involvement in activities related to the Special Session, Mustafic was also invited as a speaker for the panel on 'Equal opportunities for youth' at the First Regional Forum on Youth: Security, Opportunity and Prosperity, organized by UNECE (UN Economic Commission for Europe), ILO, OHCHR, UNAIDS (the Joint UN Programme on HIV/AIDS), UNICEF, UNDP, and UN DIESA between 26–28 August 2002 in Palais de Nations in Geneva (UNECE 2002). At this time, she was no longer working for the ERRC but was still involved in Romani activism.

Chapter 5

Interaction with the UN System Using Informal Strategies

This chapter concentrates on the second component of POS – the prevailing strategies traditionally adopted by authorities towards political contention, which define their degree of inclusiveness towards non-state actors. It describes and analyses the prevailing informal UN strategies of inclusiveness and their utilization by Romani activists. The secondary aim of this focus on informal strategies is to allow us to document the beginnings and the extent of attempts for interaction with the UN system, which could not be portrayed in Chapter 4.

The Prevailing Informal Strategies of Inclusiveness

These strategies considerably broaden the political opportunities provided by the UN to NGOs. The UN administration has been relatively favourable to the intervention of NGOs. It has 'facilitated access to its political structure by broadening the categories of organizations that can claim consultative status and making their lobbying easier once they have been admitted to the UN' (Passy 1999: 155). It has also granted consultative status in some policy areas to organizations which are not transnational, and has allowed NGOs to participate in conferences formally closed to them (e.g. 1992 Rio World Conference and WCAR).[1] The UN administration also facilitates the work of NGOs, for example by offering financial support to some organizations who could otherwise not afford to attend UN commissions and working groups, by improving communication and information flow between UN-related organizations through publishing their newsletters, by giving administrative support for NGOs through special offices (e.g. for translations and typing of reports), and by offering them spaces for meetings, networking and preparation of common statements (Passy 1999: 155).

Some states have started to rely on NGOs when drafting texts that they formally advance. They either consult NGOs during the drafting, or even ask NGOs to draft the text themselves (Fagot Aviel 1999: 158). These informal strategies have enabled NGOs to go beyond the limits of their consultative status by drafting resolutions and universal declaration proposals and other types of UN norms, helping to set agendas and influencing the work of UN world conferences through preparatory processes (Passy 1999: 157; see also Klimova 2003: Chapter 7). The UN NGO Liaison Service has increasingly financed the participation of NGOs (especially those from developing countries) in UN conferences and fora such as meetings of the ECOSOC Commissions (UN Doc. A/53/170).

Although NGOs have no formal access to the GA, practice has evolved to allow a certain degree of informal participation by them in the work of the GA's Main Committees and several of its subsidiary bodies. For instance, NGOs participate in the work of Special Committees (namely the Special Political and Decolonization Committee (Fourth Committee) and the Special Committee on the Situation with regard to the Implementation of the Declaration on the Granting of Independence to Colonial Countries and Peoples) in their capacity as petitioners. This access is based upon receiving permission from the Committee to either address it or otherwise participate in its work (UN Doc. A/53/170). Since its nineteenth special session, the GA also accredits large numbers of NGO as observers. Some NGO representatives addressed the GA at the plenary meetings of its nineteenth special session, held in June 1997, to review the implementation of Agenda 21. At the twentieth special session of the GA, held in June 1998, NGOs were invited to make an input into the draft guiding principles of drug demand reduction adopted by the GA. This included many NGOs not associated with either the ECOSOC or DPI but having working relationships with, or being listed in the directory of, the UN International Drug Control Programme (UN Doc. A/53/170). Although at the moment such participation only occurs on an *ad hoc* basis, more and more proposals are being discussed within the UN for permitting NGO representatives to sit on main committees and subcommittee meetings, receive official documents and make oral interventions (Mingst and Karns 2000: 66). Passy explains that this inclusive attitude comes from the UN's need for NGOs practical grassroots knowledge, for diffusion of normative frameworks elaborated within UN political structure through NGOs and for legitimization of its work (for details see 1999: 155–157). In other words, the role of NGOs in the UN system is increasing due to the variety of useful roles they perform. They are a 'key source of information and technical expertise on a wide variety of international issues from the environment to human rights,' often obtaining grassroots information unavailable to governments (Mingst and Karns 2000: 66). They advocate for specific policies, and provide alternative channels for political participation by mobilizing the public. They are critical for distributing assistance in disaster relief and to refugees, and for other operational tasks as well as monitoring the implementation of human rights and environmental norms (Mingst and Karns 2000: 66).

The Utilization of the Informal Strategies of Inclusiveness by Romani Activists

I found no evidence that Romani activists benefited from any of the above-described informal strategies of inclusiveness, except in relation to participation in world conferences (considered in detail in Klimova 2003: Chapter 7) and the UN GA Special Session (see pp. 83–8). There are two possible explanations for this. First of all, they were probably unaware that they could receive financial and technical help from UN administration, as their requests for such help were never answered positively (see e.g. pp. 93–99). Instead they relied on other NGOs for technical help, computer access or office space (Gheorghe 4 December 2002). The second explanation relates to Riggs and Plano's cautious note that the influence of NGOs within the UN does not depend solely on the degree of access. To exercise influence, NGOs must provide some concrete assistance to UN bodies in executing their programmes, or have good standing with nation-state governments, or provide high quality and timely research (Riggs and Plano 1999: 48–49). As the IRU's concrete assistance to UN bodies has been very minimal, their standing with nation-state governments is only favourable in a couple of countries and also usually temporary, and, although their research might be timely, it is usually not highly professional, they do not enjoy significant influence at the UN and therefore are less likely to benefit from informal privileges (see pp. 137–140).

Nevertheless, Romani activists did engage in a number of informal strategies to increase its access to the UN system. The following sections describe three situations in which they utilized informal strategies. First, prior to the IRU obtaining the consultative status, informal strategies were the only means for the access of Romani activists to the UN. Second, due to the limitations of the formal access facilitated by the consultative status described earlier (p. 69), Romani activists continued to engage in a number of informal strategies, in order to pursue goals beyond the limits of this status. Third, Romani activists were limited to using informal strategies within bodies in which either the IRU had not gained consultative status, and hence was not accorded formal access, or no consultative status is offered. Given the informal nature of the activities described (often personal unrecorded contacts), it is impossible to compile an exhaustive list of them. The chapter therefore describes those that I managed to find records of.

Using Informal Strategies Prior to the IRU Obtaining the Consultative Status

Before obtaining consultative status and being advised on their rights and points of access, Romani activists were rather confused about what the UN is and how it works. Cibula claims to have repeatedly met, in his capacity of the 1971 Congress representative for the UN in Geneva, Dr Brasha [sic] from the UN, whom he informed about the situation of the world's Roma and with whom he looked for possible solutions to their problems (Cibula 1997). He did in fact meet with Alan A. Brash in late 1972 or early 1973[2] and was asking him to organize the 1978 Congress under the auspices of the UN. Unfortunately, Dr Brash and Cibula spoke no common language, resulting in confusion on Cibula's part. Contrary to Cibula's belief, Brash was the Director of the World Council of Churches (which eventually did partly fund the 1978 Congress) and had not worked for the UN. He tried to explain this to Cibula in a letter dated 9 March 1973, writing:

> Your letter, however, confuses me as well. You are suggesting that the conference of leading representatives of gypsies and those interested in their culture should be held and that the World Council of Churches should take initiatives about organizing it. Obviously this would not be an easy thing for the World Council of Churches to do, but you make the matter even more complicated by saying that you want it to be under the United Nations, and of course I have no authority whatsoever to call a meeting under the United Nations. It might in fact obviously have certain advantages if such a group were convened by the UN rather than by such a body as the World Council of Churches, which is in some ways not so representative as you require. Also our specifically Christian position might be an embarrassment to some participants and this would be unfortunate.
>
> If, however, you want an initiative by an UN agency, I think your only option is to approach some agency directly [...] this would be a very different thing from asking us to do an impossibility, namely organize a conference actually under the UN umbrella itself (Brash 1973).

Nevertheless, even after receiving this letter, Cibula believed that he approached some UN agency. He added Brash's letter to his file with a hand-written note, 'the first letter of contact with the UN in Geneva' (see Brash 1973). In fact, in Cibula's letter to Puxon he says that he has acted upon Puxon's recommendation to contact the ECOSOC and has negotiated with Brash. Apparently, Cibula did not realize that the body which Brash represents is a religious body (despite the point quoted above in Brash's letter) because in his letter to Puxon he says that he was advised to contact another organization, but does not want to do it because the organization is too Christian (Cibula 1973). Cibula's interpretation of another event is probably similarly confused. He claims that, in 1987, nomadic Lovari Roma decided to revolt and gather in front of the UN in Geneva. However, they had no permission for this protest and caused a traffic-jam, blocking three highways around Basel. Cibula claims to have been asked by the UN and the Bern authorities to go and act as a mediator. Since the conflict was already very sharp, Cibula's only chance was to take out his violin and play. After everyone calmed down, a small Lovari delegation was allegedly allowed to present its demands outside the UN buildings (Ott 1995). It is, though, unlikely that the UN would contact Cibula to act in such case and, therefore, this story must instead be seen as a cute anecdote. Other Romani leaders have not fared much better than Cibula. They managed to target UN bodies with their requests, but not to move them into action, partly because at times they approached bodies with no mandate to help with these requests, as now detailed.

In Interaction with the Commission   The first contact with the Commission was reportedly made by the IRC which, in 1968, sent it a petition for recognition of the world's Roma as a nation, also requesting international acknowledgement of the persecution Roma have been continuously experiencing since the 15th century (Tipler 1968: 61). Evidence of such a petition was however not found in the UN Archive (Blukacz-Louisfert 3 January 2003). Further plans for co-operation were made at the 1971 Congress. Its social commission agreed that a draft report on the situation of the world's Roma should be sent to the UN, and specific acts of discrimination or persecution should be raised through the IRC with the Commission, upon the request of Romani organizations in particular countries (Puxon 1975: 108). Neither of these plans was fulfilled before the IRU gained consultative status.

In Interaction with the Division of Human Rights (the Division)[3]   The first contact with the Division was made at the end of the 1960s, when several times Rudolf Karway of the International Gypsy Rights Mission (IGRM), one of the early international Romani organizations (for details see Klimova 2003: §2.3.1.3) unsuccessfully approached the Division with his letters. He was ensured that his concerns would be dealt with (Cecatto 1969), but this was about the most positive reply he ever had. Reportedly Karway also deposited dossiers at the UN offices (Liegeois 1976: 146), but the UN Archives contain no materials related to Karway or the IGRM.[4] The first consultation between the Division and Romani activists took place in Geneva on 11 April 1978, within the framework of the 1978 Congress. Officers of the IRU consulted with the Director of the Division, Theo van Boven, urging him to ensure the full implementation of the Resolution 6 (XXX) (see pp. 40–41). They also presented him with a paper entitled *The Legal Situation of Roma in Western Europe*, prepared by Madam Marthe Bilmans (Har Kaushal 1980: 31). I have interviewed van

Boven about this meeting, yet, given the length of time that had passed, he had no recollection of it. In addition, no records of such meetings were kept for two reasons: Roma were not an important issue at that time and given the political climate of the time records of such meeting could compromise the leaders in their countries (van Boven 13 December 2002).

In Interaction with the Secretary-General and his Special Representatives   Besides the letters to Waldheim mentioned earlier (p. 79), two other organizations approached the Secretary-General without having consultative status – the IGRM and the ERRC. Not discouraged by earlier evasions, Karway of IGRM wrote directly to the Secretary-General in November 1969 (p. 94). He explained that Roma are persecuted for political and racial reasons all over the world, and therefore their problems can be settled only by the UN. The Commission [sic] should force the states that ratified the Geneva Refugee Convention to apply it to the Roma. On top of that he suggested how international passports for Roma could help to alleviate the problems of Romani migration and asked for a personal audience to discuss this issue (Karway 1969b). However, no evidence of any of this correspondence was found in the UN Archives (Blukacz-Louisfert 3 January 2003).

In July 1999, the pro-Romani ERRC addressed a letter to the Secretary-General Kofi Annan to express concern at the lack of protection provided by NATO forces in Kosovo to the Romani civilian population there (ERRC 1999c). Then, in October 1999, the ERRC wrote to Bernard Kouchner, Special Representative of the Secretary-General and Head of the UN Interim Administration Mission in Kosovo (UNMIK Kosovo), expressing concern at recent published threats to the life of Veton Surroi, editor of the Kosovo daily Koha Ditore, and 'an outspoken proponent of inter-ethnic tolerance' (ERRC 1999d: 90). In November 2000, this was followed with a letter expressing alarm at the killing of four Romani/Ashkali returnees in the village of Dosevac/Dashevc near Prishtina, Kosovo (ERRC 2000b). None of the letters were answered, but the ERRC believes that this latest letter contributed to bringing about a temporary halt to returns of Roma to Kosovo. Until this incident, the international community refused to acknowledge that Roma in Kosovo were targeted on racial grounds (Cahn 24 February 2003) (see also pp. 47, 101–2).[5]

Using Informal Strategies to Pursue Goals Beyond the Limit of Consultative Status

Even with consultative status, the results of using informal strategies by Romani activists were insignificant, apart from increasing their publicity, as now detailed. They consisted of private meetings with UN officials, letters to UN officials, other written appeals, participation of UN administration and UN member state representatives at World Romani Congresses, and giving press conferences at UN headquarters.

Private Meetings with UN Officials   The only recorded meeting with a UN official since the IRU gained consultative status is the second consultation with van Boven of the Division immediately after the 1981 Congress on 22 May (Puxon 1981; van Boven 1980). The new IRU President Sait Balic and Vice-President Romani Rose met with him to pledge for recognition of the Roma as a national minority (News and Reviews 1981; Puxon 30 November 2002). As has happened several times before and after, they were told that such recognition is actually not in the competence of the UN, but of individual states (van Boven 13 December 2002).

Letters to UN Officials   I tracked down only two occasions of direct letters to UN officials. In 1992, IRU officials resorted to rallying support for adoption of resolution 1992/65 by sending letters to the delegates of member states attending the 48th session of the Commission (see p. 35). These letters reminded delegates of the Subcommission Resolution 1991/21, a copy of which was enclosed with the letters, and argued that the Commission should follow this resolution during its 48th session by examining its recommendations and adopting it as the Commission's resolution (1992/65) (see pp. 41–2). The letters also argued that the adoption of such a resolution would contribute to addressing the root causes of Romani East-West migrations, which had become a topical issue (see e.g. Matras 2000). The IRU officials expressed the hope that the delegation would support their lobbying efforts by adopting the 1992/65 resolution (Gheorghe and Hancock 1991b). This, along with other IRU efforts, paid off, as the resolution was passed (see pp. 121–3).

Nicolae Gheorghe also wrote on behalf of the IRU to the Director of the CHR, asking him for support for a seminar and workshop on the social, legal and political status of Roma that would bring together Romani activists from various countries, experts on specific human rights issues, and representatives of nation-state governmental organizations, IGOs and NGOs (Gheorghe 1991a: 6). The seminar was eventually realized in Snagov, but under the auspices of the Ethnic Federation of Roma in Romania, PER and the Romanian government (see PER 1994).

Other Written Appeals   Virtually every time there was an important meeting of IRU officials which produced a written document with demands, these demands included requests to the UN. For example, when the IRU co-organized a conference on Romani issues in 1991 ('East confronting West: Regional and Local Policies concerning Romanies,' Rome, 20–26 September), the press release of this conference announced that the participants had called for the UN and regional organizations to monitor state policies towards Roma, and to adopt a common approach to global Romani problems (such as those of Romani migrants and refugees from the Balkans). They also considered that Roma should be included in multi- and bi-lateral initiatives within the framework of international programmes such as the low cost housing program of the UN Centre for Human Development (Press Release 1991: 3–4).

It appears that generally documents such as this were not sent directly to the UN offices; rather it was hoped that the messages would reach the UN via general media. There were, however, some exceptions. For example, the 1999 declaration of the participants in the Balkan Roma Conference for Peace and Security (Sofia, 18–19 June) was sent directly to the UN Secretary-General, the UNHCHR, and a number of European officials (ERRC 1999b: 66). The declaration called upon IGOs to ensure: the safe return of Roma to Kosovo, no forced returns, asylum rights for Kosovo Roma, accounting for the precarious situation of Roma in Kosovo in all stabilization agreements, recognition for Roma as a national minority and their equal treatment in Yugoslav law, and adequate political participation of Balkan Roma (for the entire declaration see ERRC 1999e: 48–49).

Another form of written appeal that the IRU produced was information letters. For example, in 1992, Hancock prepared a Report for the International Year of World's Indigenous Peoples in the IRU's name. This report informed about the worldwide Romani population, its history and problems, and warned of an imminent second genocide of Roma if their situation was not addressed. It also declared that, in order to increase the Romani voice in world politics and achieve a higher profile within the UN structure, the IRU had resolved to establish formal relations with *other* organizations of indigenous peoples (Hancock 1992).[6] This report was accompanied with a foreword from Hopson saying that the IRU supports 'any world movement which would enable all Indigenous People of the World to gain Observer Status at the United Nations' and 'the efforts of the Hopi people to present their ancient Peace Message to the Peoples of the World at the United Nations' (Lacroix-Hopson 1992a).

Participation of UN Administration and UN Member State Representatives at World Romani Congresses

The 1971 Congress took place without the participation of UN officials or delegates because it was constituted somewhat unofficially (see Klimova 2003: §2.3.1.4). However, reportedly an observer from the British UN Association was present (Puxon 1971). The 1978 Congress witnessed a significant presence of UN administration, probably because of its convenient location in Geneva. Since Waldheim did not honour Cibula's request of making the opening speech at this Congress (as mentioned in Chapter 4), it was officially opened by Nagendra Singh, Indian Vice-Chairman of the International Court of Justice in The Hague (Rishi 1992: 114). She was a substitute for Vijaylakshmi Pandit, the head of the Indian Mission to the UN and former President of the UN GA, who had originally been envisaged as giving the speech (Puxon 1978c). Ghare Khan, the Indian Ambassador to the UN at Geneva, and Raymonde Martineau from the NGO Liaison office were also present.[7] UNESCO officials came to listen to the plenary session of the Romani Language Commission. Necmeddin Bammat, the UNESCO Assistant Secretary, also addressed the Social Commission. He gave a sympathetic speech in which he mentioned the special connection between the UN and Romani culture, arizing from both being internationalist. In his opinion, Roma were a case where the ideals of the UN had to be applied. He also mentioned the Declaration on the rights of small nations adopted by the UNESCO meeting in Nairobi 1976 and read a long message from UNESCO Secretary-General, Amadou-Mahtar M'Bow, which argued that Romani culture needs to be preserved (Acton 1979: 11).[8] He also outlined three principles upon which any possible future co-operation with UNESCO should be built. Firstly, the initiative for co-operation must come from the Roma themselves, and should not only be a response to UNESCO's actions. Neither UNESCO nor any other organization should impose its vision on the Roma, because this would make the co-operation artificial. Secondly, Roma and their culture are living and must not only be treated as historical objects for study. They have linguistic and identity problems as well as educational and social problems which need to be addressed. Thirdly, Roma need an international body for co-operating with IGOs. This congress was the first step, bringing together Roma from all over the world in a democratic fashion. M'Bow's message emphasized the importance that UNESCO co-operates with Romani leaders, and not only with academics who write books about Roma (Allocution 1978). This speech actually shows the influence of the discourse of the discourse of Romani activists on the discourse of the UN officials because Romani activists have always empha-sized that non-Romani academics should not be considered representatives of the Roma and that IGOs also need to pay attention to the Romani people, not just the Romani culture and history (see also pp. 103–9). This book is, however, concerned with the official UN discourse, not with the discourse of individual officials.

Van Boven was also invited to participate in the 1978 Congress but sent George Brandt, Chief of Research, Studies and Prevention of Discrimination instead (Acton 1979: 11) and did not respond to Cibula's request for UN rooms or their support (van Boven 1978). He explains that, at that time, his office operated with a small budget and few facilities, and there was a lack of meeting rooms and funds even for internal UN matters. He recalls Brandt's attendance at the Congress, but said that this was not followed up with any report or briefing to the Division (van Boven 13 December 2002). Van Boven was also invited to the 1981 Congress, but replied with regret that the Division's financial resources did not allow for such travel yet that it would be the Division's pleasure to receive the Congress's delegation afterwards (van Boven 1981) (see pp. 95–6). Raymonde Martineau had to decline the same invitation, but wished the Congress success and asked to be informed of its results (1981b). Similarly, Pouchpa Dass, the Indian Director of the UNESCO's International Fund for the Promotion of Culture, declined, because the Executive Board of UNESCO was meeting simultaneously, but wished the Congress success (Dass 1981). Eventually, Triloki Nath Kaul, Indian Executive member of UNESCO, attended the Congress and delivered greetings (Agenda 1986).

The 1990 Congress was originally planned to take place in Bern between 9–11 December 1989 and Cibula claimed to have obtained promises of attendance from Horst Keilau of the UN CHR and Virginia Sauerwein, UN NGO Liaison (Cibula 1989). In fact he claimed, in a letter signed by himself and Kappenberger, that this Congress would take place upon the request of the UN in Geneva 'who wish to be informed of the composition of the world presidium' (Romani Union 1989). Probably this simply meant that the UN NGO office had requested a recent list of IRU officers and UN delegates. In Cibula's words, for reasons of internal infighting the Bern Congress was boycotted two weeks before (Cibula 1997), finally taking place in 1990, in Serock near Warsaw. Kazimierz Zygulski, Chairman of the Polish UNESCO Commission, participated in this Congress, where he delivered a speech allegedly assuring the Roma of all possible assistance from UNESCO in improving their lot (Prashar 1990/91: 44–45). This is yet to come, since UNESCO's assistance to Roma has been limited (see pp. 50–1). Other UNESCO representatives present were Victor Koptilow, Leon Wascinski and Esteban Cobas-Puente (Djuric et al. 1991).

Once again, the 2000 Congress (Prague) took place without the official presence of UN administration and delegates. The organizers had invited representatives of the UN NGO Office in New York but none attended (Nazerali 19 December 2002). However, a number of ambassadors from western countries and the European Commission attended and delivered speeches (for details see Acton and Klimova 2001: 172–173). Also, Constance Thomas of the ILO sat in some of the sessions (but without actively participating), after learning about the congress while visiting Prague on a business trip. Upon her return she reported to the ILO that the IRU could become a future partner for co-operation (Thomas 29 October 2002).

Giving Press Conferences at UN Headquarters   During its history, the IRU managed to give two press conferences at the UN headquarters, one in Geneva and one in New York.[9] On 11 April 1978, on the occasion of the second Congress, the first official press conference took place at the UNESCO office in the Palais de Nations, Geneva, but reportedly only seven[10] members of the congress were allowed to enter due to the UN regulations. Others, including representatives of small Romani papers, were not allowed entry. In protest, they carried out an impromptu 'anti-press conference' in the UN staff's canteen (Acton 1979: 12). At the official press conference, Yul Brynner explained the aims of the IRU and its desire to co-operate with the UN and other NGOs (UN Doc. E/C.2/1993/R.4/Add.2: 25).

On 5 June 2001 Scuka and Pietrosanti held a press conference at the UN headquarters in New York, following their audience with Annan earlier that day. The press conference was sponsored by the Czech MFA. They informed the press that that morning they had had an historic meeting with the Secretary-General and detailed the topics discussed (see p. 80). During the conference, Pietrosanti emphasized that, had the federal vision of Europe come true, Roma would no longer be a minority in the EU. In his opinion, giving an answer to the Romani nation's request for status would not only show acknowledgement and respect for enduring discrimination and 'a forgotten Holocaust', but would also answer many questions the international community faces today (UN 2001a). (See pp. 22–7.)

Using Informal Strategies within Bodies Where Consultative Status not Obtained or not Applicable

Although the majority of UN funds, agencies and programmes offer formal relations to NGOs, as mentioned earlier (p. 63), the interaction of Romani activists with most of these bodies has been very minimal and consultative status or formal relations were never achieved (with the exception of UNICEF; see pp. 82–5). Romani activists therefore resorted to informal strategies when wanting interaction with these bodies, as now detailed.

In Interaction with the UNHCR   The UNHCR office allows NGOs to participate as observers in both its Executive and Standing Committees. A UNHCR/NGO Consultation regularly precedes the Executive Committee meeting. The UNHCR also has a more operational relationship with NGOs involved in humanitarian and relief operations, whom it funds for implementation of projects within the Plan of Action for 'Partnership in Action', adopted in Oslo, 1994. On top of that, 'both the Emergency and Technical Sections of UNHCR have a number of formal stand-by arrangements with NGOs for the provision of staff in the early days of an emergency' (UN Doc. A/53/170). Through these operational relations, the UNHCR is also involved in NGO capacity-building for the purposes of rehabilitation and development (UN Doc. A/53/170). Although the UNHCR grants consultative status on the basis of an NGO's status with ECOSOC, it also pragmatically co-operates with any NGO that can be beneficial to refugees, provided that such co-operation is humanitarian and social, not political. The UNHCR's co-operation with NGOs also extends to participation in symposia, study sessions, seminars, meetings and congresses organized by NGOs (Jaeger 1982: 172 and 174).

Therefore, in theory the IRU does have formal access to the UNHCR, yet it has not utilized it. Indeed it was not the IRU's members but rather the RNC and local Romani activists who targeted the UNHCR the most. They largely resorted to the unconventional technique of direct protest, hence the interactions are described in this chapter, not Chapter 4. That the IRU has also used informal strategies when interacting with the UNHCR probably results from its demands being too political for them to be raised through the formal channels. In addition, IRU representatives might not have even been aware that the ECOSOC status also gives them a status within the UNHCR, as this was not emphasized in the information they received upon obtaining the ECOSOC status.

I found only one report of conventional meetings between Romani activists and the UNHCR. In February and March 1991, Nicolae Gheorghe from the IRU repeatedly visited the UNHCR office in Geneva and spoke to officers from the Division of the Protection of the Refugees in Europe (Ulli von Blumnethal, Anique Greiser, and Cengiz Aktar) and to Hans Thoolen from the UN Center for Documentation on Refugees. These meetings were arranged by the wife of Louis Picard (of the ILO) who worked at the UNHCR (see p. 111). They discussed problems related to the increasing number of Romani refugees from former Yugoslavia and Romania coming to Western Europe, and the need for information on the situation of Roma in their countries of origin. Gheorghe presented them with a report on the situation of Roma worldwide that he had compiled together with Ian Hancock (Gheorghe and Hancock 1991a). They agreed that it would be helpful to prepare an information document on this phenomenon and the legal and humanitarian means to address it (Gheorghe 4 December 2002; Gheorghe 1991a: 7). Although no such documentation was produced by or in co-operation with the UNHCR, Gheorghe later took on this issue in his capacity as the Advisor for the Contact Point for Roma and Sinti Issues (CPRSI) of the OSCE (see e.g. Klimova 2001a). The UNHCR, for its part, decided to hire an independent consultant to produce a report on Romani migrations in 1993 (see p. 46). The consultant however interviewed a number of Romani activists, including Gheorghe, when gathering information (for the full list see Braham 1993: Acknowledgements). The only other evidence of co-operation found was that, at the nation-state level, in 2001 the pro-Romani NGO Info-Roma in Slovakia became an official partner for implementation of a UNHCR programme in the area of community services, legal assistance/protection, and agency operational support (UN Doc. EC/48/SC/CRP.9).

However, the UNHCR is the only body from the UN system which has been a target of direct protest actions by Romani activists. On 9 November 1990, Rudko Kawczynski, Chairman of the RNC, led a march of some three hundred ex-Yugoslav Romani asylum-seekers from Germany to Switzerland to apply for asylum at the UNHCR headquarters in Geneva and 'to demonstrate against the organization's Roma refugee policy' (RNN 2001). They were, however, not allowed to cross the Swiss-German border. Using their coaches, they blocked one lane of the Basel border crossing for seven days in a non-violent protest, while Kawczynski and his colleagues from the RNC (including the RNC's solicitor, Christian Schneider) proceeded to the UNHCR office. The UNHCR officials reportedly encouraged the RNC to apply for the protection of the Romani asylum-seekers in accordance with the Geneva Refugee Convention, as an alternative to applying according to German law. The RNC did launch such application, on behalf of over 100 persons, with the

Federal Ministry of Interior in Bonn, arguing that the Geneva Convention should take precedence over German law. This was never acknowledged and the applications were not processed according to the Geneva Convention (Matras 26 November 2002). Nevertheless, the protest and related action reportedly eventually resulted in more than 2000 Roma from former Yugoslavia receiving permission to stay in Germany, possibly saving their lives.

However, police in the border town of Loerrach charged Kawczynski with 'coercion' (disturbing peace) for partially obstructing the border crossing. Kawczynski was found guilty, but the case was appealed several times and was finally brought before the German Constitutional Court in 1994, which did not issue the ruling for some seven years. Regardless of this, on 20 October 2001 Kawczynski reportedly received a letter from the Loerrach prosecutor instructing him to start serving a fifty-day sentence in prison. Romani leaders have speculated that the timing of this was related to a protest and a press conference against German deportation practices that was organized by Kawczynski and joined by more than sixty Romani organizations during the WCAR in September 2001 (see Klimova 2003: §7.3.3) (RNN 2001; ERRC 2001d). Kawczynski reacted to this charge with the following words: 'Our action protected the lives of some 2000 Roma from Kosovo and Jugoslavia [sic] – as Germany decided not to deport them. For that I am happy to go to jail! Let us not be afraid of them – they may take away our freedom – but they can't break our solidarity!' (Puxon 2001). Nevertheless, Romani and pro-Romani activists started a campaign on his behalf, rallying among other things on the ironic fact that Kawczynski was to be imprisoned at Neuengamme, the site of a former Nazi concentration camp where Roma had been killed during the Holocaust. This campaign, which was also joined by non-Romani NGOs and IGOs such as OSCE and CoE, was successful in delaying Kawczynski's imprisonment until the ruling of the Federal Constitutional Court on 31 January 2002 (RNN 2001; Kawczynski 2001; ERRC 2001d). This ruling has apparently not taken place, as of the end of 2003.

In July and August 2002, Roma from the Katlanova and Shuto Orizari refugees camps repeatedly demonstrated against bad living conditions in the camps and 'unfulfilled promises' from the UNHCR (such as help in granting refugee status and safe return to Kosovo) in front of its office in Skopje, asking to be transferred to camps in Western Europe, Canada or the USA. They asked for help from the UNHCR to leave Macedonia and to be accommodated in a richer and more stable western country (RNN 2002a) until it was safe for them to return to Kosovo.[11] Besides the unsuitable conditions in the camps, they argued that they were suffering a similar trauma in Macedonia as they had previously suffered, because the conflict between Macedonians and Albanians resembled that between the Serbians and Albanians in Kosovo (RNN 2002b). Reportedly, one of the reasons behind these protests was that some 200 Romani families from the two camps won US immigration visas in the visa lottery. The protesters thought that these visas had been secured by the UNHCR and requested that the same was done for them (RNN 2002a; RNN 2002c). The leaders of the protest declared that the reason for the protest was the discrimination against Romani refugees in comparison to other groups. They stated that, while 90 per cent of refugees from the Malioci group left for third countries, only 1 per cent of Roma were able to do so (Eliyahu 2002a). This report also detailed some of the Romani complaints against the conditions in the camps. Although, at most, only 100 to 350 Roma joined the protest on any particular day (RNN 2002a; Eliyahu 2002b), the leaders claimed to act on behalf of the 3000 Romani refugees that were currently in Macedonia (Eliyahu 2002b, Drom Center 2002a).

On the first day of the protest, 29 July 2002, the UNHCR representative William Toll met with seven Romani representatives, who raised the following demands: granting the Roma refugee status as opposed to temporary protection; relocation to a third, safe and richer country; and, once conditions allowed, the right for collective return to Kosovo, accompanied with property restitution, compensation, protection from assault, bringing to justice those responsible for committing crimes against Roma, guaranteeing education of children in the desired language and equal opportunities in health care and employment. Toll however reportedly refused to consider the possibility of relocation to a safe third country, ignoring the arguments of unsuitable conditions in Macedonia (Drom Center 2002a). Instead he recommended that they ask for asylum in Macedonia (Tuzla Roma Association 2002). As this was unacceptable to the Roma, the protests continued. Around 6 August 2002, the UNHCR and Skopje police reportedly discussed the necessity of dispersing the protesters by force, because they were blocking access to the UNHCR. The demonstration leaders interpreted this step as an UNHCR attempt to prevent them from exercizing their right to protest (Berisha 2002). They also claimed to have been barred from public buses in order to be prevented from joining the demonstration, to have received threats from the UNHCR (who allegedly had given the Skopje police a list of the demonstration leaders), and to have suffered harsh treatment by the Albanian policemen, causing one female protester to have a heart attack and another a miscarriage (Eliyahu 2002b; Romapage 2002). The protests finally ceased on 29 August 2002 after the demonstration leaders obtained a promise from Toll that he would discuss their demands with international political and humanitarian organizations (RNN 2002b).

Ariel Eliyahu, the IRU President's Advisor for the Middle East,[12] e-mailed a letter of protest to the UNHCR in support of the Romani refugees' demands on 31 August 2002. On 2 September 2002, he received a reply explaining that the 'UNHCR is presently engaged in a dialogue with the Government [of Macedonia] to find long-term solutions to the problems of the remaining refugees under temporary protection after the status expires on 28 September' and that 'FYR Macedonia has shown that it will be able to ensure the protection and safety of the Roma refugees in this country after 28 September' (Eliyahu 2002c). The letter also pointed out that '[f]or those individuals who cannot repatriate, UNHCR considers that local integration is the most relevant durable solution. The office is therefore actively engaged in a dialogue with the Macedonian authorities to promote the facilitation of local integration' (Eliyahu 2002c). This letter shows that the protests had little effect, with the UNHCR continuing to deal with the situation in the same way it had before the protests started. Jean-Claude Concolato, the head of the UNHCR Focal Point on Roma, points out that such protests are very common among such refugees. When some of them are resettled (or are believed to be resettled, as in this case), the rest demand the same (Concolato 16 December 2002). The dissatisfaction among the refugees resulted in vandalism of the camp and the office of the local UNHCR Romani mediators (Misljija and Muharem 2002). On 10 December 2002, to mark the UN International Human Rights Day, the Refugee Committee (an *ad hoc* body) organized a one-hour peaceful demonstration in front of the Shuto Orizari refugee camp to protest that the UNMIK and UNHCR were ignoring their difficult situation. The announcement of this demonstration was reportedly sent to the UNHCR, UN Security Council, and UNMIK (Drom Center

2002b). The protests were likely to continue throughout 2003 and the UNHCR there-fore decided to close down the Shuto Orizari refugee camp, the nucleus of the protests, by the end of March 2003 (Misljija and Muharem 2003).

Regarding UNHCR's co-operation with Romani political organizations such as the IRU or RNC, Concolato explained that such co-operation is not possible because it is bound to be political, yet their co-operation with NGOs (including those with ECOSOC status) is on a strictly non-political basis. He has explained this to the IRU, RNC and other Romani leaders when they have approached him during international meetings. Moreover, the UNHCR cannot support the current demands of the IRU and RNC – revizing the 1958 Geneva Convention to reflect the specific conditions of the Roma.[13] According to the UNHCR this is an irresponsible political demand. The UNHCR believes that the Geneva Convention is a useful humanitarian instrument and its revision would, in the current political climate, impose yet more restrictions on the rights of refugees, as opposed to expanding these rights. Therefore it is best not to start the revision debate. Furthermore, the UNHCR believes that it is unrealistic to request special status only for Roma because many other groups, such as Kurds, Muslims in Europe, etc., would soon demand their own special status, leading to an unnecessary proliferation of special instruments. Similarly, the UNHCR does not approve of the general demands by Romani activists. The Declaration of Nation is based on what, for the UNHCR, is a discredited principle of ethnic, as opposed to civic, state, and could in fact turn against the Roma; some states are only too keen to transfer all their responsibility for the Romani population to Romani leaders, who, however, are not in the position to take on such responsibilities. Also, the UNHCR (as well as other actors in the international community) do not appreciate the threat of the coming of a Romani Malcolm X that is sometimes made by some of Romani activists during international meetings and in the media (Concolato 16 December 2002). Instead, the UNHCR Focal Point on Roma co-operates with the non-political bridge people (NGO workers, Romani advisors, social street workers, governmental author-ities, teachers and artists), providing them with advisory and financial assistance (see § p. 43). Such co-operation allegedly guarantees that the UNHCR's assistance is adapted to the needs of targeted beneficiaries, rather than being diverted to (for example) the 'political benefits of a local, self-appointed leader, or to the financial interest of a small group' (UNHCR 2002a).

The pro-Romani ERRC has also had some limited co-operations with the UNHCR, by participating in its conferences in Hungary and Ireland. On 11 July 1997, the ERRC participated in a conference on 'Human Rights and the Media' organized by the UNHCR and Constitutional and Legal Policy Institute (COLPI) in Budapest (ERRC 1997). On 25 October 2001, the ERRC made a presentation on the issue of state protection of Roma in Romania at a meeting for asylum adjudicators in Dublin that was organized by the UNHCR (ERRC 2001b).

In Interaction with the UNESCO   The relationship of UNESCO with NGOs was originally guided by provisions in its constitution. In 1960 the General Conference expanded these provisions to allow for various categories of formal relations. In 1995, new provisions 'did away with the 'hierarchy' inherent in the previous ones and placed greater emphasis on operationality, direct action in the field and closer contact with grass-roots organizations' (UN Doc. A/53/170). Under the new provi-sions, UNESCO co-operates with NGOs at all levels (international, regional, subre-

gional, nation-state, local and grass-roots) under what are termed 'operational relations' in order to increase its concrete action in the field. 'Formal relations' are maintained with important international NGOs who regularly meet with UNESCO
officials, both at the global level and through regional consultations (UN Doc.
A/53/170).[14] Granting of the status of formal or operational relations does not take
place through applications, rather UNESCO offers such relations to organizations
with whom it has been successfully co-operating informally for a significant period
of time (UNESCO 2001). In many countries, UNESCO also maintains contact with
NGOs through its National Commissions. NGOs can benefit from co-operation with
UNESCO by receiving fellowships and scholarships, contracts for writing and publications, and subsidies for international exchange (Riggs and Plano 1994: 47).

The requests of Romani activists for co-operation with UNESCO reflect their
desire to promote Romani culture, language and education; tasks that are, in the case
of most nations, usually performed by the state. In the case of the Roma, most states
have largely ignored these tasks until recently, perhaps with the exception of education, which was however carried out in a culturally insensitive manner. It is therefore
unsurprising that UNESCO was the first UN body with whom Romani activists
attempted to establish formal relations, although the fact that UNESCO's headquarters are located in Paris, where most of the earliest international Romani organizations (WGC, GIPSAR, IRC – see Klimova 2003: §2.3.1) also had their headquarters,
might have played a role. The goal of establishing formal relations has, however, not
yet been achieved,[15] despite gaining ECOSOC consultative status. In relation to this,
in September 1993 Main was informed in her interview with N'Deye Fall from the
Paris UNESCO headquarters that the IRU application for consultative status was on
hold, and had never been officially presented for a number of reasons. The IRU's
leadership was unable to achieve the required unanimous decision, the organization
was paralysed by internal politics and problems with the current President, and lack
of financial and human resources prevented it from dealing effectively with
UNESCO (Main 27 February 2003). However, Marcel Courthiade, the IRU's
plenipotentiary to UNESCO since the 1990 Congress, recounts the problems with the
IRU application in the early 1990s differently. According to him, Fall was extremely
uncooperative and insisted that the IRU had to fulfil unreasonably high criteria to get
the status, such as having 200 active nation-state associations, spread more or less
equally through all five continents. However, Fall never produced an official document with such guidelines, despite numerous requests. Consequently, the IRU eventually gave up. In Courthiade's opinion, at the moment such status is, in any case, not
crucial to the IRU, for it would only serve to increase their prestige. Nevertheless, the
IRU will probably attempt to apply again in the future, after it has strengthened its
activities of interest to UNESCO (Courthiade 18 March 2003). In fact, IRU leaders
agreed at a recent meeting in Vienna (April 2003) to revive co-operation with the
UNESCO (Courthiade 16 April 2003).

Although in 1993 the UNESCO headquarters possessed two full files of correspondence with the IRU (Main 27 February 2003), when the author repeatedly
contacted the headquarters in 2002, its officials insisted that they had no information
on co-operation and status negotiations with, or funding provided to, the IRU or other
Romani organizations (Abtahi 21 January 2003; Maguire 28 October 2002 and 21
January 2003; Ferrier 11 October 2002). This book therefore has to rely on information provided by Romani activists themselves.

The first, very informal contact of Romani activists with UNESCO was the participation of WGC officers in the 1963 annual UNESCO garden party (Puxon 1975: 58). In 1965, Vanko Rouda of IRC gained prominence in a debate on Romani issues during a French symposium at the UNESCO Palace. This symposium resulted in the passing of a resolution condemning the French anti-Romani law of 1912,[16] and also in the calling for the provision of caravan sites. Rouda was then invited to join a commission set up at this symposium for the international day 'For peace and against racism'. This raised Rouda's hopes, and he planned to achieve NGO consultative status at the UNESCO for the IRC. To this end, he reportedly made written enquiries and met with Pouchpa Dass in a friendly atmosphere, but the French civil service allegedly blocked his efforts to achieve the status (Puxon 9 September 2002). Rouda had also hoped to use the UNESCO Palace for the first Congress, which he then planned for 1966 (Puxon 1975: 91). During this time, UNESCO's interest was also sustained with two articles by Romani linguist and historian Jan (Vania de Gila) Kochanowski in two UNESCO-related publications, *UNESCO Features* and *Diogenes* (see Megret, Undated). The second time that the IRC approached UNESCO was in 1970, to consult on educational matters after some success in consultations with the CoE (Puxon 2000: 101–104). Its officers (both Roudas and Puxon) met with several departmental heads in April 1970, and explained the linguistic barriers between Romani children and the curricula of state schools. They described the alternative educational models (caravan schools) developed by the IRC, such as the *Romano Drom* caravan schools in Britain.[17] They suggested that UNESCO could assist in the development of literacy materials for Roma and in the training of Romani teachers (Puxon 1975: 69–70 and 88; Puxon 2000: 104). They were well received, but no specific action came out of these meetings (Puxon 3 November 2002).

There were, however, great hopes for co-operation with UNESCO in the early 1970s. Posters announcing the 1971 Congress implied that, based on current negotiations, the obtaining of consultative status with UNESCO was imminent (World Romani Congress 1971). The faith in UNESCO's help was such that, in 1971, the Congress resolved that funds resulting from expected war reparations from West German, East German and Austrian Governments (which were never obtained) should be given to UNESCO to spend on educational programmes for Romani children. The hope was that Romani illiteracy could be eradicated with the help of UNESCO. Two further negotiations with UNESCO, similar to those in 1970, were held in 1971. Negotiations for consultative status continued into 1972, but were still being hindered by French opposition (Puxon 1975: 97, 101 and 131). Negotiations were renewed before the second Congress, starting in 1977 (News and Reviews 1978: 45). The IRU had consultations with UNESCO officials in Paris on several occasions and, as a result, Bammat attended the 1978 Congress (UN Doc. E/C.2/1993/R.4/Add.2: 23) (see pp. 97–8). After the Congress, Jan Cibula sent M'Bow a letter informing him about the IRU's goals that were agreed at the congress. These included close future co-operation with UNESCO in protecting and developing Romani culture, gaining consultative status with UNESCO, building institutes for Romani language and culture, Romani libraries and universities, and teaching Romani to school children. The letter recalled M'Bow's encouraging telegram of 6 April 1978, which now 'gives Cibula the courage' to present the IRU's aims to M'Bow. It ended with a request that M'Bow suggest how these goals could be achieved with the help of UNESCO (Cibula 1978h). I, however, found no record of such UNESCO's suggestions. The Congress also hoped to obtain UNESCO's assistance in drafting and implementing guidelines for the recognition of Romani culture and language by various state educational authorities (Puxon 1978b: 9). Consequently, the IRU discussed submission of an educational and cultural programme to UNESCO for financial assistance (Rishi 1980: 15). For this purpose, Cibula claims to have met with M'Bow on 25 April 1978, explaining to him 'the needs and wishes of the Romani people'. They also discussed future educational possibilities and the preservation of Romani cultural values. Reportedly, M'Bow again assured Cibula of his support, as he had previously done through Bammat at the Congress (Cibula 1978c; Rishi 1981b). It is, however, unsure if this meeting really took place. Given the fact that Cibula's letter to M'Bow described above also dates 25 April 1978, this could be another example of Cibula's loose interpretation of facts to make them sound more important, with the only contact with M'Bow being through this letter. Among other things, UNESCO was also asked to sponsor a multilingual Romani dictionary prepared by W.R. Rishi. This sponsorship, however, fell through, despite the fact that N.T. Kaul was enlisted to support the idea (World Romani Congress Activities of its Presidium 1980: 35) (see p. 98). The 1971 Congress idea of a UNESCO fund based on reparations was not abandoned. Jusuf and Puxon again met with Pouchpa Dass on 26 October 1979 in Paris, and agreed that part of UNESCO would be able to act as Trustees for a reparation fund if reparations were received (World Romani Congress Activities of its Presidium 1980: 39; Puxon 26 November 2002).

On 2 November 1983, during the Romani International Festival in Chandigarh, several members of the IRU signed a letter attesting that Huguette Tanguy, secretary of the French Romani Union, should be the permanent representative of the IRU at UNESCO (see also p. 137).[18] Since then, Kochanowski has also been signing letters as the plenipotentiary of the IRU at UNESCO (Kochanowski 1985: 3), claiming to be nominated as such by the IRU executive (see Megret, Undated).[19] In 1986, he claimed that the French Romani Union had UNESCO support for organizing the fourth Congress in Paris in October/November 1986 (Rishi 1986). Moreover, on 22 February 1986, an IRU Presidium meeting reportedly took place in Paris with the support of UNESCO (Cibula 1986). The Congress was, according to Kochanowski, postponed until summer 1987 (Rishi 1987: 6) due to terrorist attacks perpetrated in Paris, the change of French government and 'excuses and difficulties' raised by the IRU's highest officials, Rose, Djuric and Balic. This somewhat concurs with allegations that, although preparations by the French Romani Union were well under way in Paris, the Congress in Paris never took place due to the lack of support from the rest of the IRU Presidium (The Paris Congress, Undated). Eventually it only took place in 1990, in Serock near Warsaw, with some symbolic (non-financial) support from UNESCO. At this congress the first Romani primer was presented, within the framework of UNESCO's year against illiteracy (Djuric et. Al 1991: 3–4). A meeting on standardization of Romani was held prior to the Congress (5–6 April), and was also symbolically sponsored by UNESCO, whose representative delivered a greeting to it (Standardization of Romani Language 1990/91: 27). The congress's education, culture, language and information commissions were all to seek urgent negotiations with UNESCO (Acton 1990/91: 56–57).

The French chapter of the IRU also tried to secure money for Romani projects from UNESCO on their own, from the early 1970s onwards. They asked for money to establish an international Romani culture centre and to conduct studies of Romani language and integration projects. They maintain that their efforts were sabotaged by confessional French organizations. Kochanowski claims that after he submitted a project to UNESCO in the early 1970s (the project had already been initiated in the 1960s), which obliged France to abrogate discriminatory laws against Roma, he was put on a black list and all further projects submitted by the French chapter of the IRU were ignored. Instead non-Romani NGOs have been taking all the UNESCO money for Romani projects, which according to Kochanowski were based on his ideas but did not acknowledge his input (Kochanowski 1981/82: 21 and 35). For decades, Kochanowski has been trying to obtain a consultative status at UNESCO, mainly by writing letters to UN and French governmental offices accusing everyone (pro-Romani NGOs such as Etudes Tsiganes, research centres such as Centre de Recherches Tsiganes at Rene Descartes University, and IRU officials) of stealing money that rightfully belongs to the Roma. To this he has added personal accusations against both Romani and non-Romani NGO officials (including IRU officials) regarding their collaboration with Nazis[20] and falsification of signatures and titles, etc. (see e.g. Kochanowski 1997). Although some of Kochanowski's accusations might have been justified, they are more an expression of what Hancock calls the Romani national disease *hamishagos*, which 'makes [the Roma] want to hinder, instead of help, [their] own who are getting ahead' (Hancock 1988: 12). But is this really the Romani national disease or simply one of the human vices? Kochanowski's aggressive behaviour could also be a result of the frustration that he, and many other Roma, experience about their past (and at times present) treatment by society, thus leading to the so-called 'victim culture' which is characterized by denouncing everything and everyone non-Romani as hostile and discriminating against the Roma (see e.g. van Baalen 2000: 55).

At times, Kochanowski has convinced other IRU officials to join in with these campaigns. At a meeting in Bern on 10 December 1989 he signed, along with Djuric, Cibula, Aleka Stobin and Stevica Nikolic, a press release declaring that the IRU was the only organization in the world that had the right to represent Roma and that non-Romani organizations – such as Etudes Tsiganes (France), Centro Studii Zingari (Italy), Romani Cultural Centre in Heidelberg (of the Central Council of Roma and Sinti, Germany), Opera Nomadi (Italy), Romanestan Publications (UK), Centre de recherches tsiganes (France), and Gypsy Lore Society (USA) – must be prohibited from representing Roma. On the last day of the 1990 Congress (12 April), he also convinced the IRU President Djuric to sign a letter to the Director of UNESCO asking him to prohibit Etudes Tsiganes from representing Roma at the UNESCO, using, very impolitely, the informal pronoun 'toi' to address the Director. In the same informal way, the UNESCO Director was asked to prohibit the 'criminal' organizations Etudes Tsiganes (and their representative Marcel Cortiade, who, in passing, was by then an elected IRU officer) and Centre de Researches Tsiganes (Jean Pierre Liegeois) from representing Roma at the UNESCO and from receiving project money. This letter was drafted by the newly established (and soon failed) EUROM on 1 November 1990 (see Klímová 2003: §2.3.1). The letter also requested that the IRU be admitted to the C list (consultative status), with Kochanowski and Tanguy as permanent representatives (all these documents are reprinted in Kochanowski 1997: 17–19). As of 2000, Kochanowski still claimed to be the IRU plenipotentiary for the

French delegation to UNESCO. He also claimed to actually have some influence at UNESCO. For example, he announced that he had obtained support for the internationalization of Romani from various UNESCO delegations (France, Spain, Portugal, Chile) (1997: 13). However, his only accomplishment with UNESCO was publishing yet another article in UNESCO's *Diogenes* (see Megret, Undated). His interaction with the UNESCO officials ended up rather unfortunately, as he reportedly physically attacked the officer in charge of relations with NGOs (Falls' predecessor).[21] Overall, his actions actually accomplished the exact opposite of what he wanted. It made his complaints reality – the door for the IRU's and other Romani organizations consultative status at UNESCO were closed (Liegeois 11 October 2002).

Fortunately, the damage had mostly been done at the French UNESCO National Commission, and the IRU was still able to benefit from co-operation with other National Commissions. For example, in the early 1990s, UNESCO funded a Romani school in Moscow where children can study Romani history and language (Lemon 1995: 18). Similarly, the Yugoslav National Commission for UNESCO partly sponsored the International Symposium on Romani Language and Culture held on 9–11 June 1986 in Sarajevo, organized by the Institute for the Research into Relations between Nationalities and supported by the IRU (News and Reviews 1986: 43). The participants of this seminar adopted a number of points related to Romani language and culture, and resolved that these would be sent to UNESCO and other IGOs in order to receive financial and other help. One of these points proposed establishing a fund for research and standardization of the Romani language within the UNESCO or a similar IGO (Conclusions of the International Symposium 1986). Such a fund was never established, but, in 1989, UNESCO supported the first IRU Romani summer school in Belgrade with a donation of 10,000 USD (UN Doc. E/C.2/1993/R.4/Add.2: 31). Although the IRU has never been offered formal relations with the UNESCO headquarters, recently some National Commissions have considered including Romani representatives in their deliberations. For example, at the Senate seminar following the 2000 Congress, Jaroslava Moserova, the head of the Czech UNESCO National Commission, offered Romani activists her help in obtaining representation in UNESCO. She explained later that she had meant representation in the National Commission, because that was the only way in which Roma could be included. She made this offer publicly because her efforts to attract individual Czech Romani leaders to attend the meetings failed (Moserova 24 November 2001). Yet another opportunity missed by Romani activists.

In its 1993 request for re-classification, the IRU summarized the following as its major results of co-operation with UNESCO to that date. In 1979, it received 5,000 USD for the translation of the book Destiny of Europe's Gypsies into Romani, under the title Bibahtale Bersha (UN Doc. E/C.2/1993/R.4/Add.2: 31).[22] In the late 1980s, the IRU project on 'Romani summer school' received the support of six National UNESCO Commissions within the UNESCO programme Education and Toleration, and expanded to include activities in the field of the UNESCO programme to combat illiteracy (UN Doc. E/C.2/1993/R.4/Add.2: 31). However, in the early 2000s, all National Commissions approached have declined the request to fund further years of the summer school (Courthiade 18 March 2003). In 1994, Courthiade's NGO Rromani Baxt also co-operated with UNESCO's 'Innocenti' Center based in Florence by carrying out field research on the schooling problems of Romani children in six settlements in Albania (Rromani Baxt Albania, Undated: 1).

The most recent documented contact between the IRU and UNESCO was a 1995 resolution sent by the IRU to the UNESCO (and the Council of Ministers of the EU) appealing for support for an IRU-organized World Congress for Peace at Sarajevo (planned for 9–15 May). Its aim was to contribute towards the solution of the Balkan problems and the ending of the war in Bosnia-Herzegovina, bring about peace, reconciliation, revival of democracy and improvement of the inter-state and inter-ethnic relations, as well as the rights of national minorities in the whole Balkan region.[23] It was hoped that, besides financial means, the UN would support the conference by sending a delegation. The resolution also indicated that such a step could revive the Peace Movement on the continent, and asked the UN to proclaim 1995 the Year for Peace. Plans were also made for introducing a European Peace Prize under the name of Willy Brandt, 'an outstanding anti-fascist fighter and Nobel Peace Prize winner'. For the purposes of helping achieve peace throughout the world, the IRU set up its own foundation in the name of Mahatma Ghandi (World Congress for Peace at Sarajevo 1994). The IRU attempted to gain the UN's support through Nina Sibal, the Indian Permanent Representative to UNESCO, who replied that UNESCO could not support such an initiative, as the IRU was not associated with UNESCO. Furthermore, she pointed out that 1995 had already been declared the UN Year of Tolerance (World Congress for Peace at Sarajevo 1994). The conference never took place. While this request was simply an attempt to raise funds for an event where Romani activists could gather, it was quite cleverly presented as a Balkan peace effort. It however failed to suggest any constructive contributions to this effort. Moreover, its authors did not do their homework beforehand – for example, checking whether it was not too late to request a specific world year theme for 1995. Thus the negative answer was not surprising.

In Interaction with the ILO The ILO involves civil society through employers' and workers' organizations, who are represented in nation-state delegations on an equal footing with governments as full-fledged members of the organization's decision-making bodies, such as the International Labour Conference and the ILO Governing Body. Their representatives participate equally in regional and sectoral meetings. The Constitution of the ILO also provides for consultative relationships with 'recognized non-governmental international organizations, including international organizations of employers, workers, agriculturists and cooperatives' (UN Doc. A/53/170). The consultative relationship takes place through three categories:

1) general consultative or regional status for international NGOs with a significant interest in a wide range of the ILO's activities,
2) ILO's Special List of NGOs for NGOs which demonstrate an evident interest in at least one area of the ILO's work and
3) international NGOs invited to participate in ILO meetings of special interest. NGOs with general status are allowed to participate in all ILO meetings and also in regional meetings for those with regional consultative status (UN Doc. A/53/170).

Romani activists have no representation in the ILO because its social partners are only trade unions and employers. Although some Romani professional associations have existed at the local level since the early 19th century (see e.g. Kaminski 1980: 137–138; Marushiakova and Popov 2001b: 76–79; Marushiakova and Popov 1997:

29; Marushiakova and Popov 2001c: 374), transborder initiatives have only started to take place this century.[24] As of today, Romani organizations have not joined in with the trade unions to lobby for the improvement of the situation of their people. The International Labour Office itself is open to co-operation, and its officers occasionally talk informally with Romani representatives delivering statements at the sessions of other UN bodies in Geneva. However, if co-operation is to be formalized, the initiative must come from the activists themselves (Thomas 29 October 2002).

So far the only co-operation took place within the framework of the Commission of Inquiry on Romania (see pp. 51–2). While carrying out the investigation, on 11 October 1990 Professor Vukas of the Commission met (upon Gheorghe's recommendation), with Ion Cioaba, Vice-President of the Organization of Roma of Romania, the President of the Union of Drivers of the county of Sibiu and an IRU official. In addition, Gheorghe was one of the five witnesses that the Commission invited to the hearing. Gregor Camarasan, from local administration in Cluj and who has been in frequent touch with the Romani community in his area, was among the thirteen witnesses presented by the complainants (ILO 1990a and 1990b). Excerpts from their testimonies on Roma were cited throughout the Commision's final report. The witnesses emphasized the special, dispersed character of the Romani community and explained that Romani identity is unfortunately not defined in positive cultural terms but in negative social ones. Since Romani nationality is seen as synonymous with inferior social standing, most members of the community are reluctant to identify themselves as such. Roma are the subject of widespread prejudice and negative images in the society and their contribution to economy is seen as marginal. The socialist regimes saw their economic activities as parasitic and attempted to forcefully assimilate them. In connection to education and training, the witnesses explained that the Romanian state does not provide Roma with the necessary social conditions to permit their access to education and culture. Many families are simply too poor to afford textbooks, or even clothing suitable for school. While no official discrimination in education existed, the attitude of teachers towards Romani children was often derogatory or indifferent. Gheorghe pointed out that Roma cannot achieve equality in education and training without affirmative action. Roma who have acquired skills by practising traditional trades are unable to take on official jobs because their qualifications are not sanctioned by a diploma. They can only be employed as unskilled labour, assigned to the most arduous and menial tasks with no prospect of promotion. The witnesses also testified to Roma receiving lower wages than other Romanians for work of equal value and to discrimination in employment promotion (ILO 1991). These witnesses were very effective in convincing the Commission, for virtually all of their complaints are reflected in the recommendations issued by the Commission (see pp. 51–2). Gheorghe also states that the Ethnic Federation of Roma presented specific proposals for remedying the problems of Roma in Romania to both the Romanian government and the ILO (1991: 6). The Commission's report, however, does not mention receiving these proposals. It only mentions that it invited the following NGOs to submit materials: Amnesty International, International Commission of Jurists, International Federation of Human Rights (IFHR), Minority Rights Group (MRG), and Helsinki Watch. No materials of the IFHR (with whom the Ethnic Federation of Roma in Romania co-operated) are mentioned in the report.

Gheorghe followed up his initial contact with ILO officers during his visit to Geneva in February and March 1991, meeting with Louis Picard, who was writing the Commission's report (Gheorghe 1991a: 6). Gheorghe and Picard had in fact become friends during the investigations in Romania, thus opening several new doors to Gheorghe, both at the ILO and the UNHCR (Gheorghe 4 December 2002). (See p. 100.) For instance, during his visit Gheorghe met with Lee Swepston, a legal expert at the human rights division of the ILO and one of the promoters of the ILO 169 Convention, with whom he 'explored the legal and practical implications for the specific case of Roma, resulting from the various concepts which are framed in different human rights documents' (Gheorghe 1991a: 6). Gheorghe recalls that the ILO was keen to 'assimilate Roma into the indigenous category,' while at that time the Romani activists preferred the label national minority (perhaps due to the influence of their Yugoslav faction). In Gheorghe's opinion, applying the category of indigenous people was unreasonable because, he believes, Roma do not fulfil the requisite definition (Gheorghe 4 December 2002). The latest co-operation between some Romani activists and the ILO occurred in 2001, when the ILO sponsored an exhibition of Romani art in its headquarters in Geneva. This act amounts to a significant recognition, as it was the first time that the ILO sponsored such an event for a specific ethnic group (Thomas 29 October 2002).

In Interaction with the WB   The WB's dialogue with NGOs was institutionalized in the early 1980s and has primarily been guided through the NGO-WB Committee. Formed in 1982, the committee's 'meetings provide a formal, international arena for policy discussions among senior bank managers and twenty-six NGO leaders from around the world. The NGOs determine the membership through a staggered election process, which allows for annual rotation and diversity of NGO representation' (UN Doc. A/53/170). The NGO Unit of the WB is housed in the Social Development Department, and works with Resident Missions and headquarters offices on NGO-related issues and broader civil society participation in the WB's activities. In addition, an 'NGO thematic group brings together representatives from each region and the central vice presidency to facilitate discussion of matters related to both operational and policy work with NGOs' (UN Doc. A/53/170). The Bank also involves NGOs in the implementation of its projects. Recently 'there is also a growing trend to increase upstream involvement of NGOs in project preparation' (UN Doc. A/53/170).

As of yet Romani activists have not been significantly involved in the WB's co-operation with civil society. A number of local and nation-state Romani and pro-Romani NGOs (most notably from Hungary and Slovakia) have, however, been able to negotiate financial support for their education, employment, media and health care related projects through the Small Grants Program managed by Country Offices in the field. The IRU has also benefited from the Small Grants Program by receiving support for both the 2000 Congress and the 2001 World Romani Festival held in Prague. The WB seems to value the co-operation with the IRU, announcing on its website that Kyuchukov, the current General Secretary of the IRU, has been involved in their Child welfare project for Bulgaria (WB, Roma Page).

In October 1999, an official eight-member IRU delegation[25] met with Maureen Lewis from the Human Development Sector of the WB.[26] They introduced the IRU as 'an organization prepared to help solve the economic and social issues of the Roma' (IRU 1999b). They offered to co-operate with the WB in planning an international economic conference for representatives of CEE governments, and outlined the IRU's Stabilization Program for CEE Roma which aimed at creating an economic class among Roma who, with the assistance of the WB and nation-state governments, could produce employment for Roma and compete in the open market. They also explained that even capable Romani businessmen experience great difficulty obtaining loans from banks or states, and suggested that the WB makes its loans to states conditional on their creation of a Romani Development Fund in each country. These funds would be financed by the WB and other international financial institutions. Note that trying to gain such leverage from the WB is a common strategy among social movements. The human rights movement has tried but failed. In contrast the environmental movement has been successful in instigating stronger environmental conditions in loans, yet has not always been able to enforce them (Keck and Sikkink 1998: 202). According to the IRU, the results of this visit were the following: creation of a preparation team for the International Economic Roma Conference, and further development of the Stabilization program and nation-state stabilization and development programs (IRU 1999b). Two Romani international economic conferences actually have taken place since, co-organized by the Association of Romany Entrepreneurs and Private Persons in the Czech Republic (SRPS) and the IRU, but without WB support (Baran 6 November 2002). Nevertheless, the plan for a WB-sponsored conference was not abandoned and such a conference took place in June 2003 in Budapest, in co-operation with the OSI, leading to the Decade of Roma Inclusion (2005–2015). This event, however, occurred too late for inclusion in this book. Overall, although none of the other IRU demands were fulfilled, at least it managed to obtain WB funding for some of its activities, as discussed in the preceding paragraph. In 2000, the IRU inquired about participation in the WB annual meetings in Prague. Dena Ringold from the WB, who had previously met with Scuka and Nazerali personally during meetings in the US and Strasbourg, expressed her hope that the IRU could participate in the meetings' session on poverty, which would include discussions on Romani issues, but stressed that at this point it was not yet clear how many NGOs would be able to participate (Ringold 2000). Eventually the IRU was not invited (Nazerali 19 December 2002).

On 15 April 1999, the pro-Romani ERRC also met with WB representatives, from its Human Development Unit, to discuss the economic situation of Roma in CEE (ERRC 1999d: 90). Then, on 28 July 1999, it sent WB officials (Rory O'Sullivan, WB representative of the Joint WB/European Commission (EC) Office for Southeast Europe, and Oliver Bodin, the EC representative of this body) a letter urging international authorities to undertake all possible measures to overcome the exclusion of Roma from local aid distribution, and to involve Romani representatives in bodies charged with damage assessment and reconstruction fund distribution in Kosovo (see ERRC 1999f). This letter was not answered (Cahn 24 February 2003).

In Interaction with the UNDP   The UNDP has no formal accreditation procedures for NGOs. Instead, it draws up memoranda of understanding and co-operation agreements for specific areas with them. In June 1997, the UNDP (and UN Population Fund) Executive Board adopted rules of procedure allowing it to invite NGOs with ECOSOC consultative status to participate in its deliberations (UN Doc. A/53/170). Interaction is enabled by the UNDP's Civil Society Division, which 'supports the capacity building need of CSOs [civil society organizations] by providing them with access to accurate information and appropriate skills' (UNDP, About Civil Society Division). At the same time, it assists different parts of the UNDP in working more closely and effectively with NGOs. From 2001 the UNDP's co-operation with NGOs intensified, in order to deliver 'the promises of the Millennium Declaration as well as realizing the UNDP human development goals' (UNDP, Policies and Procedures).

Yet, as of 2002, there has not been a significant interaction between Romani activists and the UNDP. Only the pro-Romani ERRC has participated in several UNDP events. In 1998 (1–5 September) the ERRC participated in the UNDP conference on human rights celebrating the 50th anniversary of the Universal Declaration on Human Rights in Yalta, Ukraine (ERRC 1998b: 70). In November 1999, the ERRC took part in two UNDP events in Almaty, Kazakhstan, serving as a resource person and speaking on freedom from discrimination at the UNDP 'Training Workshop on Human Rights and Sustainable Human Development' and speaking on the situation of minority rights in CEE at the 'Fifth UNDP International Workshop on Ombudsman and Human Rights Institutions' (ERRC 1999d: 90). The launch of the UNDP report on Roma in CEE in early 2003 however promises to stimulate co-operation between Romani organizations and the UNDP (see pp. 49–50). In preparing the report, the authors have reportedly consulted Romani communities and organizations in Bulgaria, Romania and Slovakia and '[t]he first findings of the survey were discussed with them during direct meetings …. organized by local community organizations and the [UNDP] nation-state coordinators' (Ivanov 21 February 2003). At the pre-launch meeting of the report on 13 January 2003 in London, Kalman Mizsei, Assistant Secretary-General and Director of UNDP's Bureau for Europe and the CIS, reportedly declared that '[b]acking from Romani organizations will be essential to help realize the aims of a new [UNDP] programme for Roma [in CEE]' (Puxon 2003). (Note that this testifies to the UN's need for NGO help in advocating for its policies.) To this end, the UNDP 'will hold a number of forums with Roma across Europe to stimulate implementation of the report's main recommendations' (Puxon 2003). Christelle Chapoy, UNDP (London) Public Affairs Officer, invited Puxon,[27] as the TERF co-ordinator, to chair the pre-launch meeting and suggest Romani representatives that should be invited. Upon his recommendation, five representatives attended.[28] The author of the report, Andrey Ivanov, UNDP Human Development Advisor, was also present. The Romani leaders used this occasion to lobby for the current major concern of their organizations – the deportations of failed Romani asylum-seekers from the UK and other EU countries. They appealed to the UN to intervene to stop these deportations, reportedly obtaining Mizseu's promise to take up this issue (Puxon 2003).

It remains to be seen whether he keeps his promise on this issue as well as the one on holding fora across Europe. In January 2003, the only other meeting with Romani activists related to this report was one held with the Slovak Roma Press Agency (Prolong 29 January 2003). According to Ivanov, at the moment one of the major barriers to broader participation of Roma in the implementation of the report is the fact that the report was only produced in English. The UNDP is therefore currently translating the report into local languages in order to hold follow-up meetings and discussions in the respective countries (Ivanov 21 February 2003). Thomas Acton, Professor of Romani Studies and long-time supporter of Romani political mobilization, however warned Romani leaders to be cautious of cooperating towards the implementation of the report. In his opinion,

[D]oubtless Roma groups will want to work with this report and take what political advantage of it that they can. They may have to pay a high price for doing so. [...] It can be seen that it is one of the most important official documents on Roma for a generation, and unless some of its assumptions and conclusions are deconstructed rapidly, will prejudice the tone of debates on Roma, not just in Eastern Europe, but even more inappropriately in Western Europe and the Americas, for decades to come. [...] [T]he report is fundamentally hostile to the movement of Romani emancipation that has been growing since the first World Romani Congress in 1971. Instead of emancipation it backs the moves for 'integration' in the countries concerned, and although it follows politically correct terminology in saying it is for integration rather than assimilation, in effect it suggests that the West should throw its weight and its money behind those actually assimilative government policies. [The report firmly declares] that the solution to the Gypsy problem is policies that will change the nature of the Roma themselves to fit them in to the new client mini-nation-states of Eastern Europe. Racism is acknowledged and formally condemned – but seen as an understandable reaction to the way Roma are, an increasingly impoverished under-class. [...] [T]he authors fail to realise they are reproducing almost completely the authoritarianism and assimilationism of the former communists towards the Roma, omitting only their egalitarianism and formal anti-racism (Acton 2003).

Conclusion

This chapter suggests that the UN system has been looked upon as the main target for co-operation and lobbying from the early days of global Romani activism. All the nascent international Romani organizations had co-operation with the UN as their goal, and made various unsuccessful attempts towards this end. These attempts were often marred by ignorance of the inner workings of the UN system, with appeals being made to inappropriate bodies (e.g. in the cases of the IGRM asking the Division and the Commission to enforce the Geneva Refugee Convention or the IRC asking the Commission to give Roma the status of a nation).

The chapter described a number of informal strategies used by Romani activists to increase access to the UN system, although the majority had little impact or results, except in increased publicity. Private meetings with, and letters to, UN officials never resulted in any concrete action, with the exception of contributing to the passing of resolution 1992/65. Participation of UN administration and member states delegates in Congresses served the function of sensitizing them to Romani demands and creating potential allies out of them. Yet these allies were hardly ever used to help Romani activists achieve concrete goals (perhaps with the exception of some UNESCO funding for IRU events and projects). Therefore, the main benefit of this participation was that it increased the IRU's prestige and legitimacy of being a democratically elected organization. Although the IRU's democratic representation is questionable (see e.g. Acton and Klimova 2001: 188–195), many officials attending the Congresses were sympathetic to and supportive of the IRU's attempts at democratic elections (see e.g. comments by Bammat and Thomas). The IRU's press conferences at the UN headquarters and its written appeals were also just a means of increasing publicity. Unlike some other NGOs, Romani activists did not manage to be considered an important enough partner in terms of their expertise to be given significant privileges and be, for example, invited to join in elaborating UN norms. With the exception of deliberations over the ICRC which were, however, only joined by the IRU's non-Romani representatives (p. 82).

Romani activists were even less successful in co-operation with UN funds, programmes and specialized bodies. Although most of these bodies offer official consultative status, the IRU only managed to obtain it with UNICEF. Long-term negotiations for status with UNESCO have not yet yielded results. Utilization of consultative status with the UNHCR (which the IRU holds by virtue of its ECOSOC status) has been largely marred by the IRU's political aspirations. Some activists decided to replace formal negotiations by direct protest in the form of demonstrations, yielding mixed success. No other UN body has been a target of direct protest by Romani activists. There were plans to demonstrate, on 8 April 2001, in front of the UN headquarters in New York within the framework of the Romani National Day, in support of Point 5 of the 2000 Warsaw Recommendations to the NGO Forum of the WCAR calling for the UN to confer the status of a non-territorial nation on the Romani people (see Klimova 2003: §7.2.2, Klimova 2001b: 22). However, because of the lack of people able to attend the event, the demonstration was cancelled and a small gathering instead took place at the Union Square (Klimova 2001c). Overall, co-operation with the UN funds, programmes and specialized bodies has mostly been limited to negotiating occasional funding. Romani activists have especially not taken advantage of the existing opportunities for co-operation with the ILO and WB.

At the same time it must be said that there has been some kind of informal contact with all the UN funds, programmes and specialized bodies that have shown an interest in Romani issues. At the moment, the connection between this interaction and the inclusion of Roma on the agenda for projects of these bodies is only hypothetical. In this case, the causal relationship between the actions of Romani activists and those of the UN is not likely to be strong (i.e. the actions of Romani activists were not among the main causes moving the UN to action). Nevertheless, the chapter did establish connections between Braham's UNHCR report (which led to the inclusion of Roma on the UNHCR's agenda, acknowledging them as subject to economic deprivation, social instability, and racially-motivated violence and putting forth a number of specific recommendations, see Table 3.1) and the UNDP Roma Regional Human Development Report (which reiterated Roma as an agenda item for UNDP projects, acknowledged them as a development issue and in need of positive discrimination and provided a number of recommendations on positive discrimination measures in five CEE states, see Table 3.1) and consultations with Romani activists, whose testimonies and suggestions are reflected in the reports. Similarly, it found a clear link between the report of the ILO Commission of Inquiry on Romania (which partially led to Roma being included on the ILO's agenda for addressing discrimination in employment and providing a number of specific recommendations to address discrimination against Roma in Romania, see Table 3.1) and the testimony of Nicolae Gheorghe, then an IRU official, as most of his complaints were reflected in this Commission's recommendations. Although these actions did not take place upon the initiative of Romani activists, they did influence UN agenda-setting and discourse positively.

One could argue that given the leadership's small size and limited political experience even these informal contacts represent a significant achievement. Establishing working relationships and gaining access to information is in itself not easy. Yet it is not enough, the relationships need to be developed and information utilized. It remains to be seen if Romani activists use them to their benefit in the future. If we compare the achievements gained through formal and informal strategies, Romani activists achieved much more through formal access (if we include oral and written interventions). However, this does not necessarily mean that formal access must be the best way forward, since, as argued earlier, informal strategies can be a greater source of influence than using formal access. Nevertheless, the Romani activists only had limited achievements using informal strategies. That this was so was probably a direct result of their behaviour. The interactions described in this chapter do not show a great deal of professionalism, especially in the early days of global Romani activism. While it is possible that the early interactions in some ways helped the activists gain experience and professionalize, even upon obtaining formal access they still displayed a great degree of amateurism. The greatest achievements (in terms of one person's work) were accomplished by Nicolae Gheorghe, who displayed the most professional behaviour of all the Romani activists involved in interactions with the UN system. While he was frequently in touch with some of the early Romani and pro-Romani activists such as Grattan Puxon, most of his lobbying training came from non-Romani NGOs and UN administration (as detailed in the next chapter). Therefore while it is (or at least was) not necessary to display highly professional behaviour in order to gain formal access, professional behaviour is necessary to capitalize on the access, with the personal qualities of the individual lobbyist being among the most important factors for success. Our analysis suggests that, while the most professional Romani and pro-Romani activists such as Gheorghe and the ERRC staff concentrated their energy on using formal access and only occasionally supplemented it with informal strategies, the less professional activists did not get further than informal access. Ideally formal and informal strategies would be used in conjunction to reinforce each other, however, the current human and financial resources of Romani and to a certain extent also pro-Romani activists do not allow for such a scenario.

Notes

1 For the latter see Klimova 2003: Chapter 7.
2 He informed Grattan Puxon of this meeting, stating that they discussed the international Gypsy problems (Cibula 1973).
3 The Division of Human Rights was renamed Centre for Human Rights in 1982. Since 1994 it has been headed by a High Commissioner, with the office subsequently renamed as the OHCHR (UNIHP, undated).
4 On my behalf, the staff of the UN Archives in Geneva conducted a search of UN files for evidence of interaction with IGRM, but found none (Blukacz-Louisfert 3 January 2003).
5 To a certain extent, this development could be considered a discursive and procedural change, but it has not occurred primarily within the UN system.
6 It is interesting to read such an argument coming from Hancock, for he completely rejected the benefit of co-operation with indigenous organizations in 2000, at a conference in Greenwich where I advocated such approach (see Klimova 2000). Hancock's arguments then were that comparing Roma to indigenous peoples is a form of exoticism which degrades Roma to the status of tribal people. This sharp change of opinion could have been a reaction to the European Romani leaders' rejection of Hancock's and Hopson's attempts to join the IRU forces with the indigenous movement (see pp. 97, 111).
7 See title-page photo in *Roma* 4, no. 2 and 3 (July 1978 and January 1979); Puxon 1977c.
8 Acton misspells Bammat's name as Baumart.

9   In addition, there was an unofficial 'press conference' in the surroundings of the UN building in New York after the IRU was conferred the consultative status in 1979. This was a substitute for the speech Cibula was 'not allowed' to deliver during the meeting of the UN Committee on NGOs (see p. 79) (Cibula 1979f).

10 Yul Brynner (USA), Saip Jusuf (Yugoslavia), Aniruddha Joshi (India), Bogdan Kwiek (Sweden), Juan de Dios Ramirez Heredia (Spain), Grattan Puxon (the UK), W.R. Rishi (India), and Jan Cibula (Switzerland) (See caption under the title-page photo in *Roma* 4, no.2 and 3 (July 1978 and January 1979)).

11 This demand was raised also within the OSCE fora. See Klimova 2001a: 21.

12 Note that there is not much substance behind this title, as with many other IRU titles.

13 This demand was also raised by Romani activists within the OSCE fora (see Klimova 2001a).

14 In fact, in UNESCO's opinion, the ECOSOC would also benefit from distinguishing between formal and operational relations (see UN Doc. A/54/329, §21).

15 Although various IRU documents might mistakenly say that official relations have been formed (see e.g. Djuric et al. 1991: 4; Cibula 1979c) or that the IRU has had a membership in UNESCO since 1986 (Hancock 1991b: 2). This simply means that the IRU has, at various times, met with UNESCO officials. Some academics nevertheless accept or do not question the IRU's claim to having representation in UNESCO (see e.g. Barany 2002: 259).

16 In 1912, the French government introduced the *carnet anthropometrique*, a document containing personal data, photograph and fingerprints which all travelling populations had to carry (Timeline of Romani History 1998).

17 They also submitted a memorandum about these models.

18 I have an electronic copy of this letter on file.

19 In this capacity, he participated in an expert meeting on studies of ethno-development and ethnocide in Europe in Karasjok (Norway) organized by the Human Rights and Peace Section of UNESCO (His paper 'Causes et conséquences du nomadisme des Tsiganes d'Europe' (Causes and consequences of European Gypsy nomadism) was published in the conference proceedings (SS-83/CONF.616/4 (a) and can also be viewed at http://perso.wanadoo.fr/balval/).

20 In fact, Kochanowski himself was accused of collaboration with Nazis by Valdemar Kalinin, a Lithuanian Romani writer, during the 2000 Romani Studies Greenwich conference which I attended.

21 Information from a confidential source.

22 This grant was administered by Thomas Acton via Romanestan publications. The translation was finished in 1988 and the book was published in 1990 (Acton 23 March 2003).

23 This idea was revived by Nicolae Gheorghe, in his capacity as the OSCE Advisor on Roma and Sinti Issues. He suggested that Romani NGOs at the Lodz Congress 2002 (purported world congress) ask the OSCE to sponsor such event (Klimova 2002b).

24 For example the Association of Romany Entrepreneurs and Private Persons in the Czech Republic (SRPS) has, in co-operation with the IRU, organized two International Romani conferences on employment, professional education and entrepreneuring (2001 and 2002). While the first one was largely a Czech and Slovak affair, the second had an increased participation from other countries (Novoselsky 2002; Baran 6 November 2002).

25 Wiktor Famulson (President) and his wife, Emil Scuka (General Secretary), Ivan Vesely and Stefan Palison (members of IRU Presidium), Stanislaw Stankiewicz (Vice-President), Barry Fisher (IRU lawyer) and Sean Nazerali (translator and Scuka's assistant) (IRU 1999b).

26 This visit was a part of the IRU's New York and Washington, DC tour during which they visited a number of organizations – Richards & O'Neil, LLP; New York Times; the OSI, Radio Free Europe, Voice of America, German Marshall Fund of the United States, OSCE, NGO department of the UN, US Department of State, Holocaust Memorial Museum and the Czech Embassy in the United States (IRU 1999b).

27 Who is not aware how the UNDP found out about him (Puxon 28 January 2003).

28 Ladislav Balaz, chairman of TERF; Roza Katowicz, chairwoman of the Roma Support Group (RSG); Boris Muntyanu, former President of the Odessa Region Romani Congress; Cliff Codona of the National Travellers Action Group (NTAG); and Peter Mercer, chair of East Anglia Gypsy Council and IRU Parliament member for UK (Puxon 28 January 2003). As with the WCAR (see Klimova 2003: §7.6.2), Codona tried to use the publicity of this event to help his campaign against the eviction of his family from Woodside caravan park. When I presented my findings about the interaction between Romani activist and the UN system for the Crosstalk Society at Corpus Christi College in Cambridge on 21 January 2003, two members of the audience proudly told me that the Roma now have a representative in the UN. It is a famous Rom from Northampton who was nominated by Tony Blair. Later Puxon explained to me that this story refers to Codona's participation at the UNDP meeting which was taken up and highly distorted by the local press (Puxon 23 January 2003).

Chapter 6

UN Interventions and Allies of Romani Activists

This chapter examines the UN configuration of power in relation to the Romani activists' allies, while also detailing the activists' interventions at the UN for which allies were sought. Firstly, the third POS dimension is introduced – the configuration of power and structure of political alliances within the UN system. Secondly, the activists' oral and written interventions at the UN are analysed to determine whether links exist between these and the UN agenda-setting and discursive developments that relate to Roma (identified in Chapter 3), and if the activists themselves were influenced by UN discourse. Thirdly, the chapter analyses the alliances that the activists built to promote their goals at the UN, both through the interventions described here as well as the strategies addressed in chapters 4 and 5.

Configuration of Power and Structure of Political Alliances

While in the framework of Kriesi et al. the configuration of power refers to political parties, Passy maintains that it refers to states at the international level. Applied to the UN, the configuration varies between its different structures and election periods, because not all nation-states are present in every UN structure and are usually elected only for limited periods. For example, in the ECOSOC fifty-four states are elected for a period of three years. The degree of acceptance of NGOs and the scope of opportunities for their lobbying depends on which states are elected. Some states are more open to particular issues, based on how threatening they see them. When the state sees an issue as non-threatening, or even compatible with its nation-state interest, it can become an ally of the NGOs by facilitating their lobbying, supporting the resolutions they draft, disseminating their reports, favouring these issues in political debates, and drawing attention to them, perhaps even exerting pressure on other states (Passy 1999: 157–158). Having influence on nation-state governments thus leads to increased influence within the UN administration (Riggs and Plano 1994: 48).

Equally, because the representatives of nation-states are not always present in the UN, its administration has great autonomy. In particular, the UN administration drafts resolutions, sets agendas of conferences, working groups and commissions, prepares universal declarations, etc. (Passy 1999: 158). Therefore, the administration itself is a source of powerful allies for NGOs. Passy does not include this point in the configuration of power, however I believe that configuration of allies within the UN administration is an integral part of the UN configuration of power. As Reinalda, Arts and Noortmann argue, IGOs (and by implication their administration) should not 'be regarded as puppets of their main nation-state(s) ... [because they] to a certain extent act as more or less autonomous entities' (2001: 2). In addition, although the configuration of allies among the NGOs is not an integral part of the UN configuration of power, it does play a role by allowing less established NGOs with a lower consultative status to lobby through their more powerful NGO allies. The utilizations of all the components of the configuration of power by Romani activists are now illustrated with individual cases of intervention, and analysed further.

The Oral and Written Interventions by Romani Activists and Usage of Configuration of Power

Romani activists targeted most of their interventions at the Subcommission and, to a lesser extent, the Commission, WGPM and CERD. In only one case did it submit an intervention to the ECOSOC. The majority of its interventions at the Subcommission and Commission (and the one at the ECOSOC) were either made in, or due to, co-operation with allied NGOs who had a higher consultative status. Indeed, until 1993 this was necessary because the IRU did not have an automatic right to speak. Even after 1993, it often needed the resources and, perhaps, the motivation of allied NGOs to bring their speakers to the Commission. The following paragraphs describe these interventions and the co-operation with allies when intervening at each of the above UN bodies.

The ECOSOC

The only intervention by Romani activists at the ECOSOC was a written statement submitted by the IRU and thirty-four other NGOs in 1979. This statement supported the Commission's resolution E/CN.4/L.1416/Add.2 from 6 March 1979 inviting the Preparatory Committee for the New International Development Strategy to consider the integration of human rights in the development process, and requested that the International Development Strategy (for the Third UN Development Decade) explicitly mentions that the achievement of human rights is one of the main parts of the development process (UN Doc. E/1979/NGO/16). This petition was unsuccessful (see UN Doc. [ST/]DPI/689). The human rights dimension was not incorporated until the Fourth UN Development Decade because, until then, the Cold War prevented serious discussion of human rights in this context (UN Doc. A/45/41: Annex I, 18; van Boven 13 December 2002). The intervention was prepared at the general assembly of NGOs with ECOSOC consultative status that the IRU had attended (see p. 70). Hence, the IRU simply joined an initiative from other NGOs that was compatible with its goals. However, development issues have not been a priority in the IRU's lobbying at the UN as of yet.

The Commission

No interventions at the Commission were made purely on the initiative of Romani activists. The earliest interventions (in 1991) were made with the encouragement, support and co-operation of the IFHR. The more recent ones were the result of co-operation with the TRP and an initiative by the International Save the Children Alliance (ISCA). All the interventions are now detailed.

In relation to Resolution 1992/65, Entitled 'Protection of Roma (Gypsies)'   The first chance of Romani activists to address the Commission was in 1991, when the IFHR offered their automatic right to speak to Nicolae Gheorghe from the IRU. Gheorghe attended the Commission's sessions in 1991 and 1992, and his lobbying activities resulted in resolution 1992/65 (see p. 35). The first intervention Gheorghe delivered orally was on 25 February 1991 under the agenda item 19 (Rights of persons belonging to national, ethnic, religious and linguistic minorities). He concentrated on the need to involve the international community in guaranteeing that Roma can fully enjoy all human rights, including social, economic and cultural. He reminded the Commission of Resolution 6(XXX) and opined that since its passing there had been some progress in achieving basic freedoms and cultural rights for Roma in some countries (see pp. 40–1). He declared that, since 1989, Roma in many countries achieved political rights but also became the subjects of racial violence and discrimination, as illustrated in Voyame's report and the reports of NGOs such as the Raoul Wallenberg Association and Romani Phralipe (see pp. 36–7). He detailed some specific types of human rights violations against Roma and argued for granting collective rights to Roma, combating prejudice, promoting equal rights, including the right to development and recognition of Romani identity in order to remedy the situation.[1] He asked the Commission to encourage Special Rapporteurs to pay due attention to the conditions in which Romani communities live, to urge governments to continue taking measures that promote the rights of Roma and to recommend that governments request UN advisory services and technical assistance for this purpose, to consider tasking the CHR with designing a special project for this purpose (including a seminar and a workshop), and to recommend that interested IGOs and NGOs consider promoting the participation of Roma in protecting their rights (UN Doc. E/CN.4/1991/SR.40: 4–7). This statement was also prepared in a written form but was not officially circulated by the UN (See IRU and IFHR 1991).[2]

On 4 March 1991 Gheorghe delivered another oral statement on behalf of the IFHR and the IRU, under agenda item 21 (Advisory services in the field of human rights). He lobbied for more involvement of NGOs in the work of the UN and reiterated his earlier point that there was a need for transnational policies in relation to Roma. He argued that it was important to continue advisory services under the regular budget and the Voluntary Fund for drafting new constitutions in CEE; disseminate information not only among governmental actors but also within the general public; involve NGOs in the work of the Commission, especially in the initiation and implementation of projects for specific peoples or areas of human rights; and explicitly include the criterion of NGO participation in the guidelines prepared by the CHR for the assessment of requests for advisory services and technical assistance. He suggested that European governments should individually or collectively request advisory services for the realisation of human rights of Roma, and repeated his request for organizing (under the auspices of the CHR) a seminar on the economic, social and cultural problems encountered by Roma (UN Doc. E/CN.4/1991/SR.50: 2). Many of the general points included in this intervention resulted from discussion with the CHR deputy director Alfredsson Gudmundur who, according to Gheorghe, introduced him to the concept of anti-discrimination and taught him the jargon used at the Commission (Gheorghe 4 December 2002).

On 10 April 1991, the IRU submitted a written statement co-authored by the IFHR under the agenda item 12 (a question of the violation of human rights and fundamental freedoms in any part of the world, with particular reference to colonial and other dependent countries and territories), mostly detailing various types of violations of the human rights of Roma. The intervention frequently cited Joseph Voyame's report (UN Doc. E/CN.4/1991/30). It also briefly introduced the Romani people and recapitulated previous UN decisions in relation to them. It asked the Commission to consider all the proposals that Gheorghe had previously made orally,[3] as well as recommending that interested governments and NGOs consider ways and means for increasing the Roma's own participation in protecting their rights (for the full text see UN Doc. E/CN.4/1991/NGO/51).[4] Gheorghe also re-drafted the Subcommission's resolution 1991/21, adding preambular references to the governments' responsibility of safeguarding human rights in their countries and to Voyame's finding that the marginalization of Roma constitutes an important minority problem (see pp. 36–7). He also added the recommendation that governments request advisory services to ensure protection of the rights of Roma, and that the Commission considers ways in which Romani organizations could contribute to such protection (Gheorghe 1991b). However, during his first lobbying year he did not manage to find a government to sponsor his draft resolution. He was more successful a year later, as detailed in the next paragraph. Note that this cannot be explained just by the configuration of power because the composition of the Commission did not change much between 1991 and 1992. From the newcomers to the Commission in 1992, it was only Bulgaria that sponsored resolution 1992/65. In addition, three (Greece, Norway, and Romania) of the nine sponsoring countries of the resolution were not Commission members in 1992, they were only represented as observers (see OHCHR, Undated).

On 2 March 1992, Gheorghe delivered an oral statement on behalf of the IRU under the agenda item 21. He advocated that CEE states must incorporate provisions combating racial discrimination in their legislations, and urged the Commission to devise a coherent programme to tackle the specific problems of Roma and encourage CEE governments to avail themselves of advisory services with a view to solving Romani problems. He also offered the advisory assistance of the IRU. In the introduction of his intervention he commended the work of UN advisory services, especially the evaluations carried out by Voyame. However, he emphasized that some of the new constitutions and legislations adopted by CEE states with UN assistance still fail to define and combat racial discrimination, oppose racist attitudes and promote human rights of minorities. He also welcomed recent European and UN initiatives on Roma, including Resolution 1991/21 that he said was of great importance to the IRU (UN Doc. E/CN.4/1992/SR.50/Add.1: 25–26).

Some of Gheorghe's requests to the Commission were translated into the resolution, although he was less successful than with the Subcommission the previous year (as will be shown shortly). For, while the Subcommission translated most of his demands and even his exact wording into resolution 1991/21, the Commission only accepted some demands, which it watered down. Specifically, instead of urging all the Commission and Subcommission Special Rapporteurs to pay special attention to Roma, this attention was only to be accorded in one study. The demand for measures to be taken in consultation with Romani communities was ignored, and the measures were limited only to those eliminating discrimination, as opposed to also guaranteeing protection and security. In addition, a call was made just for *adopting* those measures, losing the emphasis on implementation. The only step in which it was more progressive than resolution 1991/21 is that it (as Gheorghe requested) specifically named the body that should provide advisory services – the CHR. Gheorghe's demand for the CHR designing a special project for this purpose (including a seminar and a workshop) and recommendation that interested IGOs and NGOs consider promoting Romani participation in protection of rights of Roma were, however, both ignored. Romania eventually took it upon itself to organize an international conference on the topic proposed by Gheorghe, in co-operation with PER, as it was anxious to prove good treatment of its minorities while its application for CoE membership was considered (Gheorghe 4 December 2002; for report of this conference see PER 1994).

In Gheorghe's opinion, the only valuable part of this resolution is its title; the rest is virtually useless (Gheorghe 4 December 2002). He recalls that his lobbying was marred by opposition from the German government, which tried to water down the resolution as much as possible so that it would not apply to Romani asylum-seekers present in Germany (see pp. 100–1). In the opinion of other Romani activists and, reportedly, also another European delegate at the Commission, this was a blatant display of German anti-Romani racism (Germany Refuses to Sign 1992: 4). Gheorghe initially asked the Indian delegation to propose the resolution which he had drafted, but they were unwilling to initiate such a resolution unless it was supported by at least five countries. Gheorghe then managed to obtain the sponsorship of three CEE countries (Gheorghe 4 December 2002) – Bulgaria, the Czech and Slovak Federal Republic, and his native Romania. Austria, France, Greece, Italy, Norway and Portugal became additional sponsors (see UN Doc. E/CN.4/1992/L.72).

While the sponsors hoped that the draft resolution might be adopted without a vote, the German representative insisted on voting. He explained that the specific focus on Roma was inappropriate because many other groups live in similar conditions. He also said that Germany does not recognize Roma as a minority and cannot institutionalize positive discrimination in favour of them because many Roma live in Germany illegally and might be expelled. The representative of the USA was also not in favour of the resolution, but for the opposite reason. He believed that it was too restricted and only required states to protect their residents, as opposed to all those who live on their territory. Due to these two concerns, the vote on the resolution was postponed from the 52nd meeting to the 54th meeting (UN Doc. E/CN.4/1992/SR.52, 2–3).

During the 54th meeting, seeing that the resolution was likely to be passed, Germany wanted to introduce an amendment specifying that the resolution would only apply to Roma who have traditionally lived in the state as its subjects. This amendment was, though, voted against (see UN Doc. E/CN.4/1992/SR.54). The IFHR succeeded in obtaining the voting support of Latin American countries as a trade-off for negotiations on other issues, and the resolution was passed despite German opposition (Gheorghe 4 December 2002). The German representative then circulated a declaration to the Commission members that, in Germany, Roma are neither considered a minority nor discriminated against, and that all persons who are in the country illegally can be expelled (see UN Doc. E/CN.4/1992/SR.54).

With regret, Gheorghe remembers none of the other IRU officials gave their support for his lobbying attempt. He had appealed to the President Djuric, Vice-President Rose and others for help, but was left alone, supported only by his colleagues from the IFHR (Gheorghe 4 December 2002). This shows that, within the UN framework, non-Roma can be more reliable allies in promoting Romani goals than other Romani activists. One of the reasons is perhaps that, for these non-Roma, human rights concerns are a priority as they are not bogged down in internal Romani politics.

Miscellaneous   Unrelated to resolution 1992/65, the IRU submitted another written statement on 1 February 1991 under the agenda item 20 (Rights of persons belonging to national, ethnic, religious and linguistic minorities), calling for the adoption of an international auxiliary language as a means of solving the communication problems among nations that hinder the achievement of world peace. As this statement is written in an untypical tone for the IRU and contains a quote coming from the Baha'i World Centre, it was probably drafted by Marko Kappenberger, who attended this Commission session (see p. 71) (see UN Doc. E/CN.4/1991/INF.1: 40). The IRU representatives listed as participating are: Kappenberger, Cibula, Gheorghe and Cioaba. Gheorghe, who came with Cioaba, was however not aware of Kappenberger's and Cibula's presence or the intervention submitted by them. The same goes for the Subcommission's session one year earlier (see p. 133) (Gheorghe 4 December 2002). This shows how little co-ordination there has been even among the leading figures in the IRU. The intervention suggested that the IRU could be an example for the nations of the world because it uses 'its own international auxiliary language' which helps reduce human rights violations. It stated that the IRU was looking forward to the World Conference on Human Rights (although it eventually did not attend it). At the end, gratefulness was expressed to all who fight prejudice and so contribute to making our planet a safe and happy place (see UN Doc. E/CN.4/1991/NGO/25).

Between 1992 and 1998 there were no IRU interventions at the Commission, despite it having an automatic right to speak from 1993. Cibula and Kappenberger had stopped representing the IRU at the UN, whilst Gheorghe found the UN process too long-term and tiresome. He instead diverted his activities to the OSCE, which was more open to Romani issues (Gheorghe 4 December 2002). This strategy has indeed proven very useful for Gheorghe as he managed to rise to an important position within the OSCE relatively fast (partly because the OSCE is a smaller and less rigid body than the UN). His OSCE position in turn opens him doors to UN delegates and administration. Meanwhile, the IRU had no one to replace them, until Pietrosanti from the TRP stepped in (see p. 141 on Pietrosanti's affiliation with the IRU).

On 25 March 1998, Pietrosanti made an oral intervention on behalf of the TRP and IRU, presenting a number of ideas later embedded in the Declaration of Nation (see pp. 22–27). He claimed that the 20 million strong Romani nation has been ignored by media, governments and international organizations and argued that Roma are a unique example of a global nation which does not wish to become a state because their characteristics and culture cut across the traditional concepts of nation and state. In his opinion, the only answer to the problems of violations of Romani rights was the enforcement of international law. He also urged the Commission to request the Special Rapporteur to submit a report at the next session on the Romani nation and the discrimination it experiences (UN Doc. E/CN.4/1998/SR.11: 5–6; for the entire speech see Pietrosanti 1998). On 30 March 1999, Pietrosanti made another oral intervention on behalf of the TRP and IRU, lobbying for both the recognition of Roma as a constituent nation of the UN and state support for establishment of Romani schools, in which Romani culture, tradition, language and values could be transmitted to

Romani children. He also repeated his request that the Commission charge the Special Rapporteur with delivering a special report on racial discrimination against Roma at its next session, and requested that a specific item on the Romani nation be included in the agenda of the forthcoming WCAR. Some steps were taken towards realising both of his latter two proposals but eventually neither was fulfilled (see p. 40 and Klimova 2003: Chapter 7). Although another speaker, Julia Ekstedt speaking for the ISCA, also raised Romani issues during this session, the Commission issued no statement or document addressing Roma (see UN Doc. E/CN.4/1999/SR.8). Eksted 'presented information about the ways in which the right to education of Roma/Gypsy and Traveller children was being compromised or violated in a number of European countries' (Save the Children 2001a: 11). As a result, various people present at the Commission's meeting were interested in receiving publications about this topic, thus motivating the ISCA to carry out its project 'Denied a Future?' (Save the Children 2001a: 11).

To make more impact at the next session, the ISCA decided to give youth Romani activists the opportunity of participating in the Commission session as part of a new project. This project aims to bring young people to the Commission to raise issues that are important to them and so gain practical experience of advocacy, lobbying and networking at the UN (Laftman, Motala, and Albery 2001). In its first year, the ISCA gave this honour to Nadia Foy, a young Scottish Traveller,[5] who, on 24 March 2000, delivered an oral intervention on the right to education for Roma, Gypsy and Traveller children. She argued that many such children experienced discrimination, segregation and prejudice in many European educational systems or were actually denied access to education, in violation of a number of UN treaties (UN Doc. E/CN.4/2000/SR.8: 2). She recommended that governments implement existing international and nation-state law and, in consultation with Romani, Gypsy and Traveller representatives, take specific measures to ensure that these children do not suffer from discrimination and instead benefit from minority rights in relation to the learning of their mother tongue, culture and history, and that governments provide basic information on the educational attainment of such children (for the UN summary of the speech see UN Doc. E/CN.4/2000/SR.8: 2;[6] for the entire speech see Equal Opportunities Committee 2001). Although her speech did not lead to any action by the Commission, it later resonated with CERD (see p. 135). Foy looks back at her experience of speaking at the UN as 'a unique opportunity'. She recalls that

[a]s a young Gypsy it was such a privilege for me to read out the declaration, to think that all those people from all the different countries were listening to me. [...] I think I was a bit surprised at how much work we did at the U.N., it seemed like we never sat down, or if we did it was with an MP or delegate trying to 'influence' them. Even the 'cocktail party' we gatecrashed was an experience – always trying to talk to people and raise their awareness. I was really surprised at how many people didn't know there were Gypsies in Scotland, or the fact that I'm fair. I think that in itself raised a lot of awareness and challenged views.

Being there really gave me a different outlook on life [...] I think it was good for people to realise that there is still so much discrimination in Scotland and the rest of the U.K. It was really important for people in authority to know that. I learnt a lot about how decisions are taken and how to try to get change for the better. In Geneva I really felt like I was able to make a difference for all Gypsies, maybe only a little bit but every little helps and it is so important that Gypsies are doing it for themselves (Equal Opportunities Committee 2001).

The ISCA also organized a well-attended fringe meeting in which it introduced its ongoing project 'Denied a future? The right to education of Roma/Gypsy and Traveller children in Europe' and had Roma from Romania, Bulgaria, Scotland and Hungary speaking about the situation in their countries (Foy and Lloyd 2002).

In 2001 the ISCA brought Andrea Mohacsi, a Romani youth delegate from Hungary, to the Commission's session. However, she did not get to speak at the session, only at a fringe meeting on 22 March 2001 and at one of the meetings of the Children's and Women's caucuses.[7] That year Pietrosanti also returned to the Commission, this time solely on behalf of the IRU, making another appeal for a revolution in international relations and the UN system that, he claimed, was necessary for promoting the interests of all Europeans, not just all Roma. This time he used the term trans-statual as opposed to a transnational nation which needs a trans-statual rule of law. He also reminded the Commission of the Declaration of Nation and of the Memorandum signed with the Czech MFA which supports the recognition of Roma as a nation (see pp. 22–7, 80). Probably because of his failure the previous year to convince states to support Romani schools, he now also urged the international community to invest into educational programmes for Romani children (for the entire speech see Pietrosanti 2001). It was not possible to check if there was any reaction to Pietrosanti's speech because, by the end of 2003, the UN summary record for this session had not been issued. Nevertheless, it is unlikely that such a visionary statement resonated well with the Commission.

At the Subcommission

Before 1993 the IRU managed to deliver a number of interventions, despite not having the automatic right to do so. However, only those that were either made in, or due to, co-operation with NGO allies – MRG and IFHR – resulted in any UN action. Those are detailed first. After 1993, the IRU almost achieved another success, in co-operation with a number of non-Romani NGOs, yet the Subcommission's call to action was blocked by the Commission. All the other interventions evoked no responses.

In Relation to Resolution 6 (XXX) of 31 August 1977   The Subcommission was the first UN body to accord representatives of Roma[8] a hearing, which is unsurprising as it was among the first UN bodies to interact closely with NGOs (UN Press Release 2001a). Three members of the 1971 Congress Presidium (Cibula, Jusuf and Puxon) managed to obtain an invitation to the Subcommission session on 31 August 1977, where Capotorti's report was discussed and the first ever resolution mentioning Roma was passed (see pp. 40–1). The invitation was obtained upon the initiative of Benjamin Whitaker, a Subcommission member, British Labour MP and Director of the MRG. When Whitaker established the MRG he had considered it important that the organization would not only deal with minority problems abroad, but also those in the UK. Therefore, with his colleagues, he tried to establish which minority was the most discriminated against and least popular in the UK, and concluded that it was the Roma. Therefore he contracted Puxon to write a report about their situation (Whitaker 26 February 2003). (See also Puxon 1973.) It was on the basis of this report that Whitaker decided to raise the issue at the Subcommission. For this purpose he drafted a resolution and found four more sponsors from other

Subcommission's members. He tried to find a sponsor from each continent, to ensure wide support for the resolution if it came to a vote. Consequently, three of the sponsors (Caicedo-Perdomo and Ortiz Martin as representatives of Latin American states and Sekyiamah as a representative of African states) were not familiar with the plight of the Roma, but were enlisted to ensure a majority vote. The Indian representative Ram Bhagat was the only sponsor with some interest in the Roma (Whitaker 26 February 2003), and was instructed to support the resolution by the Indian Prime Minister Morarji Desai upon lobbying from the IRC officials. Puxon and Jusuf met Desai in London on 14 June 1977 (News and Reviews 1977b: 32).[9] Reportedly the IRC contacted the Indian Mission at Geneva upon Desai's suggestion. The Indian representative then took up the matter of the resolution that the IRC wanted to have presented at the Subcommission (Jusuf 1981: 24–25). According to Puxon, this draft of the resolution, drawn by him and Desai, included the definition of Roma as a national minority of Indian origin – unlike Whitaker's original version. Desai reportedly supported this definition upon meeting Puxon's Romani wife Sanije, whose Indian appearance impressed him, as he had never met any Roma before. Puxon visited Desai again the evening before the Subcommission's meeting to ensure that India would fully support this resolution (Puxon 1 March 2003). According to Whitaker, India's role in passing the resolution was, however, supportive, rather than initiatory (Whitaker 26 February 2003).

The draft resolution was discussed by the Subcommission on 31 August 1977 (see also pp. 40–1). Puxon, speaking on behalf of the MRG and the 1971 Congress, detailed Romani persecution, including the still unremedied Holocaust. He also mentioned a then recent CoE resolution, recommending measures to improve the living conditions of Roma and Travellers and to protect them from discrimination (Parliamentary Assembly of the CoE 1969), which remained unimplemented.[10] He argued that Roma want the same rights as other minorities, namely recognition of their language and culture and the status of minority denied to them by most countries. He expressed the hope that Capotorti's study would lead the Commission to further action to protecting the rights of minorities, including the Roma (UN Doc. E/CN.4/Sub.2/SR.795: 11–12). He also circulated both his previously published report on the situation of Roma (Puxon 1973) and a written statement, emphasizing the plight of the world's Roma and their links to India[11] and the support they had recently received from India's governmental officials (for details see India Supports Roma 1978: 16), publicizing the activities of the IRC, the 1971 Congress and affiliated nation-state organizations, and arguing that Roma are the largest non-territorial national minority in Europe and that their national movement dates back to their liberation from slavery in Romania in the mid-19th century (for the full text of this appeal see Puxon 1977d). According to reports in the journal *Roma* published in India, Puxon concluded his speech by saying that Roma look to the UN and India for their emancipation (News and Reviews 1977a: 33–35; India Supports Roma 1978: 3–17). This information, except that Roma are a non-territorial nation, however does not occur in the UN summary records of this meeting (UN Doc. E/CN.4/Sub.2/SR.795: 11–12).

There were no further comments relating to Roma at this morning session, except Whitaker's introduction of the resolution (UN Doc. E/CN.4/Sub.2/SR.795). The resolution was then passed at the afternoon session, although the request to be recognized as a nationality of Indian origin was lost due to opposition from CEE countries experts (see pp. 40–1). However, the perhaps more important goal of calling upon states to guarantee Roma equal rights was won – thus the first hearing of Romania activists at the UN was crowned with success, although this was primarily due to their NGO/UN expert ally Whitaker. The 1978 Congress declaredly took the publicizing of this resolution among the world's Roma, and the pressing of governments to implement it through nation-state organizations, as its primary tasks (Rishi 1978: 5).

In Relation to Resolution 1991/21, Entitled 'Protection of Minorities'   It was another fifteen years before Romani activists succeeded in pushing for another Subcommission resolution to mention Roma. It was Gheorghe's oral statement delivered on behalf of the IRU and IFHR on 29 August 1990, under agenda item 4 (Review of further developments in fields with which the Subcommission has been concerned), which, together with Gheorghe's lobbying of the Subcommission's members, resulted one year later in resolution 1991/21, entitled 'Protection of minorities' (for the full text see Danbakli 2001: 265–266). Gheorghe detailed the negative (and a few positive) effects of democratic transition on Roma and the feeling of insecurity they created among them, warning the Subcommission of the potential dangers of such a situation. He said that the Romani community expected governments to develop comprehensive policies on Roma, in co-operation with Romani representatives, as the Subcommission had requested for minorities in general on the basis of proposals made by Capotorti. He requested that the Subcommission ensures that governments who benefit from UN advisory services and technical assistance include measures on the elimination of discrimination against Roma in their programmes. He also requested that the Special Rapporteurs dealing with minorities accord special attention to Roma (UN Doc. E/CN.4/Sub.2/1990/SR.32). All of these requests were included in the resolution 1991/21, adopted on 19 August 1991, which consisted chiefly of these requests and a preamble-type text (see pp. 41–2).

One day after the adoption of this resolution, Gheorghe was already thinking of its more specific implementation. On 20 August 1991, he delivered an oral statement (UN Doc. E/CN.4/Sub.2/1991/SR.20) under agenda item 18 (Protection of Minorities). He welcomed the reference Special Rapporteur Asbjorn Eide had made about the essential role of NGOs in elucidating issues related to conflict resolution, and made a number of suggestions to the Special Rapporteur and the Subcommission. These were: 1) the Special Rapporteur should pay special attention to a) the case of non-territorially based peoples and transnational minorities, taking the world's Roma as an ideal case, in order to reflect new political realities which call for international institutions to take responsibility for peoples and minorities who do not have an ethnic government of their own; and b) to the evaluation of various commissions on Romani and other minority issues (such commissions should use the guidelines advanced by Asbjorn Eide); and 2) the Subcommission should a) call on governments to recognize the problems of potential danger of large scale violence against the Roma in situations of instability in some Eastern European countries and the need for measures towards a solution; b) consider organizing a debate and a seminar on Romani issues concentrating on the roots of prejudice, hostility, inter-ethnic tensions and means towards equality and peaceful co-habitation; c) recommend the inclusion of Romani issues on the agenda of the UN Conference on Human Rights in 1993 and invite Romani NGOs to participate in this event; d) call on governments to allocate special funds for the implementation of the special measures needed to reduce the existing gap between Roma and the majority in education, employment, housing and health; and e) recommend that governments allocate a specified amount of resources for projects concerning Romani communities when concluding bi-lateral treaties. Gheorghe also drew attention to the recent plight of Romani refugees and asked for the improvement in the living conditions in home countries as a long-term solution (Gheorghe 1991b). Note that not all of these recommendations were transcribed into the UN summary record. Unlike those made the previous year, none of these proposals were acted upon. During this session, Gheorghe also submitted a compilation of cases of human rights violations against Roma under point 10 of the Subcommission agenda (Administration of justice and human rights of the detainees). (This submission is mentioned in Gheorghe 1991d; for the full text see Gheorghe 1991c.) Although the cases were not relevant to the agenda item, Gheorghe wanted to use any possible chance for submitting them. These cases do not appear in UN records on the official written statement submitted, but Gheorghe insists that he did submit them (Gheorghe 4 December 2002). The fact that they are not included in the UN records, however, shows that his strategy of trying to submit evidence under an irrelevant topic (attempted because it was not possible to submit it under a relevant one) was not successful.

In Relation to the Initiative for a Rapporteur on Roma   Again, it took a long time before Romani and pro-Romani activists achieved some action by the Subcommission, in a case concerning the initiative for a Rapporteur on Roma. This initiative started with the repeated requests of Pietrosanti in the 1998 and 1999 sessions of the Commission that the Commission charges the Special Rapporteur with delivering a special report on racial discrimination against Roma and on the phenomenon of the Romani nation (UN Doc. E/CN.4/1999/SR.8; UN Doc. E/CN.4/1998/SR.11). In 1999, the first steps towards institutionalizing such a post were taken by the Subcommission which, as an independent expert body, is bound to be more receptive to the plight of vulnerable groups than the Commission, itself composed of governmental delegates. Then, during its annual review on 14 August 2000, the Subcommission discussed Romani issues in detail, based on the findings of a preliminary study by the Subcommission expert Sik Yuen (see pp. 39–40). During the afternoon session of 14 August 2000 Pietrosanti addressed Romani issues, calling for representation of Roma at the UN on a par with other nations, and for an institutional reform of the EU and UN. He argued that the Roma are not a minority but a nation (sharing the same origin, language and traditions) consisting of over fifteen million individuals. (Note that two years earlier he claimed twenty million, see p. 124.) This entire nation was represented in the UN system by merely one NGO – the IRU. In his opinion, Romani demands for representation in the UN without becoming a state underlined one of the major issues at stake in the current international debate on the adequacy of the state system in a globalized world. He also reminded the Subcommission about the suffering of Roma in Kosovo and argued for institutional reform in the EU which would ensure the rule of law for each individual, irrespective his nationality and ethnicity. This, according to him, was also the dream of the Romani nation. He urged the Subcommission to address the issue of whether the current institution of state was properly equipped to deal with the challenges of the modern world. He also called on the Subcommission to develop the dream of the Romani nation further (UN Press Release 2000a; UN Doc.

E/CN.4/Sub.2/2000/SR.19: 11–12). As his statement was rather ideological, aiming to initiate a change in current thinking about international relations, no specific action was mentioned or taken by the Subcommission (see UN Press Release 2001b; UN Doc. E/CN.4/Sub.2/2000/SR.19: 11–12).

The discussion continued during the evening session, in which a number of NGOs also addressed Romani issues, and endorsed the elaboration of Sik Yuen's report on Roma. As they were all non-Romani NGOs these interventions are not mentioned here (for their summary see UN Doc. E/CN.4/Sub.2/2000/SR.20), except for two relevant exceptions. The International Movement against all Forms of Discrimination and Racism (IMADR) also spoke in the name of the Zentralrat, its partner Romani organization. The speaker supported arguments made in a written statement prepared by Romani Rose, the Chairman of the Zentralrat, for the purposes of the informal meeting with CERD members the next day, criticising the working paper presented by Sik Yuen for echoing a number of prejudices such as that Roma do not show respect for the laws of the countries they live in. Nevertheless, the IMADR also supported the continuance of Sik Yuen's work. Sik Yuen rejected the IMADR criticism, pointing out that this was a misinterpretation of his words. His report mentioned examples of existing prejudices but did not sanction them (UN Press Release 2000b). He stated that he 'had tried at all times to be objective and fair and, in all fairness, he had to state that the Roma themselves often courted criticism and acted uncooperatively in ways that did not help their cause. Only if all sides respected the rules could understanding and progress be achieved' (UN Doc. E/CN.4/Sub.2/2000/SR.20: 5). His argument comes back to one of the inquiries of this book – the extent to which IGOs try to impose their discourse and rules of the game on the non-state actors they interact with – and to Goodwin's suggestion that an agonistic system of international relations would be better able to accommodate the demands of Romani activists because it would allow them to determine the rules of the game according to the terms of their own culture as opposed to those already established by dominant actors (see p. 25). Romani activists often complain that Roma are forced to abide by rules and conventions that were negotiated without their participation.

The second exception that I want to mention is the intervention by Clementine MacDonald speaking for the ISCA. MacDonald was a part of a larger ISCA delegation to the UN in Geneva, with three other Irish and Scottish Travellers (Michelle Stewart, Patrick Mongan, Mark Donohue) and two Romanian Romani youths (Delia Grigore and Lavinia Olmazu). All of the delegation members got to make a presentation at one of the fringe meetings the ISCA organized, or at the CERD and the Subcommission (see pp. 125–6, 130–1, 135–6). Together, the Travellers prepared a declaration about 'their own views on life' and 'the way they get treated' as Travellers (for the entire text of the declaration see Equal Opportunities Committee 2001).[12] The declaration, read by MacDonald on 14 August 2000, welcomed Sik Yuen's paper and expressed support for 'any further actions aimed at promoting and protecting the human rights of Travellers, Roma/Gypsies', especially regarding education. The declaration opened by explaining that the delegation came to the UN to try and persuade those in power to bring an end to the discrimination that Traveller communities have suffered for centuries. It maintained that Roma and Travellers have long been ignored by states, regarded as a 'problem' because of their nomadic nature. It likened some campsites provided for Travellers to concentration camps or reservations, and complained of the verbal abuse, denial of adequate medical attention, substandard and segregated education, suspicion by the police and disparagement in the media that Travellers are exposed to. It argued that, despite legislative progress in some countries, in practice little had changed in recent years (Oral declaration in Equal Opportunities Committee 2001). It requested that the Subcommission urges Governments to legally recognize the right to a travelling life and access to health and education for Travellers, actively involve Travellers and Roma in all decision-making that affects their lives, and promote an international public education campaign for removing prejudice towards Travellers and Roma (Equal Opportunities Committee 2001; UN Doc. E/CN.4/Sub.2/2000/SR.20: 2–3). Similarly to Foy, MacDonald saw speaking at the UN as an eye-opening experience (see p. 125). She recounts it as follows: 'I was really proud to say my bit for my culture and I am pleased that people noticed me along with all the other NGOs. I had my five minutes and I was surprised at the response I got for my little say. […] I just hope that every NGO's five minutes makes a difference' (Equal Opportunities Committee 2001).

Two days later Grigore, another member of the ISCA delegation, had a chance of delivering an oral statement. She posited that the current problematic situation of Romani children in Romania was the direct consequence of six centuries of slavery. Although slavery was abolished in 1856, in her opinion 'the authorities had continued their unequal treatment of the Roma in the civil, social and political spheres' through institutionalized discrimination which had not ceased even after Roma had been recognized as a national minority in 1990 (UN Doc. E/CN.4/Sub.2/2000/SR.23, 14). She detailed the problems Romani children experience resulting from the Romanian educational assimilation policy, and explained that this policy is the reason why the Romani movement in Romania opted for building a nation on a non-territorial basis. She called on the Subcommission to recommend that the Romanian Government take a number of educational and anti-discrimination measures in relation to Roma. These were to:

> sign the various international agreements and take measures in accordance with international law; include provisions in domestic legislation to prohibit discrimination in education; set up a partnership on an equal footing between the Roma representatives and the authorities to ensure that the Roma took an equal part in preparing and evaluating education policies; support, including by making the necessary credit available, an educational system that took the Roma into consideration (multicultural programmes, the building of crèches in Roma communities, primary school education in Romany, etc.); and support intercultural education (a national campaign to combat racial discrimination in schools, the adoption of multicultural curricula and the preparation of teaching materials on Roma history and culture, etc.) (UN Doc. E/CN.4/Sub.2/2000/SR.23, 14).

Although Grigore's statement did not mention the initiative for a Special Rapporteur on Roma, it did, nevertheless, testify to the request for the UN to pay attention to Romani issues. Whilst the IRU achieved some success, with steps towards institutionalising a Special Rapporteur on Roma being taken upon its request, it might have spoiled the chances of this initiative being taken any further by suggesting an unsuitably political direction for the Rapporteur, as opposed to endorsing his efforts addressing discrimination against Roma within the framework of the Subcommission's competency.

As mentioned earlier (p. 129), the initiative for a Special Rapporteur on Roma came from the IRU, through Pietrosanti. The result had a mixed reception among the

Romani community. While pleased that Romani issues were finally accorded attention, some objected to the fact that the expert came from Mauritius and had probably never had any direct contact with Romani communities, seeing it as paternalism to have Roma studied by yet another non-Rom. Others however thought that his distance might lead to less bias (see the discussion on Romani chat list Patrin between 23–26 August 2000 under the subjects Expert on Roma, (Expert) – Yeung, Yeung Kam Yeung Sik Yuen and Sik Yuen – a turning point).

Miscellaneous   Besides the already mentioned successful or semi-successful interventions, the IRU made six more interventions – four oral and two written – at the Subcommission *after* achieving consultative status. However, these interventions evoked no response from the Subcommission. Nevertheless, they are briefly detailed in this section for historical record.

On 28 August 1981, the IRU submitted a written statement under agenda item 6 (A question of the violation of human rights and fundamental freedoms, including policies of racial discrimination and segregation and of apartheid, in all countries, with particular reference to colonial and other dependent countries and territories: report of the Sub-commission under Commission on Human Rights resolution 8 (XLVIII)). This statement described the long-term persecution (including Holocaust) of Roma, said to be a nation scattered throughout the world, and informed about the aims of IRU and the 1981 Congress. It appealed to all countries to accept Roma and give them the financial and economic possibilities to organize themselves, and requested that the Subcommission promote the protection of the rights of Roma in order to avoid genocide against them (for full text see UN Doc. E/CN.4/Sub.2/NGO/99).

On 30 August 1982, Cibula delivered an oral statement on behalf of the IRU under agenda item 6. He informed the Subcommission about the 1981 Congress, the aims of the IRU and Romani contributions to other nations (mainly in art, music and handicraft), and thanked the UN for granting the IRU consultative status. He demanded recognition of Roma by all social and public institutions and as a nationality, repeal of unjust laws, right of assembly, financial protection for the IRU, abolition of brutal and arbitrary police measures against Roma and of disparaging epithets such as Gypsy, Tzigane, or Zigeuner (see endnote 1 in Chapter 2), recognition of Romani Holocaust, and both collective and individual reparations from Germany (UN Doc. E/CN.4/Sub.2/1982/SR.13: 16–17). A year later, on 24 August 1983, Cibula delivered another, very similar oral statement on behalf of the IRU. Perhaps the only difference was that he informed the Subcommission about the holding of all three Congresses (UN Doc. E/CN.4/Sub.2/1983/SR.10: 15–16). (See Klimova 2003: §2.3.1.4–5.) At neither of these two Subcommission sessions did anybody comment on Cibula's remarks and the Subcommission took no related action.

No further interventions were made at the Subcommission until 25 August 1989, when Tom Odley, leader of the British Romani Union, delivered an oral statement under agenda item 7 (The new international economic order and the protection of human rights). He detailed the persecution of Roma and pointed out that Roma had no wish to be represented by self-styled Gypsy experts who were not Roma but simply members of the 'Gypsy industry,' seeking either personal profit or political benefit from exploiting the suffering of Roma (see also pp. 106–8). He said they wished to be accorded the basic human rights enshrined in the Universal Declaration of Human Rights (UDHR), including the right to live in freedom and dignity as a nation among nations (UN Doc. E/CN.4/Sub.2/1989/SR.28: 6–7). The tone of his speech was slightly more aggressive and less diplomatic than the IRU's other interventions. Again, nobody commented on Odley's remarks at this Subcommission session and the Subcommission took no related action. Some claim that Odley's Union is a fascist front organization with no formal connection to the IRU (Acton 23 March 2003). Nevertheless, Odley was successful in convincing either the IRU, the UN or both that he has the right to deliver an intervention in the IRU's name.

On 21 August 1990, the IRU submitted a written statement under the agenda item 6. This statement indicated that the IRU had consultative status II. It is unclear whether this claim was just the result of a typographical error, the confusion of IRU representatives, or an attempt to trick the system in order to submit a written statement without being asked to do so. It mostly echoed the points made in their written intervention to the Commission on 1 February 1991. In addition, it maintained that, despite progress made, prejudice and genocide attempts towards Roma are still common. It urged that we should strive 'towards a world of commonwealth uniting all nations, with a world legislature with representatives elected by and dedicated to humankind, and an international force and a world tribunal to safeguard peaceful unity in diversity for all' (UN Doc. E/CN.4/Sub.2/1990/NGO/27: 2). It further pointed out that Roma suffer from racial prejudice which leads to human rights violations, social unrest, war and even genocide (UN Doc. E/CN.4/Sub.2/1990/NGO/27: 2). This statement was probably again Kappenberger's work, for it contained another quote from the Baha'i World Centre, this time on racism. As with Pietrosanti's speech made ten years later, this statement argued for a global change and therefore did not fall within the competence of the Subcommission (see p. 130).[13] Note that, as with Pietrosanti ten years later, Kappenberger tried to hijack the Romani cause to pursue agendas promoting the globalisation of governance.

Hancock also reports that he presented a preliminary report on his visit to Romania at the Subcommission in August 1991, and that John McCarthy (its head) assured him that the Subcommission would act upon the full report (when presented) in its weekly meetings with Romanian representatives (Hancock 1991d: 5). However, I found no mention of Hancock's intervention in UN summary records, although he is included in the list of participants for this Subcommission session (UN Doc. E/CN.4/Sub.2/1991/INF/1: 24). His final report was never presented to the Subcommission but was reportedly published in UNICEF NGO periodicals (Hancock 13 February 2003).

At the WGPM

As the WGPM requires no consultative status for interventions, a number of nation-state Romani NGOs have managed to have their voice heard. Due to the open access, co-operation with allies was not so crucial. Although Romani NGOs have attended the WGPM since its second session, their first intervention only came at its sixth session, in May 2000 (see p. 42). In this, a representative of the Romani CRISS emphasized that police protection and access to employment in public institutions or government administrations was often inadequate and that a disproportionate number of Romani children were sent to special schools for mentally disabled children. She also denounced recent international initiatives to improve the situation of Roma as insufficient because Roma 'continued to suffer widespread discrimination and prejudice, evidenced in considerable social exclusion, and high levels of poverty, illiteracy and unemployment,' supporting her statement by citing Roma-related passages of the 1999 European Commission report on Bulgaria, Czech Republic, Slovakia, and Romania. She suggested that, when it comes to Roma, many countries still needed to harmonize their legislatives with the requirements of international standards, especially the ICERD (UN Doc. E/CN.4/Sub.2/2000/27: §62).

At the seventh session, a number of Romani NGOs (Consejo Gitano, SATRA/ASTRA, Aven Amentza, and Roma Association of Izmail and Region) delivered oral interventions. All of them mentioned the lack of implementation of article 4.4 of the UN Declaration on the Rights of Persons Belonging to National or Ethnic, Religious and Linguistic Minorities in their countries (Spain, Romania, and Ukraine). They advocated for the use of the education system to create public awareness about Roma and promote tolerance towards them. In addition, they 'pointed to the importance of article 4.4 in combination with article 4.3 in the process of identity assertion and self-esteem-building for the Roma people themselves' (UN Doc. E/CN.4/Sub.2/2001/22). SATRA/ASTRA and Aven Amentza recommended inclusive curricula for Roma which would take account of their language, history and culture, ensuring safer learning environments. Consejo Gitano declared that the aspiration of the Roma is to live in peace and dignity, yet not in a centralized and homogenous society. They therefore advocated decentralized autonomy, but pointed out that 'certain parties' were afraid to discuss self-determination and autonomy (UN Doc. E/CN.4/Sub.2/2001/22). At the eighth session, in May 2002, the Romani youth organization Anglunipe stressed that, while the Roma had been recognized as a minority in the Former Yugoslav Republic of Macedonia since 1991, they did not enjoy full and effective participation in public life (UN Doc. E/CN.4/Sub.2/2002/19).

None of the recommendations made were translated into action within the WGPM fora. Yet these oral interventions probably did contribute to the decision of the WGPM to specifically devote some of its recommendations of the seventh session to Romani issues (see p. 42). Some of them also resonated with CERD later.

At CERD

As described earlier (pp. 77–8), the ERRC has been submitting statements (mostly written) to CERD since 1998. Although the ERRC's work at CERD has the potential of leading to the most concrete and significant improvement in the lives of Roma in individual countries, the statements are not considered in detail in this chapter because they all concentrate on very specific details of ICERD violations in particular countries, and so do not provide crucial insights into the dynamics of *global* Romani activism or its interaction with the UN. Instead, the following section concentrates on an event of significance to Romani activism at large, in which Romani, pro-Romani and non-Romani NGOs co-operated towards a successful result.

The Thematic Discussion and CERD Recommendation XVII on Roma   The thematic discussion was held on 15 and 16 August 2000 (see pp. 44–5). It was preceded by an informal hearing, during which representatives of NGOs decried the conditions of Roma to CERD members. Some CERD members suggested that at least one Romani representative should also be present and given the floor during the official thematic discussion. However, on the basis of information from the UN Secretariat, the CERD working group preparing the discussion decided that, with no international umbrella organization representing Roma having ECOSOC consultative status (i.e. the IRU was disregarded), it was not appropriate to privilege one Romani NGO by inviting it to the official discussion. Therefore, NGO participation was limited to the informal hearing (see UN Doc. CERD/C/SR.1405: 9–11; UN Doc. CERD/C/SR.1402: 6–10). This shows that, despite reiterating this point at the beginning of most of its interventions, the IRU did not manage to convince all UN actors that it is the umbrella organization representing the world's Roma. Yet, it did manage to convince some, such as Kofi Annan, as mentioned earlier (p. 80). Before the NGO statements, CERD members[14] pointed out that CERD is aware of the multifaceted discrimination Roma face, citing examples. Its chairman explained that CERD reached these conclusions during consideration of the periodic reports of several contracting parties. Lavinia Olmazu, part of the autumn 2000 ISCA delegation to the UN and also speaking on behalf of the Aven Amentza, reminded the meeting of Romani slavery and Holocaust and the racial discrimination Roma have suffered in Romania. She recommended a number of measures to be taken, especially regarding education (The Roma Center for Public Policies 2000). (See p.13.)

Michelle Stewart from the British contingent of the same ISCA delegation addressed accommodation problems faced by Travellers in Northern Ireland and Scotland. A representative of IMADR and the Zentralrat argued that Roma should no longer be classified as 'marginal social groups' and treated as 'social problems' responsible for their own plight. He suggested that protection of Roma and Sinti is also a matter for international organizations, complaining that the Framework Convention on National Minorities and the European Charter for Regional or Minority Languages are not applied adequately to Roma, and requested international resources for supporting Romani organizations in their fight against racism and discrimination (Rose 2000). Mihaela Gheorghe, a representative of Romani CRISS, further detailed the inequality and discrimination against Roma in Romania. She also put forth recommendations relating to state protection of the equality in employment, and adoption of anti-discrimination and minority laws, including those prohibiting and sanctioning verbal discrimination (for the full text of the statement see CRISS 2000).

A representative of the non-Romani NGO Medicins du Monde drew attention to both the alarming health situation in many Romani communities and the efforts made by Romani NGOs to address this situation because of the indifference of states to these problems. A representative of the Roma-Lom Foundation (Bulgaria) described marginalization of Roma in Bulgaria. Veronika Leila Szente, a representative of the ERRC, made ten detailed recommendations.[15] A representative of the non-Romani NGO Greek Helsinki Monitor (GHM) addressed the problem of Romani evictions in Greece, some of them related to the 2004 Athens Olympic Games, and asked the international community to stop such ethnic cleansing. The non-Romani Society for Threatened Peoples (STP, Goettingen) had a representative address the problem of Roma in Kosovo. A representative of the Croatian Romani Union argued that Romani refugees from CEE should be granted asylum in Western Europe as refusal of this was against international law. A representative from the non-Romani NGO MRG International (Hungary) described the discrimination that persisted in Hungary despite the existence of laws prohibiting it. A Central Unified Salvation of Bulgaria representative outlined further discrimination against Roma in Bulgaria and police abuse of Roma. The ERRC and GHM also submitted written statements which provided details of the problems and solutions outlined in their oral statements (for the full text of these statements see GHM 2000; ERRC 2000a). Glele-Ahanhanzo echoed many of the statements made, based on the fieldwork he had conducted. He argued that states need to adopt comprehensive anti-discrimination legislations. The concept of a Romani nation was also briefly mentioned (UN Press Release 2000c).

During the discussion of the afternoon session of the thematic discussion on 15 August, the main issues raised by NGOs were recapitulated as the following: the absence of legislation prohibiting and punishing discrimination in various fields such as employment, housing, education, and access to services – or failure to apply or enforce such legislation; impunity for racial crimes against Roma; refusal by certain municipalities to accept Roma in their locality; and persecution of Roma in war-torn countries and zones of international conflict. It was also recalled that the discussion with NGOs identified some 'good practices,' at least in terms of the adoption of programs aimed at improving the situation of Roma and the eradication of discrimination against them, if not in terms of effective implementation. The CERD members debated the NGO proposals, most of all those presented by the ERRC. They also expressed satisfaction at both the optimism and the constructive approach of the Romani representatives and concluded that this informal meeting was very fruitful (UN Doc. CERD/C/SR.1422). Later one of the CERD members pointed out that

> [i]t was regrettable that there had not been sufficient time set aside for questions and answers during the previous day's informal meeting, all the more so since the very competent answers given to the few questions put by the Committee members appeared to indicate that such a dialogue would have been very helpful indeed (UN Doc. CERD/C/SR.1423: 8).

One of the questions this CERD member wished to discuss (but could not for lack of time) was the question of 'whether recognition as a national minority or as a nation would be desirable, a matter which was subject of debate within the Sinti and Roma communities themselves' (UN Press Release 2000c). The Romani and Travellers representatives, at least those from the ISCA delegation, also had very positive impressions from the exchange with CERD members. Stewart recalls with satisfaction: 'Apart from reading bits from my speech I also got the opportunity to ask questions, and put across my point of view, in some of the Committee meetings. [...] The UN officials I spoke to from the sub-Commission and CERD were very understanding' (Equal Opportunities Committee 2001).

During the discussion on 16 August various CERD members again emphasized a number of points the Romani NGOs had made earlier. These were: there was a lack of political will to improve the situation of Roma in many countries, any efforts for improvement must be undertaken with the full co-operation and participation of Roma, institutional discrimination combined with prejudice existed in many countries, and the establishment of market economies led to the deterioration in the situation of Roma (UN Doc. CERD/C/SR.1423, 2–7). One CERD expert pointed out that the present dialogue was fruitful because it was being carried out with representatives of Roma, while in the past CERD had only engaged in dialogue with states (UN Press release 2000d). (In this case, the Romani representatives perhaps contributed to the goal of greater inclusion of NGOs in CERD's future work as CERD members appreciated their input.) In the afternoon, CERD adopted by acclamation general Recommendation XVII (UN Press Release 2000e). (See pp. 44–5.)

The Recommendation took account of almost all of the problems presented by the NGOs. Ones that it specifically decided not to address were the situations of evictions in Greece and refugees in Kosovo. It also did not recommend granting Romani refugees asylum in western Europe, as the Croatian Romani Union had suggested, but did urge for non-discrimination in asylum procedures, as requested by the UNHCR (see p. 64). The CERD Recommendation incorporated virtually all of the recommendations made by the ERRC,[16] except the ones related to specialized monitoring, investigative and prosecuting bodies (item 6) and the application of international instruments (item 10). It also incorporated about half of Aven Amenza's recommendations, excluding those on self-esteem, pre-school education, religious education, support for an international Romani educational network, and multicultural education. All of the recommendations from Romani CRISS were incorporated, except the one relating to minority law. However, criticisms and recommendations from the IMADR and Zentralrat were not incorporated.

General Usage of Configuration of Power

This section briefly covers how the configuration of power was used for the delivering of interventions and lobbying for resolutions that were described earlier (pp. 120–137). However, it also analyses how Romani activists used the configuration of power in events covered in Chapters 4 and 5. Among the UN member states, the two most important allies of Romani activists have been India and, more recently, the Czech Republic.[17] The IRU used India as their ally for obtaining ECOSOC consultative status. It also tried to use Indian influence to gain UNESCO consultative status, but in vain (see pp. 105–6). Although consultative status was not achieved, Puxon concluded that it was largely a result of India's intervention that UNESCO became interested in Roma in 1970 (Puxon 13 June 2001). The IRU actually claims that the POS provided by the configuration of power was unfavourable to them, with their efforts being marred by the influence of French civil servants and 'congressional organizations'. India's role in this primarily came from the personal connections of Padmashri Weer Rajendra Rishi, the IRU's Honorary President, who was an Indian diplomat and personal friend and former interpreter of the former Prime Minister Jawaharlal Nehru (see Roma 1992: Chapter 2). Rishi cultivated the Romani-Indian connection by establishing and running the half-yearly journal *Roma* as the IRU's official organ (since 1974) as well as the Indian Institute of Romani Studies (since 1973), both at Chandigarh. He also organized two International Romani festivals in Chandigarh (in 1976 and 1983). During the first occasion, he arranged an audience for Romani leaders and artists with the then Prime Minister Indira Gandhi and the then President of India Fakhruddin Ali Ahmed (Roma 1992: 111–117). Rishi's presentation of Roma as messengers of Indian culture, language and traditions throughout the world appealed to Indian nation-state interest, and, during the incumbency of Jawaharlal Nehru and Indira Ghandi, India was willing to act as the kin state of Roma and support Romani *cultural* demands (see e.g. speeches made at the first International Romani festival in Chandigarh in Ali Ahmed 1976; Prime Minister Praises Roma's Freedom of Spirit 1976; Sharma A. 1976). However, India's support has always been limited to cultural, not political, issues.

With Rishi's advancing age, the IRU-Indian link weakened in the 1990s; the 2000 Congress was the only Congress with no Indian presence at all. Indian delegates were actually invited but could not attend because of too short a notice (Nazerali 19 December 2002). However, in 2001 the connection was renewed when a thirty-three-member delegation of Romani activists undertook a week-long visit to India. They participated in two conferences, one in New Delhi and one in Chandigarh, and visited religious and historical places of their 'forefathers' (Pramod 2001; Press Information Bureau Releases 2001). On this occasion they met with India's Prime Minister, Atal Behari Vajpayee. The IRU's President Scuka asked the Indian government to help Roma in socio-cultural and political fields and to act as 'the moral protector of the Romani people around the world' (Pramod 2001; Press Information Bureau Releases 2001). The Prime Minister assured the delegates that India would support their cause if the matter was raised in the UN or any other international forum, and that it was ready to help Roma and extend its co-operation with the IRU through more frequent and effective interactions in the future (Pramod 2001; Press Information Bureau Releases 2001). This is quite an extreme example of what Bauboeck calls 'extra-territorial nation-building' or the attempts of country governments or political elites to control their nationals aboard or at least stay connected with them, which might lead to the introduction of external citizenship (see Bauboeck 2002: 7–14). The Roma were also 'given the option of official recognition as an Indian minority and were offered the same status given to all Indian emigres as Indian minorities abroad, including passports' (PER 2003: 13). Scuka however rejected this offer, explaining that the IRU Parliament as well as Romani communities needed to be consulted before such a decision was taken. Other reasons for caution were that such recognition might lead some countries to ask Roma to return to India, or even expel them forcefully, and that with such recognition Roma could hardly claim to be a nation of their own (PER 2003: 13). This visit was followed by a visit of 'the Indian brothers' to Europe, on the occasion of a 2001 OSCE Conference (Equal Opportunities for Roma and Sinti: Translating Words into Facts, held in Bucharest, Romania from 10–13 September). One of the conference's side events was entitled the Roma India Task Force. This was to continue the discussions started at the New Delhi international conference earlier that year, concerning improved relations between the Indian Government and Romani organizations from Europe, scholarships for Roma to study in India, India's support at the international level for granting Roma legal rights and collaboration between Roma and Indian organizations from all around the world through common interests programs (Roma India Task Force 2001). However, it remains to be seen whether India really is ready to again take an active role in supporting Roma within the UN fora.

The second most obvious example of ally help from a member state occurred in 2001, when the Czech Republic arranged an audience for the IRU President with the Secretary-General. The co-operation between the IRU and the Czech Republic, specifically with its MFA, started prior to the 2000 Congress through the personal contact of Martin Palous, Czech Deputy Foreign Minister, with Emil Scuka. Palous, a former human rights activist from Helsinki Citizen's Assembly, had first started co-operating with Scuka within the framework of the Civic Forum, an umbrella civil organization and later a political party created during the 1989 regime change in Czechoslovakia. He helped to ensure support for the 2000 Congress and signed the Memorandum of Understanding and Cooperation (see p. 80). Additionally, the (then)

Czech and Slovak Republic (along with Romania and Bulgaria), was one of the CEE sponsors of the resolution 1992/65 on protection of Roma. By the mid-1990s, the Czech MFA (together with the Finnish Government), was also supporting Romani activists and issues within other international fora, such as the OSCE and CoE (see Gheorghe 2001). It has been alleged that the reason behind this support is to ensure international Romani support that would help legitimize the Czech Republic's claim of improving Romani rights and 'its urgent priority to prevent Roma by humane means from emigrating, in order to win Western European approval and gain EU membership' (Acton and Klimova 2001: 167). Others postulate, based on analysis of the Czech MFA Strategy, that the Czech Republic's aim is the Europeanisation of the Romani problem, thus shifting the financial responsibility and support from the state to the international community as well as 'shifting the criticism of the situation of Roma from human rights rhetoric to a more vague political platform, not embodied in any internationally binding documents' (Sobotka 2001). There are also speculations that the Czech MFA wishes to consult Romani leaders before they raise issues that are potentially embarrassing for the Czech Republic at the international organizations' fora (Sobotka 2001; see also Acton 2000).

Undoubtedly other CEE countries shared the Czech aim of the Europeanisation of Romani issues over the past few years. This is evident in the majority of speeches made by representatives of governments of these countries within the UN or European international platforms. This phenomenon deserves further documentation and analysis in future research. In this way the strategies of Romani leaders and those states converge, yet not to a common goal. Romani leaders started to appeal to international fora because they were not getting any help from the states and so wanted the international community to pressure states to improve the situation of their people. In order to catch the interest of the international community, they had to argue that Romani problems are an international issue. Now these states where Romani problems are the gravest are supporting the Romani claim that Romani problems are an international issue, but only to wash their hands of these problems and pass them onto the international community. Some Romani leaders are nevertheless supporting these states in making the claim that Romani problems should be addressed with European and international resources, because they understand that their states are unwilling or unable to provide sufficient funds for addressing Romani problems from their small, strained and often deficient budgets.

Occasionally, other states have supported the demands of Romani activists at the UN. For example, during the upgrade, delegates of member states who had had a positive experience co-operating with Romani NGOs in their countries also supported the IRU's application (see p. 68). Some otherwise disinterested states also used the Romani issue as a political tool, arguing for improved treatment of the Roma in other countries.[18]

In its beginnings, the IRU also seemed to have created allies within the NGO Offices in both Geneva and New York. Virginia Sauerwein, the Chief of the NFO/DIESA Section, and Raymonde Martineau, the Geneva NGO Liaison, appear to have been sympathetic to the IRU and helpful in its initial application for consultative status. In the words of Cibula, Sauerwein 'saw the necessity of IRU for Roma and for the whole society' (Cibula 1997). She also supported the appointment of a permanent IRU representative to New York, as did Robert Muller, the Assistant to the Secretary-General (see p. 71). Unfortunately, Sauerwein's successor, Farida Ayoub, lost patience with the IRU after all the squabbles over permanent representation described earlier (pp. 73–4), and thereafter exhibited an unfavourable attitude towards their representatives (Hancock 13 February 2003; Lacroix-Hopson 3 April 2001).

Before we consider alliances with non-Romani NGOs, it is appropriate to briefly address the relationship between Romani activists and the pro-Romani ERRC, whose actions have been introduced in this book alongside those of the IRU and other Romani activists. The relationship between Roma and pro-Romani organizations (which in fact predate Romani organizations) has always been uneasy, as many Romani organizations see them as a barrier to setting up a direct dialogue between them and the authorities. The ERRC is not an exception, no matter how much it would like to see itself as a part of 'the Romani movement' in whose existence it seems to believe more than many Romani activists themselves (see ERRC 2001e). As one of its aims is to cultivate 'a generation of educated Roma rights activists recruited from the Roma community' (ERRC 1996a), it does employ a number of Romani individuals. However, the highest positions in the organization are dominated by non-Roma. Romani organizations and Romani individuals throughout Europe do reportedly contribute time, money and expertise to the ERRC (ERRC 1996c). Nevertheless, some Romani activists see the ERRC as an enemy rather than a friend, despite it having been instrumental in a number of positive developments in the area of rights of the Roma. Within the UN context, it has, for example, been instrumental in bringing Romani issues to the attention of the UN human rights treaty bodies and the WCAR (see pp. 77–8 and Klimova 2003: chapter 7). Although during the WCAR the ERRC's interaction with the UN system was in co-operation with the IRU and other Romani activists (as detailed in Klimova 2003: chapters 7 and 8), this was the exception. At other times it has only co-operated with those activists that work for it. Overall, it seems that the current competition over the right to speak 'on the behalf of the Roma' is preventing a closer co-operation between Romani and pro-Romani activists, when ideally they should be allies in their attempts to improve the situation of the Roma through interaction with the UN system. So far, Romani organizations (especially the IRU, which presents itself as the voice of the Roma) have not been intervening simultaneously in the same UN fora with the ERRC, thus there has not been any open confrontation. However, we cannot exclude the possibility of this happening in the future.

As for non-Romani NGOs, the IRU indeed created some allies among them. Although not part of the configuration of power *per se*, they nevertheless helped the IRU's work within the UN. Most of the co-operation between Romani activists and other NGOs occurred within the framework of the WCAR and I detailed it elsewhere (see Klimova 2003: Chapter 7). Nevertheless, chapters 4–6 also provided evidence of co-operation with NGOs. First of all, the Bahai'i International Community provided the IRU with two assistant permanent representatives and seemed instrumental in their gaining of UNICEF consultative status. It was probably because of Kappenberger's networking at the UN that the IRU was invited to present a number of interventions in the early 1980s and 1990s (pp. 127, 132). After Gheorghe befriended Fabienne Rousseau-Lenoir and Antoine Bernard, two IFHR officials, during the 1990 OSCE human dimension meeting in Copenhagen, they convinced him to make his oral and written interventions at the Commission and Subcommission (Gheorghe 1993: 53), moreover with some of these being joint statements. They also introduced Gheorghe into the world of lobbying and diplomacy, trained him and acted as his mentors (Gheorghe 4 December 2002). In addition, the IFHR sent a mission of enquiry on Romani issues to Romania and, in 1991, Rousseau-Lenoir took the floor at the Subcommission to call for its attention to the plight of Roma in CEE (especially Romania) after the 1989 transition. She argued that Roma in Romania became scapegoats for the economic hardship following the transition, falling victim of arson, pillaging, and pogroms. This was sanctioned by a media that exposed the Roma to public condemnation, as also described by Voyame in his UN report (see pp. 36–7). She said that the authorities failed to protect the Roma, acting only occasionally upon pressure from either the Ethnic Federation of Romanian Gypsies (Gheorghe's organization) or the international community. She urged Romania to show full political commitment to addressing the situation by enacting legislative, administrative and economic measures and by developing dialogue between the Roma and the authorities (UN Doc. E/CN.4/Sub.2/1991/SR.19: 13).

Romani activists also co-operated with Human Rights Watch, which issued a number of publications documenting human rights violations of Roma in CEE (see e.g. HRW 1991, 1992, 1993, 1996a, 1996b). It also presented a number of interventions at the Commission related exclusively or partially to Roma (see e.g. UN Doc. E/CN.4/1995/NGO/17; UN Doc. E/CN.4/2001/NGO/28). Another NGO with whom Romani activists co-operated was the IMADR. A couple of IMADR's interventions were mentioned earlier (pp. 130, 135), but they delivered others as well (see e.g. UN Doc. E/CN.4/Sub.2/1998/SR.22: 7–8; UN Doc. E/CN.4/2001/SR.31: 5). Also, when acting for the TRP (i.e. pre-affiliation to IRU), Pietrosanti brought Romani issues to the attention of the Commission and Subcommission on a few occasions. The relationship between the TRP and the IRU went both ways. While Pietrosanti joined the IRU, both of the last IRU Presidents Djuric and Scuka became TRP members (Scuka 25 May 2001). Another case was the co-operation with the ISCA. The initiative came from the ISCA, who decided to offer youth Romani activists the opportunity of becoming involved in UN diplomacy. This provides an invaluable service to the cause of Romani activism, which needs young and experienced lobbyists. The ISCA also decided to champion the cause of Romani children segregated into special schools and other institutions. To this end, it has published a number of reports in its series 'Denied a future?' and organized several conferences and briefings on this topic. Within the UN fora, the ISCA highlighted the issue of Romani education most importantly at the UNESCO Education for All 2000 regional meeting for Europe and North America and during the WCAR (see Klimova 2003: §7.3.4) (Save the Children 2001a: 11–12). The ISCA's initiative should be an example for other non-Romani NGOs on how to incorporate Roma in their issue-specific campaigns.

A number of other NGOs, such as Movement Against Racism and for Friendship Among People (UN Doc. E/CN.4/Sub.2/1999.SR.21: 4), Pax Christi International (UN Doc. E/CN.4/2001/NGO/134), Organization for Defending Victims of Violence (UN Doc. E/CN.4/2001/NGO/79), and Medecins du Monde (UN Doc. E/CN.4/Sub.2/2001/SR.17: 7–8) have occasionally become allies to Romani activists by making positive interventions on Romani issues. Co-operation with non-Romani NGOs outside the UN framework has also created allies who later on raised Romani issues within the UN fora. For example the STP started to co-operate with the

Romani activists on nation-state issues in Germany and helped to co-organize the 1981 Congress. It has since kept its interest in Romani issues and has made interventions on them within UN fora (see p. 135). Main also states that the IRU co-operated with Terre des Hommes in the field of human rights (1994: Chapter 3, Part I, A1a), yet, although this co-operation was planned, nothing came out of it except an initial meeting (Hancock 13 February 2003; Hancock 1993: 5).

Co-operation with NGOs has also helped Romani activists make some crucial allies among UN experts. Benjamin Whitaker, director of the MRG and Subcommission member in the 1970s, was instrumental in passing resolution 6(XXX). Theo van Boven, an IMADR Board member, has also championed the Romani cause in his various UN appointments as Subcommission, Commission, and CERD member, and Special Rapporteur. The way various UN experts champion the Romani cause also deserves further research.

Conclusion

This chapter established links between all but one[19] of the Subcommission's and Commission's resolutions (and the agenda-setting and discursive developments connected to them, see Table 3.1) related to Roma and the lobbying and interventions by Romani activists at the UN. All these resolutions were passed upon the initiative of Romani activists and their allies, some accepting the discourse of Romani activists virtually word by word, others using it in modified forms. The initiative for establishing a Special Rapporteur on Romani issues clearly started upon the suggestion by an IRU official and was supported by interventions by Romani activists throughout, as was the CERD thematic discussion and Recommendation XVII, which addressed many issues Romani activists had been lobbying for. In the case of the CERD, the IRU (the most frequent lobbyist) was not directly involved, yet the involvement of nation-state Romani NGOs ensured that Romani voices were heard. Many of the recommendations made by these nation-state Romani NGOs were incorporated into the CERD Recommendation, although the majority of the input into this Recommendation was from the pro-Romani ERRC. The link between WGPM recommendations no. 7 and 10 and the involvement of Romani activists is less obvious, yet Romani activists did lobby the WGPM with their interventions.

Overall, the agenda-setting and discursive developments followed the direction desired by Romani activists, even if they were never as far-reaching as the activists wished. The main three demands directly voiced by Romani activists that remain unfulfilled are 1) firmly establishing Roma as a special UN issue through inclusion on the UN agenda and through institutionalising a Special Rapporteur on Roma, 2) UN support for Roma receiving collective Holocaust reparations, and 3) UN institutional reform which would allow for an enhanced status of the Romani nation, so allegedly ensuring better protection of the rights of Roma.

While Romani activists have clearly been influencing the UN discourse, their own discourse was also shaped by that of the UN. Given the fact that Romani activists had to make its interventions under specific agenda items of the various bodies, they had to adjust their demands to at least loosely fit these items. (Recall that the Gheorghe's one attempt of presenting a topic he considered important under an unrelated agenda item was not successful.) Consequently, they started to make demands simply to extend the degree of the UN's activities relating to the Roma (e.g. the work of Special Rapporteurs, advisory services, etc.). They also requested that standards agreed for other minorities are applied to the Roma (such as that minority policies should be elaborated in co-operation with minority leaders). In fact, virtually all of the UN discursive developments which were successfully initiated by Romani activists were those that built on the existing UN discourse but insisted on its application to the Roma. This supports the hypothesis posed by scholars of transnationalism that non-state actors are likely to be more successful if they couche their demands in terms similar to those of existing regimes. By extension, the Declaration of Nation discourse has, so far, been unsuccessful because it builds on a globalisation discourse promoted by academics, the civil society, individual prominent political personalities and, up to certain extent, some European institutions, but not the UN member states.

Romani activists have not been particularly successful in exploiting the configuration of power to enlist allies. Nevertheless, they achieved some success (mostly status and prestige related) with the help of India, the Czech Republic and a few members of the UN administration. Co-operation with and support from other NGOs has been crucial in bringing about the greatest achievements of global Romani activism – the passing of three UN resolutions. Non-Romani NGOs helped Romani activists by letting them speak in the name of these NGOs in cases when Romani activists were not entitled to present interventions in their own right. They also helped Romani activists convince member states or UN experts to propose and/or support the activists' draft resolutions. In addition, non-Romani NGOs started to train youth Romani activists in UN diplomacy; we might soon see the fruits of this exercise. Yet, overall, Romani activists need to increase their co-operation with other NGOs and devote more energy to exploiting the UN configuration of power if they are to achieve lasting results. Perhaps most importantly, they need to rethink their relationship with the pro-Romani ERRC which could be a powerful ally within the UN fora.

Notes

1 Note that this is the only reference to the right of development found in interventions by Romani activists.

2 A more detailed background for this statement was produced as Gheorghe and Hancock 1991a.

3 To recapitulate these were: encouraging the Special Rapporteurs of the Commission and Subcommission to pay due attention to the specific conditions of Roma in their work, urging governments to continue taking all appropriate measures to protect and promote the rights and freedoms of Roma, and assisting countries with advisory services and technical assistance on Roma (including a project on best practices on Roma and a seminar on Roma).

4 This statement is an edited version of the previously unaccepted written statement mentioned earlier in relation to Gheorghe's 1991 intervention at the Commission.

5 Whose trip to Geneva was financed by CoE.

6 This summary misspells Foy's last name as Fay.

7 The caucuses were NGO and UN agency groupings which met regularly during the Commission sessions (Laftman, Motala, and Albery 2001).

8 The representative speaking was not Romani, but was a high official of the 1971 Congress.

9 During this visit, Desai also agreed to head the Trusteeship Council that was to be established in Delhi to assist Roma (see also pp. 105–6) (Puxon 1977).

10 Puxon and a number of Romani activists had in fact contributed to the passing of this resolution. It was the first occasion when the Romani plight received a hearing by an IGO. The
   CoE report on which the resolution was based frequently refers to information submitted by
   the IRC and praises its work (see Wiklund 1969; Puxon 1975: 80–88; Puxon 2000:
   102–104).
11 Arguing that Roma were dispersed from their Indian homeland by Muslim invasions during
   the 10–13th centuries (News and Reviews 1977a: 33).
12 In her letter to the Scottish Equal Opportunities Committee, Stewart states that this declaration 'was read out to the full Commission on Human Rights,' but in reality it was delivered
   to the Subcommission (see the letter from Michelle Stewart, November 2000 in Equal
   Opportunities Committee 2001).
13 The Subcommission's mandate is limited to undertaking studies and making recommendations to the Commission concerning prevention of violations of human rights (Save the
   Children 2001b: 23).
14 Committee Chairman, Michael E. Sherifis, the Commission's Special Rapporteur on
   Racism, Racial Discrimination, Xenophobia and Related Intolerance, Maurice Glele-
   Ahanhanzo, and CERD experts Mahmoud Aboul-Nasr and Regis de Gouttes.
15 Regarding the involvement of Romani representatives in designing, implementing and
   evaluating policies to combat and prevent discrimination at all stages; political will and
   moral leadership at the highest levels of government; enacting and implementing legislation specifically prohibiting racial discrimination; positive discrimination including the
   active recruitment, identification and capacitating of Roma into the ranks of public employment, including the police, prosecutorial corps and the judiciary; specialized bodies with
   the legal power to investigate and prosecute acts of discrimination; collection of race statistics; programmes to facilitate dialogue and understanding between groups of Roma and
   various public officials, including the police, prosecutors and the judiciary; anti-racism and
   human rights education; and strengthening of international commitments (for the full text
   of the statement see ERRC 2000a).
16 See endnote 15.
17 This of course refers to building alliances for the purposes of work within the UN system.
   At the European level, Romani activists have additional allies such as Finland (see e.g. PER
   2003: 28–31).
18 See e.g. the representative of Cuba condemning the treatment of Roma in the Czech
   Republic (UN Doc. E/CN.4/2001/SR.54: 12).
19 Commission resolution 2001/9 on the right to development.

Chapter 7

Conclusion

One of the aims of this book was to bring the Roma into the international relations discourse, which has until now largely ignored them. In my opinion, the Roma currently occupy what has been termed 'a marginal site of politically significant experience'. According to Wilmer, this is a site 'where the distribution of power is embedded in internalized meanings and where the powerless remain powerless, in part, because they do not successfully challenge the meaning of terms used to describe their existence, their experiences' (1993: 33). She points out that '[m]arginalized sites are occupied by marginalized and excluded people whose demands for inclusion will change the nature of the discourse'. These sites represent the possibility of 'fundamental and dramatic changes in the conditions of world politics that are not necessarily anticipated or taken into account by more conventional theoretical orientations' (1993: 39). In the case of the Roma, it is too early to say if, and how, the nature of the discourse will be changed, or what dramatic changes, if any, their demands for inclusion will bring. Nevertheless, it is not too early to call attention to these demands as a potentially interesting political phenomenon.

Since Roma have been stereotyped as a backward, uncivilized, primitive, antisocial, unorganized and apolitical people (in the meaning of a people without politics, outside politics, disinterested in politics), their political experience was perhaps at first deemed unworthy of studying. Later it might have been ignored in relation to the study of nation-state, as well as world, politics because it does not fit any of the dominant paradigms. In comparison to political science, international relations has been even more dismissive of the relevance of the Romani experience, ignoring the very transnational nature of their experience in its preoccupation with a state-centric focus. In order to bring Roma into the discourse, I strove to break down the popular stereotype that Roma (or Gypsies, the name prevalent in the dominant/marginalizing discourse) are the parasites of society and scroungers of the welfare system, who either try to improve their lot solely through illegal means or passively expect to be taken care of. This book described and analysed their fight for inclusion in international decision-making, in terms of its results that relate to UN agenda-setting, discourse and procedural/institutional developments. Thus, while raising the level of consciousness about the situation of the Roma and their activism, this work also contributes to the debates on group rights that the UN recently started to grapple with under the label 'third generation' human rights (see e.g. Lyons and Mayall 2003; Anaya 1999), on the role of non-state actors in international relations (see e.g. Arts, Noortmann and Reinalda 2001; Ronit and Schneider 2000; Higgott, Underhill and Bieler 2000; Keck and Sikkink 1998), and over the concept of cosmopolitan governance (see Held 1995; Archibugi, Held, and Kohler 1998).

Summary of Main Findings

The main research questions answered in this book were:

1) Can we discern a voice of Romani activism in world politics? If so, how unified is it and what does it call for?
2) What influence has it had on the UN agenda-setting, discursive and procedural/institutional developments related to the Roma?
3) How, on the contrary, did interacting with the UN system affect the agenda, discourse and organisational structure of global Romani activism?

The first question was both the starting and end point. At the start, I confirmed the existence of global Romani activism, whose members have wished to become actors in world politics and have their voices heard ever since global politics became institutionalized in the League of Nations and, later on, the UN systems. I then determined that the essence of these voices is the call for equality of all nations and people, and their economic, social, cultural, civil and political rights (both individual and collective), regardless of whether they possess a state or territory and other means of political leverage (e.g. military and economic). Some of these voices are indeed a normative critique of the current political system based on nation-states and dominated by majority nations, calling for a revolution in international relations towards a non-territorial rule. Having determined the above, I had to consider the influence of Romani activists on the UN before I could establish if, and by how much, their voices are unified *and* being heard in world politics.

In order to answer this, I described the interaction between Romani and pro-Romani activists and the UN system using a UN POS analytical framework. The framework allowed us to account for the types of formal as well as informal actions that Romani activists could have and did develop within the UN system. Through descriptive inference, these actions were linked to the main UN events/actions leading to agenda-setting, discursive and procedural/institutional developments, as well as to the developments themselves. Although no clear links were established with the procedural/institutional developments, the majority of the agenda-setting and discursive developments are associated with the actions of Romani and pro-Romani activists. This relationship (which is not meant to prove direct and exclusive causality) is illustrated in Table 7.1. This finding supports Reinalda's and Verbeek's assumption that NGO influence is especially felt in agenda-setting phases of international policy-making (2001: 156).[1] According to Willetts, it is indeed 'fundamental to the existence of NGOs and to the nature of governments that NGOs should dominate agenda-setting' (1996: 46). In the case of the UN system, agenda-setting of Romani issues *has* been dominated by Romani and pro-Romani activists. We can conclude that, according to Arts' definition of political influence, Romani activism did indeed matter and has made a difference because *some* of its policy goals were achieved with regard to outcomes of UN agenda-setting and discursive commitments which were (at least partly) caused by intentional intervention of Romani activists in the UN political arena and processes. These policy outcomes were clearly more in line with the policy goals of the activists than if they had not intervened (see p. 3).

Although our analysis was not meant to quantify the exact extent of the influence of Romani activism on the agenda-setting and discursive developments, it did establish that the activists' influence could well have been a significant factor leading to such developments. In a few instances related to discursive developments, we can dare to hypothesize that the activists' actions had a major influence, with developments being both initiated by them and then closely reflecting their discourse. Yet even for these, to establish any causal relationship, a number of other factors would have to be taken into account (as acknowledged in Chapter 1, see p. 7). In fact, the lack of association between the activists' actions and virtually all procedural/institutional developments, and some agenda-setting and discursive ones (see Table 7.1), suggests that understanding such factors is necessary.

Trying to assess the significance of the activists' influence brings us back to our first research question. Was the influence significant enough to conclude that the Romani voice/voices permeated world politics? At this point, the answer has to be, 'not quite'. The developments that have taken place in the UN system have not been of major political significance, and could be linked to the activists' actions only when related to agenda-setting and discursive, not procedural/institutional, changes. Thus the activists' success was limited only to sensitising, not substantive, impacts (see Roozendaal 2001: 162 and Noortmann, Arts and Reinalda 2001: 299 for this distinction). In terms of procedural/institutional developments, no Roma-specific body or special mechanism has been established within the UN, although both have been requested by the activists, albeit very recently. Considering agenda-setting, the Roma have neither become a global issue on the UN agenda nor an official focus minority group or issue under the global agenda of human rights, despite this demand being voiced for over a decade. In relation to discursive developments, contrary to the activists' wishes, the UN member states have not made any legally binding commitments for improving the situation of the Roma. This is in stark contrast to the developments related to the indigenous peoples. Indigenous peoples are now a global agenda issue and a specific focus group for many UN bodies and agencies, having their own Permanent Forum on Indigenous Issues,[2] the International Day (9 August) and Decade of the World's Indigenous People (1995–2004), a Special Rapporteur on the situation of human rights and fundamental freedoms of indigenous people, Voluntary Fund for Indigenous Populations, Working Group on Indigenous Populations, Working Group on the Draft Declaration on the Rights of Indigenous People (hopefully producing a legally binding instrument in the near future) and a legally-binding ILO Convention (see OHCHR, Indigenous Peoples). Therefore, Romani activists have a long way to go before firmly establishing their voice in world politics. However, it is important to point out that they have started such a journey and that, from time to time, small echoes of their voices resonate in the UN fora.

According to Arts, 'political power is built on and sustained by political influence' (2001: 197), thus having some political influence is the first step. We can indeed consider Romani activists consequential and relevant actors within the UN fora as their actions have been taken into account by other actors (Roozendaal 2001: 174, footnote 1). They have been influential in respect to a number of specific outcomes. However, as Arts points out, we should distinguish between the notion of political influence and political power, with the latter referring 'to a player's more or less permanent ability to influence political outcomes' (2001: 197). In contrast, a player which has been influential 'with regard to a specific outcome is not necessarily powerful in general' (Arts 2001: 197). Yet, as Noortmann, Arts and Reinalda point out, political power is not the sole factor which makes an actor relevant in international decision-making. The fact that Romani activists have been part of the UN policy community and have been able to affect its political discourse is enough to conclude that Romani activism has mattered (2001: 302).

Not least, the laws of physics apply even within the international system; any body applying pressure on another will also feel the pressure. In another words, interaction and influence are usually mutual, even if hardly ever equal. Thus the agenda, discourse and even organizational structure of global Romani activism were also influenced by the interaction with the UN. The decision to participate in the modern international political system required a radical break of the new Romani elite from traditional forms of Romani identity and interaction with non-Romani world. In order to gain a consultative status, Romani activists had to follow the rules for such recognition, which required organizational and procedural conformity and discursive commitment. In keeping with their ultimate goal of representation in the GA, the IRU has also been reorganising its organizational structure to resemble that of a government, by creating a presidential post, cabinet, parliament, court of justice and ministries (commissariats). The agenda of global Romani activism was set to fit, at least loosely, into the agenda of various UN bodies, to facilitate interventions and negotiations. Romani activists also tried to translate their demands into the UN language and have actually been most successful in instigating UN discursive developments when doing so. This finding supports Reinalda's and Verbeek's proposition that IGOs exert a significant influence over NGOs by conferring consultative status on them, thus limiting the scope of their activities and their official positions, and attempting to make NGOs instruments of intergovernmental problem solving and objectives. It also supports the hypothesis posed by scholars of transnationalism that non-state actors are likely to be successful in gaining some political influence if they couch their demands in terms similar to those of existing regimes (as this increases the legitimacy of the demands). The analysis presented in this book also shows that Romani activists have been more successful when they were able to provide quality expertise, display diplomatic and professional behaviour, mobilize various resources and exploit the favourability of the POS (as suggested by the transnationalism and collective social action perspectives).[3] (See pp. 3–4.) The book has shown that at the moment Romani activism lacks most of the resources non-state actors usually rely on to gain influence. Romani activists interacting with the UN system are not adequately funded and briefed and, as of yet, have not gained enough experience to establish reliability, integrity and prestige. Some of them forget to be diplomatic when trying to be tough and resolute. Although there certainly are visionaries among Romani activists, their visions and objectives are not always clear and their charisma not strong enough to continue inspiring followers long-term. Their dedication and determination falters when the crusade through the labyrinthine UN procedures starts to seem too long and support from their fellow activists is not forthcoming. Patience and armament against discouragement are also not among the strongest weapons of Romani activists. Yet, the degree of stamina, dedication, determination and vision present has been sufficient to keep the Romani cause going for a few decades now and that on its own could be seen as a considerable success given the obstacles.

Future influence remains to be seen. Will either Romani activists or the UN yield? Will the UN accept that having a territory is not a precondition for a government or other actor for having a voice in its GA, perhaps at least in this, as the Roma claim, exceptional case? Will it try to channel the Romani demand for representation into an advisory body, as it did with that of the indigenous peoples?[4] Will Romani activists revert to claiming a territory for their people in order to create a conventional state? Will they accept the rule of existing states and try to have the situation of Roma improved through regular political participation and/or minority arrangements at the nation-state level? All these possibilities would require a major change in the thinking of either the UN or the current leading Romani activists, but cannot be ruled out.

The remaining question to be answered is how unified and concerted is global Romani activism. Can the actions of Romani (and perhaps also pro-Romani) activists be viewed as the actions of one collective non-state actor? Can we speak about 'the Romani voice' and 'a global Romani actor'? If so, how can such an actor be conceptualized? It has become fashionable to refer to Romani activism (at all levels up to the global) as the Romani movement (see e.g. Puxon 1981a; Mirga and Gheorghe 1997; Kawczynski 1997; Matras 1998; Puxon 2000; Foszto 2000; ERRC 2001e; Vermeersch 2002; Barany 2002). But is there really a Romani movement and if so, what kind of movement is it? The phrase Romani movement is often used in relation to the two main organizations whose actions are described in this book – the IRU and the ERRC. In the case of the IRU, scholars as well as activists often speak of a nationalist movement which, as explained earlier (see pp. 19–22), is not completely accurate. The ERRC sees itself as the main protagonists of the 'Roma rights movement'. Is there something more, a common cause, that unites both of these organizations as well as other Romani activists? Can we see global Romani activism as a new transnational social movement? In order to answer this question, we have to consider current definitions of transnational social movements. Since the study of social movements is a relatively new field, there is neither an integrated theory of movements nor a single accepted definition of what a social movement is (della Porta and Diani 1999: 14). For the purposes of this book, the following definition by Dieter Rucht, a leading social movements scholar, is accepted: 'A social movement ... is an action system comprised of mobilized networks of individuals, groups and organizations which, based on a shared collective identity, attempt to achieve or prevent social change, predominantly by means of collective protest' (1999: 207). Two other social movements scholars, della Porta and Diani, devise a similar definition but substitute shared collective identity for shared beliefs (1999: 16). We can in fact observe such an action system slowly developing among at least some segments of the Romani people in most countries where Roma live. The shared collective identity is based on the belief that, although divided into various groups, Roma are a nation which shares the same origin, language, culture and history of persecution. The social change desired is improvement of the social and political status and treatment of the Romani people. The various forms of collective protest include non-co-operation and challenging governmental authorities at various levels through indirect or direct confrontation (e.g. petitions, demonstrations, campaigns or civil disobedience, and negotiations).

How do we move from the notion of social movement to transnational social movement? Della Porta and Diani suggest that the main indicator is that transnational social movements specialize in supranational-level action (1999: 249). In Rucht's opinion the notion of a transnational social movement is less clear because the 'transnational aspect could refer to various dimensions of a movement, such as issues, targets, mobilization, and organization' (1997: 207). He suggests that the organisational criterion should take precedence and a movement should therefore qualify as transnational 'when it is essentially composed of closely interrelated groups and organizations that belong to more than one country' (della Porta and

Diani 1999: 14). These groups and organizations must co-ordinate through sustained interaction in order to mobilize for common goals. They can do so in two ways: through horizontal co-ordination between groups from different countries or through both horizontal and vertical co-ordination in the form of a centralized or decentralized international body. While Rucht would apply the term 'transnational social movement' to both cases, other authors argue that this term applies only to the former while the latter should be called transnational social movement organization. In fact, transnational social movement organizations on their own can be transnational social movements, provided that no relevant actors are left out. More often, though, they are only a part of a wider transnational social movement composed of movement organizations (transnational, regional, nation-state, local, etc.), groups and individuals (della Porta and Diani 1999: 14).

Therefore what we should be able to observe if a transnational Romani social movement[5] exists are closely interrelated individuals, groups and organizations from various countries, either all united in one transnational organization or regularly interacting and co-operating with each other towards common goals. In this sense, the IRU could be considered a transnational social movement organization (although, as we have seen, it functions more due to the effort of a few individuals, as opposed to a concerted effort of member organizations). But is the IRU a part of a larger transnational Romani social movement? From what we have seen of global Romani activism directed towards the UN system, there is no concerted effort between the various players – the IRU (or even its individual members!), the ERRC and individual nation-state Romani NGOs.[6] Furthermore, the relationship between Romani and pro-Romani organizations is uneasy to say the least. The actions of Romani and pro-Romani activists cannot thus be viewed as the actions of one collective 'global Romani actor' and there is currently no unified Romani voice at the global level. Yet the idea of creating a transnational Romani social movement has in fact been present in the minds of the founders of the IRU and the ERRC as well as many other Romani activists, and both the IRU and the ERRC have in fact striven to create such a movement. If we were to conceptualize this idea of a transnational Romani social movement, emphasizing both Rucht's organizational aspect and della Porta's and Diani's targeting aspect, it would be a movement with both transnational targets (IGOs) and transnational organization (encompassing members from several continents). Thus it could be defined as an action system comprised of mobilized networks of Romani and pro-Romani individuals, groups and organizations from several continents functioning at all levels up to the global. This action system would be based on a shared belief in Romani identity and attempts to improve social and political status and treatment of the Romani people all over the world, by means of organized actions targeting all levels up to the global.

However, as this book has shown, there is not yet any such phenomenon *at the global level*. In terms of global Romani activism targeting the UN system, we are really talking about the work of a few dedicated individuals. Thus while there is no real success story in structural terms, which is not surprising given both the financial and human resource constraints of global Romani activism and its growing pains that manifest themselves in infighting and corruption, the achievements of some of the few dedicated individuals are in fact quite impressive. Although active involvement in global Romani activism largely stays confined to a score of individual Romani elites and their non-Romani supporters who typically participate for private idealistic or pragmatic reasons, Romani activism *is* becoming a force that the UN needs to and is willing to negotiate with. This shows that, at least in the initial stages before an issue becomes well established, it is possible to exert some influence or have one's voice heard even on a quite individual basis. Although it does limit the degree of influence, it is not necessary to create a strong movement in order to instigate minor discursive and agenda-setting developments. Despite having no popular legitimacy and no strong movement behind them, Romani activists are benefiting from the general international trend of consulting minority leaders; in other words, Romani activism exists partly because the international community wants it to exist. Unable to deal with the fragmented traditional leadership structure of Romani communities, governments and IGOs are encouraging the creation of a modern unified Romani movement whose leaders they can negotiate with. As this book established, the formal and informal access to the UN system, and co-operation with allies within the system, all provide a significant opportunity for action that Romani activists have yet not taken a full advantage of; thus the potential for developing more influence is there. Thus a distinct, unified Romani voice and movement in world politics might in fact be 'a music of the future'. The development of a strong global Romani movement is, however, a precondition of the future success of Romani activism in establishing a truly influential voice, because, as we have seen, it is not possible for a few individuals who enter the scene only occasionally to fully exploit the quite wide degree of access that the UN offers for non-state actors. At the same time, I believe that, in comparison to the current situation, considerable progress could be made if the IRU (or other organizations) simply managed to adequately fund at least one truly permanent professional Romani representative to the UN.

Practical Implications

The practical aim of this book was to offer a mirror to both Romani activists and the UN by evaluating their actions. The image in the mirror is not very flattering for either. The UN has shown embarrassingly little interest in the plight of the Roma as Holocaust survivors and as victims of frequent human rights violations in virtually all countries where they live. Especially in practical terms, it has done virtually nothing for them. Admittedly, there are many global issues the UN has to deal with and this one might not be the most serious, yet it definitely deserves more attention than it has been receiving. Another finding that does not bode well for the UN is that some Romani activists find its decision-making too slow and complicated to respond adequately and in time to their pressing needs, and they therefore turn to regional organizations instead. Although the UN itself encourages delegating certain issues to regional organizations, the fact that it is bypassed due to its inefficiency should be rather alarming. Not in the least, the Romani voices are reminders of the UN's hypocrisy in claiming to represent all the world's peoples and nations, for in reality it has so far only represented the governments of its member states. Their voices challenge it to live up to the ideals it proclaims.

For the part of Romani activists, under closer scrutiny, the actions of the IRU are not much more than self-promoting, although a number of its leaders, most notably Nicolae Gheorghe and Jan Cibula, did genuinely try to use the UN to benefit their people. The IRU has concentrated its activities on constantly seeking a higher status at the UN, while not making full use of the rights associated with the status it already

has. Although demands supporting the declared goals of promotion of Romani identity and cultural rights, remedy and prevention of human rights abuses, and addressing social and economic problems have frequently been voiced by the IRU in the UN
fora, they stayed secondary to the goal of recognition of political status which the
IRU sees as a stepping-stone to the rest of its goals. Consequently, very little has been
achieved in these areas. Only miniscule financial and virtually no institutional
support for Romani culture and language and education of Romani children and
youth has been solicited directly from the UN system. The UN has not helped to
further the cause of symbolic and financial Holocaust reparations. It only recently
started encouraging states to address Romani social and economic problems and its
own funding of projects towards this end has been minimal. It is only the pro-Romani
ERRC that actually systematically brings concrete violations of the rights of Roma in
various countries to the scrutiny of the UN human rights treaty bodies. Although I
sympathize with the normative argument that Roma should have the right to participate in decision-making at all levels, it is clear that the UN will not grant this only on
the basis of the normative claim. Romani activists clearly need to devote some of
their energy, which is now mostly spent on agitating for a revolution in international
relations, to making itself practically useful for both the Roma and the UN. The UN,
as with any other exclusive club, requires credentials from potential members.
Romani activists should also realize that unless they generate at least limited
economic resources and popular support, any voice they gain will remain advisory.[7]
As Guibernau concluded, nations without states might in fact have a chance to
become new global political actors, but only if they are economically viable and
provide individuals with a strong sense of identity (1999: 180). 'The Romani nation'
has a long way to go on both fronts.

At the same time, one question Romani activists need to ask is whether their
energy is actually best spent on lobbying at the UN. Are regional organizations
perhaps better equipped to deal with the problems Roma face? European organizations have recently been exerting much more pressure on CEE governments to
improve the situation of their Roma than the UN has. This might, however, just have
been a temporary, pre-EU enlargement phenomenon, and is in any case unfairly
selective, only targeting EU candidate states when there are also abundant violations
of the human rights of Roma in EU member states. The idea of a non-territorial nation
is much more realistic within the framework of the ever-closer integrating EU than
within the UN. As Guibernau points out, within the EU, '[t]he nation-state's territory
is steadily loosing its relevance as a frame for political, economic, social and cultural
life' (1999: 157) and '[n]ation-states will in time turn into nations without states…,
since they are destined to surrender fundamental aspects of their sovereignty to an EU
Parliament or Government' (1999: 171). Hans Vollaard seconds this by arguing that
'territory seems no longer fundamental to sovereign state authority given the coexistence of the functionally-founded sovereignty of some of the European institutions'
(Reinalda, Arts and Noortmann 2001: 6). However, European citizenship would not
extend to all the world's (and, in the near future, all of Europe's) Roma. Given the
global Romani presence, the UN might in fact be the most appropriate target for
lobbying, despite its flaws. In my opinion, lobbying European (and for that matter
other regional) IGOs is an important complement to lobbying the UN, but cannot
substitute it. Therefore, Romani activists should use its association with the UN as
more than a status symbol.

The findings of this book suggest that emphasizing human rights, as opposed to a purely political, agenda, might be a better way of establishing an influence/voice within the UN system. The book demonstrated that Romani activists have only been successful in influencing the UN agenda and discourse in relation to human rights demands. All of their political demands have been ignored. Human rights or 'Roma rights' discourse is in fact the discourse which, according to Dimitrina Petrova, the ERRC director, could unite Romani activists into a movement, because it is the least controversial discourse, accepted by most (ERRC 2001e). Emphasis on human rights would, however, require a change in the thinking of the current IRU leadership or, most probably, a change of leadership itself. For, as I suggested, the leadership has typically been more interested in promoting its status at the UN than in fighting for improvements in the conditions of the people it claims to represent.

Alternatively, instead of a change in thinking, a change in the framing of the main goals of global Romani activism might be sufficient for achieving better results. Keck and Sikkink suggest that transnational advocacy is most successful when it centres around the issues of bodily harm to vulnerable groups or issues involving legal equality of opportunity, evoking normative and juridical/institutional logic (1998: 27). While concentrating on the former might be useful for Romani activists in order to publicize the plight of the Roma in a more dramatic way (since violence and physical mistreatment are in fact among the human rights abuses Roma often suffer), concentrating on the latter would be consistent with the IRU's status quest. The argument that Roma do not *de facto* have an equal opportunity to be involved in global (or even local or nation-state) decision-making resonates better than a nationalist claim for status. Another change needed is the professionalization of Romani activism, so that it can provide useful services to the UN (such as concrete assistance to UN bodies in executing their programmes or delivering high quality and timely research), in exchange for influence.

The latest UN campaign of Romani activists, carried out within the framework of the WCAR process (which I have analysed elsewhere), does give signs for hope (see Klimova 2003: Chapters 7–8). Although it was not completely free of the growing pains, it exhibited some progressive trends in global Romani activism. It had a strong human rights focus with a concrete agenda, supported by research and experience. It showed a dedication to the human rights cause that was manifested in sustained lobbying for specific, largely, although not completely, non-political demands. Most importantly, it succeeded (with the help of other actors) in putting and keeping Roma on the WCAR's agenda, even if not as an official, separate issue but rather as one of the less important victim groups. It also succeeded in having some principles for state and IGO approaches in one area of concern to the Roma – discrimination and racism – being incorporated into the conference's governmental documents (see Klimova 2003: the last row in Table 3). This marks the first instance of such a mention in a UN document *adopted by UN member states*, so representing a breakthrough in the UN discourse on Roma with a move from invisibility or implied inclusion as a minority to specific recognition. These principles can also be seen as the first step towards establishing, at least in theory, norms of good practice in relation to Roma within the UN system.

When discussing the IRU's claim for recognition as a non-territorial nation, some caution is appropriate. Since Roma have to operate in a world where national self-determination is tied to territorial state and which is dominated by nation-states, this demand is highly ambitious. States will hardly support a new concept which would impinge on their exclusive right to sovereignty over citizens of a given territory, forcing them to share this sovereignty with non-territorial institutions, and ultimately perhaps leading to their total redundancy. Consequently, Romani activists need to rely rather on the civil society to sensitize the UN and other global actors to the values of the law of humanity and global governance. As Falk argued in 1995, the challenge that the civil society faces here is formidable, yet the current window of opportunity is unprecedented (1995: 178–179). However, recent trends of a resurgence of the far right and exclusive nationalist ideas along with the tightening of immigration and asylum rules in Europe seem to be closing this window down. If some vision of non-territorial global governance could nevertheless materialize, it is perhaps appropriate to point out that Romani activists should be careful what they wish for because that wish may be fulfilled. At the present they do not have the ability to carry out tasks usually associated with governments, such as providing various (even if selected) services to the people. Thus they might be demanding more than they could cope with. This should be taken into consideration by all promoters of the Romani cause, even those who want to use it as a catalyst for other political projects.

Possible Directions for Future Research

As pointed out earlier (pp. 2–3), this research was inspired by the success of the inter-national indigenous movement at establishing a voice in world politics. The book shows that the Roma have not been nearly as successful. Given the significant simi-larities between the situations and activism of these two groups, what accounts for the *relative* success of the international indigenous activism and the failure of the Romani, especially in the light of the fact that, at the nation-state level, the indigenous peoples have not overall fared better than the Roma? Is it simply the internal charac-teristics of the activisms and their leaders? The Romani case study shows a large degree of amateurism among the Romani activists, but have the indigenous leaders been more professional? A comparison of the personal qualities and capacities of Romani and indigenous activists could shed more light on the importance of these factors for the success in negotiations with intergovernmental bodies *and* on ways for disadvantaged communities to acquire them. Is there a stronger, developed move-ment on behalf of the indigenous peoples? If so, how was this achieved and why has the same not been achieved for the Roma, given the similar time frame of their activism? Is the success of the indigenous movement simply exceptional? Wilmer suggests that one of the reasons for the success of the indigenous movement was the construction of a successful critique of modernisation and providing an alternative to it with social, psychological and spiritual technologies relevant 'to some of the most pressing personal and social problems of our times' (1993: 206). Such a critique has also been advanced and alternatives offered by the Roma, although not so much in public international fora; have they perhaps just not been vocal enough about it?

Although the idea of the nature of the international system changing towards being more responsive to normative issues and various forms of self-determination for ethnic groups, as suggested by Wilmer, is very appealing to me, it remains question-able. Can the relative gains of the international indigenous movement instead be explained in the realist terms of nation-state interest? Could the fear of secession (which is not very applicable in the case of dispersed Roma) be one of the main reasons for the concessions the indigenous movement achieved? The (still very incomplete) picture emerging from the Romani case study testifies to that more than to a global normative change. While individual diplomats, UN administration members and experts might be responsive to the normative critique of the basis for membership in the UN and sympathetic to the Romani call for inclusion in global decision-making, UN member states normally appear to support transnational Romani claims only when it is in their nation-state interest. For example, Romania took over the IRU's demand for organizing an international seminar on Roma just before its membership application for the CoE was considered; CEE states have been supporting the internationalization, or at least Europeanisation, of the Romani issue in order to externalize the costs of programmes for integration and improvement of the conditions of Roma; and Cuba discovered that the treatment of the Roma was a good excuse for criticising European governments and hence distracting attention from its own problematic human rights record (see e.g. pp. 96 and 144, n18).

This trend is in fact much more evident in relation to European institutions, an aspect that has not been explored in this book. There, it is obvious that the majority of CEE governmental programmes on Roma can be linked to the need for satisfying the Copenhagen criteria for EU enlargement, even if no detailed empirical study has yet ascertained this. Identifying the reasons for positive nation-state Roma-specific initiatives carried out upon international pressure (to see if they can be linked to nation-state interest) is therefore one possible extension of the current research.

Adopting a more country-specific approach to studying the international indigenous and Romani activism can also help us better understand the reasons for their success or failure. The global indigenous activism bore most fruits for indigenous populations in settlement/immigrant countries with the tradition of rights-based activism that the indigenous peoples could latch onto. At the same time, indigenous peoples in such countries could use the decolonisation discourse to further their cause. In contrast, indigenous peoples in countries like India enjoy no recognition from the state. The Roma are largely settled in non-immigrant countries of CEE. Having arrived in these territories later than the ancestors of what are today majority populations in the nation-states, they cannot successfully use the decolonization discourse. Similarly, the tradition of rights-based activism is still in an infant stage in CEE and cannot offer the Roma the same capital as is available to indigenous peoples in North America, New Zealand or Australia. Unlike with the indigenous peoples, there are no obvious allies for the Roma in the human rights community and no obvious niche in the dominant discourse that they could move into, especially now when many Romani activists reject the status of national minority and asserts nationhood. Perhaps another aspect in the success of the indigenous activists from North America, New Zealand or Australia at the global stage is their command of English as a political *lingua franca*. Although English is not usually their native language, coming from English-speaking countries it is their language of instruction in educational institutions. At minimum they would have had mastered it for the purposes of dealing with local authorities and populations. Therefore, they can easily present their claims in the international fora. In contrast, Romani leaders often come from CEE. Although some possess higher education (due to the promotion of selected minority elites in the communist educational system) and speak a number of CEE languages, they either have very little or no command of English or French, the main

UN languages. Quite possibly yet more factors also apply. These questions should be explored in further comparative studies in order to fully identify the reasons for the relative success of the international indigenous activism as well as the current failure of the Romani. Such studies could contribute to the growing literature on transnational activism by postulating which factors account for success. From the social movements perspective, it might also be worth investigating and comparing the reasons for the growth of global indigenous and Romani mobilization. Romani and indigenous mobilization developed along a similar timeline, but were the factors leading to their respective beginnings and growth also similar?

Preliminary research suggests that Romani activists have been more successful in instigating agenda-setting, discursive and, especially, procedural/organizational changes related to the Roma within European IGOs, most notably the CoE and OSCE. What accounts for this? Have Romani activists devoted more energy to lobbying at this level? Is the POS offered by these IGOs more favourable to non-state actors? Is it simply because the presence of Roma in Europe is more numerous and their problems more pressing than elsewhere? Another aspect worthy of comparative study in the field of intergovernmental interactions with Romani activists is the role of the European system relative to the UN system. Are the European and UN actions mutually reinforcing and complementary or the contrary?

The book started with the assumption that it would be premature to establish a causal inference about the reasons for the UN agenda-setting, discursive and procedural/organizational developments in relation to the Roma, as neither the UN's dealing with Romani issues nor its interaction with Romani activists had been properly described. As this book has covered a large part of the detailed descriptions needed, it may now be possible to identify the causes for such developments, of which the actions of Romani activists might be one, as this book suggests. Another possible extension of this research is towards a more advanced stage of influence, identified by Keck and Sikkink, by studying the effect of Romani activism on the actual behaviour of target actors (states, UN administration, etc.) (see p. 6).

Finally, as this book illuminated the phenomenon of global Romani activism, it may now be possible to use it as a case study to test a variety of international relations, social movements and nationalism theories, contributing to debates within these disciplines. For example, the Romani elites quest to forge a common transnational Romani identity impacts on the debates on transnationalization of identities and overlapping of identities and loyalties at different levels of the international system. Their attempt to create a non-territorial nation or state contributes to the debates on non-territorial/transnational forms of governance. Their political mobilisation calls for reorganization of the state-centric international system so that nations without states can gain representation. Their critique of the way that states have been marginalizing them and ignoring their rights and wishes is relevant to the debate over whether a state is the most adequate institution to satisfy people's security and identity needs. Their mobilization is an interesting case for studying the phenomenon of transnational collective action because its organization, its goals and the targets of its protest are transnational, while other actors are often termed transnational simply on the basis of one of these factors being transnational. I challenge scholars to recognize that leaving out cases which do not confirm to our current paradigms is not the way to advance our knowledge.

Table 7.1   Main UN and Romani and pro-Romani Activists' Events/ Actions Leading to Agenda-setting and Discursive Developments[8]

Year	Main UN events/ actions [C][9]	Agenda setting [C]	Discursive developments (C/A/R) [C]	Main actions by Romani and pro-Romani activists [C]
1977	Capotorti's Report [SR] Resolution 6 (XXX) [S]	Roma as a minority issue [S]	Roma presence (A), equal rights (R) [S]	Lobbying S members, helping to draft the resolution, oral intervention, distribution of written materials in support [S]
1989/ 1990	ILO Inquiry [ILO]	Discrimination [ILO]	Romanian discrimination (R) [ILO]	Gheorghe's testimony, interviews between Romani activists and the Commission of Inquiry, written material in support[10] [ILO]
1990s		Treaties, projects [TB/UNICEF/ UNESCO]		
1990 –91	Voyame's Reports [SR]	Human rights in Romania [SR]	Human rights abuses, discrimination, racism, marginalisation, minority problem (A), Romanian authorities' attention (R) [SR]	Oral and written information provided by Gheorghe [SR]
1991/ 1992	Resolution 1991/21 [S]	Prevention of racial discrimination and protection of national minorities [S]	Obstacles, vulnerability, racism, prejudice, discrimination, intolerance, xenophobia, advisory services on the topic (A), Special Rapporteurs' attention; equality, protection, security, consultation (R) [C]	Resolution drafted by Gheorghe, lobbying, oral and written interventions in support [S]
1992	Resolution 1992/65	'Minorities' Special Rapporteur [SR]	Discrimination elimination, measures, UN advisory services (R) [C]	Resolution drafted by Gheorghe,[11] lobbying, oral and written interventions in support [C]
1993	Eide's Report [SR]		Deterioration (A), OSCE and CoE prevention of discrimination (R) [SR]	Alleged written and oral information (not proven) [SR]
1993	Braham's Report [E]	UNHCR's agenda [UNHCR]	Transnational group, economic deprivation, social instability, racial violence (A), work of UNHCR, Roma-specific institutions (R) [E]	Interviews with Romani activists – information and suggestions

Table 7.1 continued

Year	Main UN events/ actions [C][9]	Agenda setting [C]	Discursive developments (C/A/R) [C]	Main actions by Romani and pro-Romani activists [C]
1997–2001	Ahanhanzo's Reports [SR]	Racism, racial discrimination, xenophobia and related intolerance	Community-building measures, segregation, anti-discrimination law, tolerance information campaigns, police attitudes, involvement in decision-making (R) [SR]	Interviews with Romani and pro-Romani activists – information and recommendations, written material provided
1999–2000	Roma Rapporteur/ Sik Yuen's working paper [S/E]	Focus min./human rights group, WCAR [E]	Discrimination (A), anti-racism laws, protection, South American study (R) [E]	Initiated by the IRU, oral interventions in support
End of the 1990s		Projects, Special Rapporteur [UNDP/WR/SR]		
1999–2002	Weissbrodt's Reports [SR]	Citizenship problems [S]	Lack of UN effort [SR]	
2000	Recommend. XVII/ thematic discussion [CERD]	Discrimination and WCAR [CERD/C]	Discrimination, disadvantage (A), violence, living conditions, UNHCHR Focal Point, WCAR (R) [CEDR]	Oral interventions leading to recommendations
2000s		Projects [ILO]		
2001	Resolution 2001/9 [C]	Right to development, vulnerable group [C]	Developmental attention (A/R) [C]	
	Recommend. no. 7 and 10 [WGPM]		OSCE and CoE non-discrimination and minority rights, treaty bodies' attention [WGPM]	Indirectly related oral interventions
	Formal opinion [ILO]	169 Convention (A/R) [ILO]		
2003	UNDP Report [UNDP]	UNDP projects	Development, positive discrimination (A/R) [UNDP]	Input from Romani activists
	Kothari's report [SR]	Vulnerable group, housing in Romania [SR]	Romania, vulnerable group, housing (A) Anti-discrimination, identity documents, national housing sector policies, consultation (R) (SR)	ERRC Memorandum

Notes

1 Note that this assumption relates to both agenda-setting and implementation phases. The implementation phase was however not examined in this book.
2 The Permanent Forum is an advisory body to the ECOSOC on indigenous issues relating to economic and social development, culture, the environment, education, health and human rights, composed of eight experts nominated by governments and eight experts appointed by the ECOSOC President on the basis of consultations with indigenous organizations and governments. It held its first session on 13–24 May 2002 at the UN headquarters in New York (for details see OHCHR, Permanent Forum on Indigenous Issues).
3 These hypotheses were also confirmed through my analysis of the WCAR process (see Klimova 2003: Chapter 8).
4 Recall that the demand for such a body for indigenous peoples was in fact championed within the UN fora by Lacroix-Hopson, the IRU representative in New York.
5 Note that the characterization of the Romani movement as social should by no means be interpreted as implying that Roma are or consider themselves to be a social as opposed to ethnic or national group. The definition of trasnational social movements is sufficiently broad to encompass the subcategories of ethnic and national movements.
6 This is, however, not to say that there is no co-operation or pieces of a common framework whatsoever. For example, the ever-increasing acceptance of the discourse of non-territorial nation among activists outside the IRU is an example of a developing common vision.
7 This is not to say that an advisory role cannot on its own be very influential. However, it seems that Romani activists are aiming higher than that.
8 Data in columns 2–4 are presented in keyword form as they are identical to those in Table 3.1.
9 Code for the UN body to which the discursive development applies: [S] – the Subcommission, [C] – the Commission, [SR] – individual UN Special Rapporteur, [E] – individual expert commissioned to do a study, [TB] – treaty bodies. For others, regular abbreviations are used.
10 The evidence about the written material is inconclusive.
11 But much altered by the Commission.

Bibliography

Achim, V. (1998), *Tigani din Istoria Romaniei*, Bucharest: Editura Enciclopedica.

Acton, Thomas (1972), 'Meetings of the Social and War Crimes Commissions of the World Romani Congress (April 25–29, 1972): A Summary Report', *JGLS,* **LI** (3–4), Third Series July-October.

—— (1974), *Gypsy Politics and Social Change: The Development of Ethnic Ideology and Pressure Politics among British Gypsies from Victorian Reforms to Romany Nationalism*, London: Routledge.

—— (1979), 'The World Romani Congress', *Traveller Education*, (14), 7–13.

—— (1990/91), 'Romani Encyclopaedists Set to Work', *Roma*, (3–4), July, 56–60.

—— (2003), 'That UNDP Report', E-mail distributed to various lists and recipients, 6 February.

Acton, Thomas, and Nicolae Gheorghe (2001), 'Citizens of the World and Nowhere: Minority, Ethnic and Human Rights for Roma', in Guy, Will (ed.), *Between Past and Future: the Roma of Central and Eastern Europe*, Hartfield: University of Hertfordshire Press, pp. 54–70.

Acton, Thomas, and Ilona Klimova (2001), 'The International Romani Union: An East European Answer to West European Questions?' in Guy, Will (ed.), *Between Past and Future: the Roma of Central and Eastern Europe*, Hartfield: University of Hertfordshire Press, pp. 157–219.

Agence France Presse (2000), *UNHCR Demands Inquiry into Kosovo Roma Murders, 11 November*, accessed 22 October 2002, available from the UNHCR website, http: //www.unhcr.ch.

Agenda of 3rd World Romani Congress (1986), Archive 1.

Ali Ahmed, F. (1976), 'Roma – Messengers of Universal Understanding and Friendship: Address by the President of India', *Roma,* **2** (2), 1–2.

Allocution de Monsieur Bhamat [sic] de l'UNESCO lors du Congres Mondial Tsigane (1978), Geneve, Archive 1.

Anaya, James S. (1999), *Superpower Attitudes Towards Indigenous Peoples and Group Rights*, Lecture delivered at the 93rd Annual Meeting of the American Society of International Law, March 24–27, Washington, D.C., accessed 27 April 2003, available from the Indian Law Resource Center website, http://www.indianlaw.org/body_superpower_attitudes.htm.

Anderson, B. (1991), *Imagined communities: reflections on the origin and spread of nationalism*, London: Verso.

Archibugi, Danielle and David Held (eds.) (1995), *Cosmopolitan Democracy: An Agenda for a New World Order*, Cambridge, MA: Polity Press.

Arts, B. (1998), *The Political Influence of Global NGOs: Case Studies on the Climate and Biodiversity Conventions*, London: International Books.

—— (2001), 'The Impact of Environmental NGOs on International Conventions', in Arts, B., M. Noortmann and B. Reinalda (eds.), *Non-State Actors in International Relations*, Aldershot: Ashgate, pp. 195–210.

Arts, B., M. Noortmann and B. Reinalda (eds.) (2001), *Non-State Actors in International Relations*, Aldershot: Ashgate.

Ayoub, Farida (1991), Chief of the NGO/DIESA, Letter to Rajko Djuric, 16 May, Archive 3.

—— (1992), Chief of the NGO/DIESA, Letter to Rajko Djuric, New York, 25 November, Document obtained from Lynnaia Main.

Bakker, Edwin (2001), 'Early Warning by NGOs in Conflict Areas', in Arts, B., M. Noortmann and B. Reinalda (eds.), *Non-State Actors in International Relations*, Aldershot: Ashgate, pp. 263–277.

Bakker, Peter, Milena Huebschmannova, Valdemar Kalinin, Donald Kenrick, Hristo Kyuchukov, Yaron Matras, and Giulio Soravia (2001), *What is the Romani language?* Hatfield: University of Hertfordshire Press.

Balic, Sait (1985), 'Letter to the editor', *Romanija,* **3** (2), June.

Barany, Zoltan (2000), 'The Poverty of Gypsy Studies, *NewsNet: The Newsletter of the AAASS (American Association for the Advancement of Slavic Studies)*, **30** (3).

—— (2002), *The East European Gypsies: Regime Change, Marginality, and Ethnopolitics*, New York: Cambridge University Press.

Barry, Gerald, (1958), 'Gypsies: wanderers for two thousand years', *UNESCO Courier,* **11** (4), April, 4.

Bauboeck, Rainer (2001), *Multinational Federalism: Territorial or Cultural Autonomy?* Willy Brandt Series of Working Papers in International Migration and Ethnic Relations 2/01, accessed 20 April 2003, available from the Malmo Hogskola Bibliotek website, http://www.bit.mah.se.

—— (2002), 'Political Community Beyond the Sovereign State, Supranational Federalism, and Transnational Minorities' in Vertovec, Steven and Robin Cohen (eds.), *Conceiving Cosmopolitanism: Theory, Context, and Practice*, Oxford: Oxford University Press, pp. 110–136.

Bauer, O. (2000), *The Question of Nationalities and Social Democracy*, ed. E. Nimni, Minneapolis: University of Minnesota Press.

Beck, U. (1999a), *What is Globalization?* Cambridge: Polity Press.

—— (1999b), *World Risk Society*, Cambridge: Polity Press.

—— (2000), *The Brave New World of Work*, Cambridge: Polity Press.

—— (2002), *Macht und Gegenmacht im Globalen Zeitalter* [Power and Countervailing Power in the Global Age], Frankfurt am Main: Suhrkamp Verlag.

Bencsi, Imre (1989), *Report on the Texas, California and Illinois Meetings of the Romani Union*, Autumn, Archive 6.

Berisha, Zenelj (2002), Romani local mediator in Skopje, Group E-mail, 6 August.

Bowring, Bill (2002), 'Austro-Marxism's Last Laugh: The Struggle for Recognition of National-Cultural Autonomy for Rossians and Russians', *Europe-Asia Studies*, **54** (2), 229–250.

Braham, Mark (1993), *The Untouchables: A Survey of the Roma People of Central and Eastern Europe: Report to UNHCR*, Geneva, March.

Brash, Alan A. (1973), Letter to Jan Cibula, 9 March, Archive 2.

Brockett, Charles (1991), 'The structure of political opportunities and peasant mobilization in Central America', *Comparative Politics,* **23** (3), 253–274.

Castle-Kanerova, Mita (2003), 'Round and Round the Roundabout: Czech Roma and the Vicious Circle of Asylum-Seeking', *Nationalities Papers*, **31** (1), 13–25.

Cecatto, G.N. (1969), Chief of the Communications Unit of the Division of Human Rights of the UN, Letter to Rudolf Karway, 22 April, Archive 1.

Chatterjee, P. (1993), *The Nation and Its Fragments: Colonial and Postcolonial Histories*, Princeton: Princeton University Press.

Cibula, Jan (1973), Letter to Grattan Puxon, 28 January, Archive 2.

—— (1978a-b), Letters to Lola Costa-Esnard, Council Affairs Officer, NGO Secretariat DIESA, 2 November (1978a) and 29 November (1978b), Archive 2.

—— (1978c), *Communication to the Presidium and to all brothers and sisters throughout the world*, Bern, November, Archive 4.

—— (1978d, e, f), Letters to Kurt Waldheim, 19 February (1978d), 3 March (1978e) and 5 July (1978f), Archive 2.

—— (1978g), Letter to Eberhard Gelbe-Haussen, Senior Information Officer, Geneva, 16 November, Archive 2.

—— (1978h), Letter to Amadou-Mahtar M'Bow, Bern, 25 April, Archive 2.

—— (1979a), Letter to Raymonde Martineau, 23 January, Archive 4.

—— (1979b), Letter to Lola Costa-Esnard, Council Affairs Officer, NGO Secretariat DIESA, 26 January, Archive 2.

—— (1979c), *Erneuerung der Delegation der Romani Union fuer UNO Genf 1980*, Bern, 7 November, Archive 4.

—— (1979d), Letter to Miroslav Holomek, 14 June, Archive 4.

—— (1979e), *Verkuerzte Verfassung ueber die Praesidialsitzung vom 3. und 4. Juni*, Archive 4.

—— (1979f), *Praesidiale Erklaerung von Romani Union, ordentliches Mitglied des NGOs ECOSOC*, Letter to Kurt Waldheim, 3 April, Archive 2.

—— (1981a), *Perspektive des III. Weltkongresses der Roma-Welt-Union-NGOs ECOSOC, Goettingen 16–20 May*, Transcript of a prepared speech, 13 May, Archive 5.

—— (1985), Letter to Virginia F. Sauerwein, Chief NGO Unit, Bern, 30 September, Archive 5a.

—— (1986), *Die Manipulationen mit ethnishen Minderheiten wie die Roma oder Menschenrechte Illusion der Menschen allgemein?* Vortrag zur Praesidialsitzung der Romani Union im Jardin de Luxemburg – Paris, 22 February, Bern, Archive 2.

—— (1989), *Pressemitteilung, RIJ Konferenz*, Bern, 27 November, Archive 2.

—— (1997), *Ziadost o prijatie do vedenia fondu holokaustu ako zastupcu Romov* [Application for the post of Romani representative on the Board of the Holocaust Foundation], Bern, 11 May, Slovak translation, Archive 5a.

Cibula, Jan, and Eynard Gilles (1978), Letter to Virginia Sauerwein, 15 June, Archive 2.

Cibula, Jan, Ivanov Gusti, Grattan Puxon, and Marco Kappenberger (1981), Letter of 13 February, Archive 5a.

Child Rights Information Network (2001), *The Berlin Commitment for Children of Europe and Central Asia*, accessed 12 January 2003, available from the Child Rights Information Network website, http://www.crin.org/docs/resources/publications/berlin2draft.pdf.

CNN (2001), International (Global Channel), *Live from the New York Studios, June 9th 2001 – 3:00pm USA East Coast Time, Jim Clancy Interviews Paolo Pietrosanti, Commissioner for Foreign Affairs of the International Romani Union*, accessed 10 November 2002, available from the Dzeno website, http://www.dzeno.cz/english/aktuality_en_01.htm.

Coakley, John (1994), 'Approaches to the Resolution of Ethnic Conflict: The Strategy of Non-Territorial Autonomy', *International Political Science Review,* **15** (3), 297–314.

CoE (2002a), *Newsletter on activities within the Joint CoE/OSCE-ODIHR/EC Project 'Roma under the Stability Pact'*, (3), January, Strasbourg.
—— (2002b), Directorate General III – Social Cohesion, and Migration and Roma/Gypsies Division, *Roma Participation in Europe – The Way Forward (Strasbourg, 21 October), Seminar Report (8 January 2003)*, accessed 15 March 2003, available through the RNN website, http://www.globetek-networks.com/roma/Participation_in_Europe.htm.
'Conclusions of the International Symposium on Romani Language and Culture' (1986), *Roma*, (25), July, 16–18.
Concolato, Jean-Claude (2000), *How to define a humanitarian approach to the Roma issue?* Prague, May, Presentation for the Khamoro festival.
—— (2002), *UNHCR Prague opening speech on the occasion of the seminar 'Housing and Roma Community' co-organised by UNHCR, DROM, Socioklub and SOZE*, Brno, 3–4 October.
Conference of Non-Governmental Organisations in consultative status with the Economic and Social Council of the United Nations (1979), Report of the 14th General Assembly, 2–5 July, Geneva, Switzerland, Archive 5b, Classmark 1751.
'Congresul Tiganilor are loc peste o luna la Bucuresti' (1933), *Tempo*, (45), 27 August.
Cortiade, Marcel, and Jeta Duka (1994), 'International Romani Union in Action', *Roma*, (41), July, 28–41.
Costarelli, Sandro (ed.) (1993), *Children of minorities: gypsies*, Florence: UNICEF International Child Development Centre.
Crowe, D. M. (1996), *A History of the Gypsies of Eastern Europe and Russia*, New York: St. Martin's Press.
Crowe, David M., and John Kolsti (eds.) (1991), *The Gypsies of Eastern Europe*, New York: Armonk.
Danbakli, Marielle (ed.) (2001), *Roma, Gypsies: Text Issued by International Institutions*, Hatfield: University of Hertfordshire Press.
Daniel, Antonin, Tomas Holomek, and Ladislav Demeter (1971), 'Svetovy kongres a festival Romu v Londyne [The World Congress and Festival of Roma in London]', *Romano Lil Zpravodaj*, (3), 21–27.
Dass, Pouchpa (1981), Director of the UNESCO International Fund for the Promotion of Culture, Letter to Grattan Puxon, General Secretary of Romani Kongreso 3, 30 March, CC/IFPC/543, Archive 1.
della Porta, Donatella, and Mario Diani (1999), *Social movements: An introduction*, Oxford: Blackwell.
Djuric, Rajko (1991), Letter to Rafeeuddin Ahmet, Undersecretary-General, 30 May, Archive 3.
—— (1992), Letter to Farida Ayoub, 30 April, Archive 3.
Djuric, Rajko, Sait Balic, Stanislav Stankiewicz, Victor Famulson, and Emil Scuka (1991), 'Lil e IV Rromane Kongresosqo Bichaldo k-o Raj Perez de Cuellar [Letter of the Fourth World Romani Congress to Perez de Cuellar], written in Warsaw on 11 April 1990', *Informaciaqo Lil e Rromane Uniaqoro*, July-August, 3–4.
DPI NGO Section, *About Us*, accessed 10 October 2002, available from the UN website, http://www.un.org/dpi/ngosection/aboutus.htm.
—— *NGOs and the United Nations Department of Public Information: Some Questions and Answers*, accessed 13 October 2002, available from the UN website, http://www.un.org/dpi/ngosection/brochure.htm.

—— *The Directory of NGOs associated with DPI*, accessed 12 November 2002, available from the UN website, http://www.un.org/MoreInfo/ngolink/ngodir.

Drom Center (2002a), 'Report from the strike of local mediator from Macedonia from region of Kosovo', Message forwarded to Romano Liloro newsgroup (romano_liloro@yahoo.com) by Ariel Eliyahu, 30 July.

—— (2002b), *10 December – Peaceful protest in Skopje, Macedonia*, accessed 22 December 2002, available from the RNN website, http://www.romnews.com.

Eide, Asbjorn (1998), 'Cultural Autonomy: Concept, Content, History and Role in the World Order', in Suksi, Markku (ed.), *Autonomy: Applications and Implications*, The Hague: Kluwer Law International, pp. 251–276.

Eliyahu, Ariel (2002a), 'Report from Shuto Orizari', Message posted to Romano Liloro newsgroup (romano_liloro@yahoo.com), 8 August.

—— (2002b), 'Macedonia – Roma protest to UNHCR', Message to Romano Liloro newsgroup (romano_liloro@yahoo.com), 10 August.

—— (2002c), 'Responce of UNHCR Skopje on the Letter of Protest' [sic], Message to the Roma Daily News newsgroup (Roma_Daily_News@yahoogroups.com), 2 September.

Emerick, Robert E. (1996), 'Mad Liberation: The Sociology of Knowledge and the Ultimate Civil Rights Movement', accessed 10 October 2002, available from the *Journal of Mind and Behaviour,* **17** (2), Spring 1996, 135–160, http://www.academicarmageddon.co.uk/library/emer.htm.

ERRC (1996a), *Statement of Mission*, accessed 22 September 2002, available from the ERRC website, *Roma Rights*, Autumn, http://errc.org/rraut1996/statement.shtml.

—— (1996b), *What does ERRC do?*, accessed 22 September 2002, available from the ERRC website, http://www.errc.org/about/does.shtml.

—— (1996c), *What is the ERRC*, accessed 22 September 2002, available from the ERRC website, http://www.errc.org/about/index.shtml.

—— (1996d), *Chronicle 96*, accessed 26 January 2003, available from the ERRC website, http://errc.org/rr_aut1996/chronicle.shtml.

—— (1997), *Chronicle 97*, accessed 10 November 2002, available from the ERRC website, *Roma Rights*, Summer, http://errc.org/rr_sum1997/chronicle.shtml.

—— (1998), 'Chronicle winter 98', *Roma Rights*, 67.

—— (1999a), 'Chronicle 99/1', *Roma Rights*, (1), 79.

—— (1999b), 'Chronicle 99/2', *Roma Rights*, (2), 66.

—— (1999c), 'Chronicle 99/3', accessed 24 January 2003, available from the ERRC website, *Roma Rights*, (3), http://errc.org/rr_nr3_1999/chronicle.shtml.

—— (1999d), 'Chronicle 99/4', *Roma Rights*, (4), 90.

—— (1999e), 'Declaration of the participants in the Balkan Roma conference for peace and security', *Roma Rights*, (2), 47–49.

—— (1999f), *ERRC Letter to Joint World Bank/European Commission Office for Southeast Europe, July 28,* accessed 13 November 2002, available from the ERRC website, www.errc.org/publications/letters/1999/bank_jul_28_99.shtml.

—— (2000a), *Racial Discrimination and Violence against Roma in Europe, Statement Submitted by the European Roma Right Center, ERRC,* August, accessed 21 November 2002, available from the GHM website, http://www.greekhelsinki.gr/special-issues-roma-un-cerd-debates.html.

—— (2000b), 'Chronicle 2000/4', accessed 10 December 2002, available from the ERRC website, *Roma Rights*, (4), http://errc.org/rr_nr4_2000/chronicle.shtml.

—— (2001a), 'Chronicle 2001/1', *Roma Rights*, (1), 106.

—— (2001b), 'Chronicle 2001/4', *Roma Rights*, (4), 113–114.

—— (2001c), 'Campaigning, conferences and meetings', *Roma Rights*, (2 and 3), 104.

—— (2001d), *Germany Threatens to Imprison Romani Activist*, Electronic press release, 12 November.

—— (2001e), 'The Romani movement: what shape, what direction?' accessed 10 December 2002, available from the ERRC website, *Roma Rights*, (4), http://lists.errc.org/rr_nr4_2001/noteb3.shtml.

—— (2002a), 'Chronicle 2002/3–4', *Roma Rights*, (3 and 4), 168–169.

—— (2002b), *Memorandum of the European Roma Rights Center concerning the right of Roma to adequate housing in Romania*, accessed 17 February 2003, available from the ERRC website, http://www.errc.org/publications/legal/index.shtml.

—— (2002c), 'Campaigning, conferences and meetings', *Roma Rights*, (2), 121–122.

—— (2003), ERRC: Roma Rights Victory in Yugoslav Torture Case, Electronic Press Release, 22 January.

Equal Opportunities Committee (2001), *1st Report 2001, Inquiry into Gypsy Travellers and Public Sector Policies, Volume 2: Evidence*, accessed 29 January 2003, available from the Scottish Parliament website, http://www.scottish.parliament.uk/officialreport/cttee/equal-01/eor01–01-vol02–05.htm.

Fagot Aviel, JoAnn (1999), 'NGOs and International Affairs: A New Dimension of Diplomacy', in Muldoon, James P. Jr., Richard Reitano, JoAnn Fagot Aviel and Earl Sullivan (eds.), *Multilateral Diplomacy and the United Nations Today*, Oxford: Westview Press, pp. 156–166.

Falk, Richard (1995), 'The World Order between Inter-State Law and the Law of Humanity: the Role of Civil Society Institutions', in Archibugi, Danielle and David Held (eds.), *Cosmopolitan Democracy: An Agenda for a New World Order*, Cambridge, MA: Polity Press, pp. 163–179.

Fernandez Jimenez, D.L. (1996), *Young Roma, Gypsies and Travellers in Europe*, Strasbourg: Council of Europe.

Feys, Cara (1997), 'Towards a New Paradigm of the Nation: The Case of the Roma', accessed 17 January 2003, available from the *Journal of Public and International Affairs*, http://www.wws.princeton.edu/~jpia/1997/chap1.html.

Ficowski, J. (1991), *The Gypsies in Poland: History and Customs*, Warsaw: Interpress.

Fings, K., H. Heuss, and F. Sparing (1997), *The Gypsies during the Second World War: From 'Race Science' to the Camps*, Hatfield: University of Hertfordshire Press.

Forte, Maxmilian C. (1995), 'The Crisis of Creolization in Trinidad and Tobago? Globalized Revitalizations, Systemic Ethno-politics, and Alter-Nationalism', *International Third World Studies*, (7), October, 41–54.

Foszto, L. (2000), 'The International Romany Movement in the 90s', unpublished MA thesis, Central European University.

Fourth World Romani Congress (1990), Draft of a letter to Perez de Cuellar, Archive 3.

Foy, Nadia, and Michelle Lloyd (2002), *Speaking at the UN*, Edinburgh, June, Document received from Lloyd.

Fraser, A. (1992), *The Gypsies*, Oxford: Blackwell.

Gelbe-Haussen, Eberhard (1978), Senior Information Officer, Geneva, Letter to Jan Cibula, 24 October, Archive 2.

'Germany Refuses to Sign Resolution Protecting Rights of Roma' (1992), *Buhazi*, (2), Winter, 4.

Gheorghe, Nicolae (1991a), *Report on the activity during the 47th session of the UN Commission on Human Rights*, Geneva, 19 February – 7 March, Archive 6.

—— (1991b), Draft project of resolution on item 12 ou [sic] 20 to be submitted to the attention of the members of the Commission on Human Rights, 47th session, Archive 3.

—— (1991c), Sub-Commission on Prevention of Discrimination and Protection of Minorities, Forty-third session, August 1991, Item 18 of the provisional agenda: Protection of Minorities, Hostile attitudes towards Roma people in Central and Eastern Europe, Archive 3.

—— (1991d), *Sub-Commission on Prevention of Discrimination and Protection of minorities, Forty-third session, August 1991, Item 18 of the provisional agenda: Protection of Minorities, Statement by the Representative of the Romani International Union*, Archive 3.

—— (1993), 'L'Union romani et les institutions internationales', *Ethnie,* **8** (15), Autumn, 50–65.

—— (2001), *Developments in international politics on Roma and Sinti affairs*, Warsaw, 2 July, Draft document prepared for Meeting of the Informal Contact Group on Roma of Intergovernmental Organisations, Brussels, 4 July and for the OSCE Conference on Roma and Sinti Issues, Bucharest, 10–13 September, Archive 3.

Gheorghe, Nicolae, and Ian Hancock (1991a), *Report of the International Romani Union on the current situation of Roma throughout the world: A report prepared under the auspices of the International Romani Union and the International Federation of Human Rights*, Archive 3.

—— (1991b), Letter addressed to the delegates to the 48th meeting of the Commission on Human Rights, 16 December, Archive 6.

GHM (2000), *Racial discrimination and violence against Roma in Greece, GHM and MRG-G, 31 July*, accessed 21 November 2002, available from the GHM website, http://www.greekhelsinki.gr/special-issues-roma-un-cerd-debates.html.

Girvan, Norman (2002), *Globalization not just Economics: The Greater Caribbean this week*, accessed 18 May 2003, available from the Association of Caribbean States website, http://www.acs-aec.org/column/index35.htm.

Goodwin, Morag (2004), 'The Romani Claim to Non-Territorial Nation Status: Recognition from an International Legal Perspective', *Roma Rights* (1), 54–64.

Guibernau, M. (1999), *Nations Without States*, Cambridge: Polity Press.

Gusti, Ivanov (1979), Letter to Kurt Waldheim, Lelystad, 12 June, Archive 4.

Haley, John (1934), 'The Gypsy Conference at Bucharest', *JGLS,* **XVIII** (4), 182–190.

Hall, R. B. (1999), *National collective identity: social constructs and international systems*, New York: Columbia University Press.

Hancock, Ian (1986), 'World Roma Mourn Passing of Yul Brynner', *Roma*, (24), January, 15–16.

—— (1987a), 'The plight of the Romani children', *Action for Children,* **3** (11), 1–6.

168   *The Romani Voice in World Politics*

—— (1987b), 'Le sort des enfants Romani', *Action pour les Enfants*, **2** (3), 1–5.
—— (1988), 'Reunification and the Role of the International Romani Union', *Roma*, (29), July, 9–18.
—— (1991a), 'The East European Roots of Romani Nationalism', *Nationalities Papers*, **19** (3), 251–268.
—— (1991b), 'What is the International Romani Union', *Informaciaqo Lil e Rromane Uniaqoro*, (1–2), 1–2.
—— (1991c), 'Gypsy History in Germany and Neighboring Lands: A Chronology to the Holocaust and Beyond', *Nationalities Papers*, **19** (3), 395–421.
—— (1991d), 'Report on Visit to Romania, 9–23 August 1991', *Informaciaqo Lil e Rromane Uniaqoro*, (3–4), September-October, 3–5.
—— (1992), *NGO Committee on the International Year of the World's Indigenous Peoples: Report of the International Romani Union*, New York, 5 March, Archive 6.
—— (1993a), Letter to Farida Ayoub, NGO Unit, DIESA, 21 April, Archive 6.
—— (1993b), Letter to Paolo Pietrosanti, 29 March, Prague IRU Archive.
—— (1998), *Unauthorized Appointment of IRU United Nations Representative*, 4 March, Archive 6.
—— (1999a), *The Pariah Syndrome: An Account of Gypsy Slavery and Persecution*, accessed 25 February 2000, available from the *Patrin Web Journal*, www.geocities.com/Paris/5121/pariah-contents.htm.
—— (1999b), *RNN Exclusive: Statement regarding my position with the International Romani Union*, accessed 11 November 2002, available from the RNN website, http://www.romnews.com.
—— (2002), *We Are the Romani People: Ame sam e Rromane dzene*, Hatfield: University of Hertfordshire Press.
—— (Undated), Curriculum Vitae, Archive 6.
Hancock, Ian, and Yaron Matras (1990), *EUROM: Romano Parlamento Evropjano/European Romani Parliament*, 10 November, Archive 6.
Har Kaushal, Hari (1980), 'Legal Status of Roma in Europe and America', *Roma*, **5** (1), January, 20–31.
Heilman, S. C., and S. M. Cohen (1989), *Cosmopolitans and Parochials: Modern Orthodox Jew in America*, Chicago: University of Chicago Press.
Held, D. (1995), *Democracy and the global order: from the modern state to cosmopolitan governance*, Cambridge, MA: Polity Press.
Heywood, A. (1998), *Political Ideas and Concepts: An Introduction*, 2nd ed., London: Macmillan Press.
Higgott, R. A, G. R. D. Underhill, and A. Bieler (eds.) (2000), *Non-State Actors and Authority in the Global System*, London: Routledge.
Hoeffe, O. (1999), *Demokratie im Zeitalter der Globalisierung* [Democracy in the Age of Globalisation], Muenchen: Beck.
HRW (1991), *Destroying Ethnic Identity: the Persecution of Gypsies in Romania*, New York: HRW.
—— (1992), *Struggling for Ethnic Identity: Czechoslovakia's Endangered Gypsies*, New York: HRW.
—— (1993), *Struggling for Ethnic Identity: The Gypsies of Hungary*, New York: HRW.
—— (1996), *Roma in the Czech Republic: Foreigners in Their Own Land*, New York: HRW.

—— (1996), *Rights Denied: The Roma of Hungary*, New York: HRW.

IGRM (1969), English translation of an undated document on an IGRM letterhead describing the work and aims of the IGRM, attached to Karway's letter to the Pope dated 27 May, Archive 1.

ILO (1990a), *IIIeme session de la commison d'enquete chargee d'examiner l'obser-vation par la Roumanie de la convention (no 111) concernant la discrimination (emploi et profession), 1958: Seance du 6 octobre 1990, 10h.00–13h.00*, (Geneva – Bucharest, 2–13 Octobre 1990), Available in the ILO Library in Geneva.

—— (1990b), *IIIeme session de la commison d'enquete chargee d'examiner l'obser-vation par la Roumanie de la convention (no 111) concernant la discrimination (emploi et profession), 1958: Seance du 6 octobre 1990, 14h.00–17h.30*, (Geneva-Bucharest, 2–13 October 1990), available in the ILO Library in Geneva.

—— (1991), *Report of the Commission of Inquiry appointed under article 26 of the Constitution of the International Labour Organisation to examine the observance by Romania of the Discrimination (Employment and Occupation) Convention, 1958 (No. 111), Vol. LXXIV, 1991, Series B, Supplement 3)*, accessed 1 November 2002, available from the ILOLEX database at the ILO website, http://www.ilo.org/ilolex.

—— (1998), *The ILO: What it is and What it does*, Geneva: ILO.

—— (1999), *The International Labour Organization and the promotion of full, productive and freely chosen employment, International Consultation concerning Follow-up to the World Summit for Social Development, Geneva, 2–4 November 1999, Employment and Training Department, International Labour Office Geneva*, accessed 28 October 2002, available from the ILO website, http://www.ilo.org/public/english/employment/strat/publ/fwsd.htm.

—— (2001), Opinion relative to the decisions of the International Labour Conference, Indigenous and Tribal Peoples Convention, 1989 (No. 169), Memorandum by the International Office, GB.280/18, GB280–18–2001–02 –0195–3-EN.Doc.

—— (2002a), *CEACR: Individual Observation concerning Convention No. 122, Employment Policy, 1964 Czech Republic (ratification: 1993), published 1999*, accessed 1 November 2002, available from the ILOLEX database at the ILO website, http://www.ilo.org/ilolex.

—— (2002b), *CEACR: Individual Observation concerning Convention No. 122, Employment Policy, 1964 Hungary (ratification: 1969), published 2002*, accessed 1 November 2002, available from the ILOLEX database at the ILO website, http://www.ilo.org/ilolex.

—— (2002c), *Principles contained in the Declaration. Equality of opportunity and treatment, Hungary. Seventh Survey on the effect given to the Tripartite Declaration of Principles concerning Multinational Enterprises and Social Policy: Summary of reports submitted by governments and by employers' and workers' organizations (Part II), Document GB.280/MNE/1/2*, accessed 1 November, available from the ILOLEX database at the ILO website, http://www.ilo.org/ilolex.

—— (2003), *Comments submitted by the International Labour Office to the Commission on Human Rights, Fifty-ninth session, Item 6 of the provisional agenda – Racism, racial discrimination, xenophobia and all forms of discrimina-tion*, Document received from Martin Oelz.

'India Supports Roma at the United Nations Human Rights Commission' (1978), *Roma,* **4** (1), January, 13–17.

IRC (Undated), *Report,* Archive 1.

IRU (1979), *Presseerklaerung,* Bern, 6 February, Archive 2.

—— (1992), Abstract sheet for the IRU, Rough draft of application for reclassification to category 2, Archive 3.

—— (1993), Draft of reclassification request for ECOSOC status category II, Archive 3.

—— (1999a), *Letter 'To whom it may concern',* Washington, 22 October, Copy included in participants' folders at the Fifth World Romani Congress.

—— (1999b), *Evaluation Report of the IRU Trip to the United States,* 16–23 October, Archive 3.

—— (2000a), *Information Sheet,* Distributed during the Fifth World Romani Congress in Prague, July.

—— (2000b), *IRU Program.* Distributed during the Fifth World Romani Congress in Prague, July.

—— (2000c), *Clenske zeme* [Member states], accessed 29 January 2003, available from the IRU website, http://www.romaniunion.net.

—— (2000d), *Kandidatske zeme* [Candidate states], accessed 28 January 2002, available from the IRU website, http://www.romaniunion.net.

—— (2000e), *Centrala IRU – Regionalni pobocky* [IRU headquarters – Regional branch offices], accessed 29 January 2003, available from the IRU website, http://www.romaniunion.net.

—— (2000f), *Presidium – Donori* [Presidium – Donors] and *Parlament – Donori* [Parliament – Donors], accessed 29 January 2003, available from the IRU website, http://www.romaniunion.net.

IRU and IFHR (1991), Commission on Human Rights, 47th session, February 25, Item 12- Gross violations of human rights in any part of the world, Current situation of the Roma throughout the world, Written statement, Archive 3.

Ivatts, Arthur R. (1974), 'Gypsies: a minority at the crossroads; education opens new horizons for nomad families', *UNESCO Courier,* (27), November.

Jackson-Preece, J. (1998), *National Minorities and the European Nation-States System,* Oxford: Clarendon Press.

Jaeger, Gilbert (1982), 'Participation of Non-Governmental Organizations in the Activities of the United Nations High Commissioner for Refugees', in Willetts, Peter (ed.), *Pressure Groups in the Global System: The Transnational Relations of Issue-Oriented Non-Governmental Organizations,* London: Frances Pinter, pp. 172–178.

Jusuf, Saip (1981), 'The Wheel of Destiny: Roma Today and Tomorrow', *Roma,* **6** (1), January, 21–25.

Kaminski, I-M. (1980), *The State of Ambiguity: Studies of Gypsy Refugees,* Gothenburg: University of Gothenburg.

Kappenberger, Marco (1985), Letter to 'Very Dear Representative of the Romani Union to the UN in NY', 30 October, Archive 2.

Karway, Rudolf (1968), *Minutes of the meeting of the elected delegates of IGRM,* 31 May, Archive 1.

—— (1969a), Letter to the Pope, English translation, 27 May, Archive 1.

—— (1969b), Letter to UN Secretary-General, English translation, Hamburg. 20 November, Archive 1.

Kawczynski, Rudko (1997), 'The Politics of Romani Politics', *Transitions*, **4** (4), 24–29.

—— (2001), 'Rudko thanks', Message forwarded to the author by Martin Demirovski, 4 December.

Keck, M. E., and K. Sikkink (1998), *Activists Beyond Borders: Advocacy Networks in International Politics*, Ithaca: Cornell University Press.

Kenrick, D. (ed.) (1999), *The Gypsies during the Second World War: In the Shadow of the Swastika*, Hatfield: University of Hertfordshire Press.

Kenrick, D. and G. Puxon (1972), *The Destiny of Europe's Gypsies*, London: Sussex University Press.

—— (1995), *Gypsies under the Swastika*, Hatfield: University of Hertfordshire Press.

King, G., R. O. Keohane, and S. Verba (1994), *Designing Social Inquiry: Scientific Inference in Qualitative Research*, Princeton: Princeton University Press.

Klimova, I. (1999), 'Protection of Dispersed Transnational Communities in Contemporary Europe: The Case of the Roma', unpublished MPhil thesis, University of Cambridge.

—— (2000), *Roma Rights, Indigenous Rights and International Relations*, University of Greenwich, 1 July, Paper presented at the Romani Studies Conference.

—— (2001a), *ODIHR Project International Consultation on Romani Refugees and Asylum-Seekers*, Background Paper of the CPRSI OSCE ODIHR, Warsaw, Prepared for the OSCE Conference on 'Equal Opportunities for Roma and Sinti: Translating Words into Facts,' Bucharest, 10–13 September 2001, Accessed 10 September 2002, Available from the Romanian National Office for the Roma website, http://www.rroma.ro/download/osce/roma_refugees.pdf.

—— (2001b), 'The 30th Romani National Day', *Analysis of Current Events*, **13** (1), February 2001, 20–21.

—— (2001c), 'The 30th Romani National Day: 8 April 2001', Accessed 10 September 2002, Available from Radio Free Europe *(Un)Civil Societies*, **2** (20), 16 May 2001, Endnote, http://www.rferl.org/ucs/2001/05/20–160501.html.

—— (2001d), *The New Political Strategy of the International Romani Union*, Presentation for the Romani Studies Seminar, University of Greenwich, 22 February.

—— (2002a), 'Romani political representation in Central Europe. An historical survey', *Romani Studies,* **12** (2), Fifth Series, 103–148.

—— (2002b), Personal notes from the II. Roma World Congress, Lodz, May.

—— (2003), 'The Romani Voice in World Politics', unpublished PhD dissertation, University of Cambridge.

Klímová-Alexander, Ilona (forthcoming 2005), 'Prospects for Romani national-cultural autonomy' in Nimni, E. (ed.), *National-Cultural Autonomy and its Contemporary Critics*, London: Routledge.

Kochanowski, Vania de Gila (Jan) (1985), 'Homage to Amari Daj: Amari Bari Rani [Telegram to Rajiv Gandhi]', *Roma*, **9** (1), January, 3.

—— (1997), 'Today's Ethnocide Conduces Fatally to the New Genocide', *Roma*, (46–47), January-July, 9–22.

—— (1981/82), 'Demystification', *Roma,* **6** (2–3), July and January, 16–39.

Koenig, Christian (1991), 'Observer status for the International Committee of the Red Cross at the United Nations: A legal viewpoint', *International Review of the Red Cross*, **31** (280), 37–48.

Kovats, Martin (2001), 'The Emergence of European Roma Policy', in Guy, Will (ed.), *Between Past and Future: the Roma of Central and Eastern Europe*, Hartfield: University of Hertfordshire Press, pp. 93–116.
—— (2003). 'The Politics of Roma identity: between nationalism and destitution', *Open Democracy*, 30 July, accessed 20 August 2003, available from http://www.openDemocracy.net.
Kriesi, Hanspeter (1996), 'The organizational structure of new social movements in a political context', in McAdam, Doug, John D. McCarthy and Mayer N. Zald, (eds.), *Comparative perspectives on social movements: Political opportunities, mobilizing structures, and cultural framings*, New York: Cambridge University Press, pp. 152–184.
—— (ed.) (1995), *New social movements in Western Europe: a comparative analysis*, London: University of California Press.
Kriesi, Hanspeter, Ruud Koopmans, Jan Willem Duyvendak, and Marco Giugni (1992), 'New social movements and political opportunities in Western Europe', *European Journal of Political Research*, (22), 219–244.
Kukathas, Chandran (1998), 'Liberalism and Multiculturalism – The Politics of Indifference', *Political Theory*, (26), October, 686–699.
Lacroix-Hopson, Eliane (1992a), IRU ECOSOC representative between 1985–2000, *Foreword to NGO Committee on the International Year of the World's Indigenous Peoples: Report of the International Romani Union*, 5 March, Archive 6.
—— (1992b), *International Romani Union's work at the United Nations*, 8 September, Archive 6.
—— (1993), *Report: Background and IRU activities at the UN*, March, Document received from Lacroix-Hopson, Archive 6.
Laftman, Eva, Ahmed Motala, and Sylvia Albery (2001), *The International Save the Children Alliance Report on the 57th session of the United Nations Commission on Human Rights, Geneva, 19 March – 27 April*, accessed 29 January 2003, available from the Child Rights Information Network website, http://www.crin.org/docs/resources/publications/SCAlliance_CHR57.pdf.
Lee, Ronald (1998), *RCAC fact sheet 6: Roma: Self-identity*, accessed 10 January 2003, available from the Roma Community and Advocacy Center website, http://www.romani.org/toronto/FS6ident.html.
Lemon, Alaina (1995), 'Roma in Russia: A Community Divided', *Transitions*, **1** (4), 12–18.
Liegeois, J-P. (1976), *Mutation tsiganes*, Paris: PUF.
—— (1986), *Gypsies: An Illustrated History*, London: Al Saqi Books.
Little, Duncan (2001), *The transformation of the NGO/UNICEF Committee for Children in the CEE/CIS and the Baltic States into a proposed Regional Network and its future involvement in the Global Movement for Children*, Chavannes-de-Bogis, Geneva, Switzerland, 2 – 3 December.
Luksic-Orlandic, Tamara (Undated), 'Roma Children in Fr Yugoslavia', accessed 15 January 2003, available from *Monitor*, Bulletin of Yugoslav Child Rights Centre, (2), http://yu.cpd.org.yu/engmon/emonit2.html.
Lyons, G. M. and J. Mayall (eds.) (2003), *International Human Rights in the 21st Century: Protecting the Rights of Groups*, Lanham, MD: Rowman and Littlefield.
Main, L. (1994), 'Logique, integration et action politique dans le systeme des Nations Unies: Le cas des Rom a travers l'Union Internationale Romani', unpublished MA dissertation, L'Institute d'etudes politiques de Paris.

Malloch Brown, Mark (2003), *Foreword, Roma Regional Human Development Report*, accessed 1 February 2003, available from the UNDP Slovakia website, http://www.ocean.sk/undp.

Marks, Gary, and Doug McAdam (1999), 'On the Relationship of Political Opportunities to the Form of Collective Action: the Case of the European Union', in della Porta, Donatella, Hanspeter Kriesi and Dieter Rucht (eds.), *Social Movements in a Globalising World*, London: Macmillan, pp. 97–109.

Martineau, Raymonde (1979 and 1981b), Letters to Jan Cibula, 12 May (1979) and 12 May (1981b), Archive 4.

—— (1981a), Untitled letter quoting Djuric's letter of 4 June, Archive 4.

Marushiakova, E. and V. Popov (1997), *Gypsies (Roma) in Bulgaria*, New York: Peter Lang Verlag.

—— (2001a), 'Historical and Ethnographic Background: Gypsies, Roma, Sinti', in Guy, Will (ed.), *Between Past and Future: the Roma of Central and Eastern Europe*, Hartfield: University of Hertfordshire Press, pp. 33–53.

—— (2001b), *Gypsies in the Ottoman Empire*, Hertfordshire: University of Hertfordshire Press.

—— (2001c), 'Bulgaria: Ethnic Diversity – a Common Struggle for Equality', in Guy, Will (ed.), *Between Past and Future: the Roma of Central and Eastern Europe*, Hartfield: University of Hertfordshire Press, pp. 370–388.

Matras, Yaron (1998), 'The Development of the Romani Civil Rights Movement in Germany 1945–1996', in Susan Tebutt (ed.), *Sinti and Roma: Gypsies in German-speaking Society and Literature*, Oxford: Berghahn Books, pp. 49–64.

—— (2000), 'Roma Migrations in the Post-Communist Era: Their Historical and Political Significance', *Cambridge Review of International Affairs*, **13** (2), Spring-Summer, 32–50.

—— (2002), *Romani: A linguistic introduction*, Cambridge: Cambridge University Press.

M'Bow, Amadou-Mahtar (1984), 'The Gypsy Destiny', *UNESCO Courier*, (37), October, 4.

McAdam, Doug (1996), 'Conceptual origins, current problems, future directions', in McAdam, Doug, John D. McCarthy and Mayer N. Zald, (eds.), *Comparative perspectives on social movements: Political opportunities, mobilizing structures, and cultural framings*, New York: Cambridge University Press, pp. 23–40.

McAdam, Doug, John D. McCarthy and Mayer N. Zald (1996), 'Introduction: Opportunities, mobilising structures, and framing processes – towards a synthetic, comparative perspective on social movements', in McAdam, Doug, John D. McCarthy and Mayer N. Zald, (eds.), *Comparative perspectives on social movements: Political opportunities, mobilizing structures, and cultural framings*, New York: Cambridge University Press, pp. 1–20.

Megret, Jean-Claude (Balval) (Undated), *Biodata of Vania de Gila Kochanowski*, accessed 15 October 2002, available from Balval's personal website, http://perso.wanadoo.fr/balval.

'Memorandum of understanding and co-operation between IRU and Czech Ministry of Foreign Affairs' (2001), Accessed 11 November 2002, Available from the RNN website, http://www.romnews.com.

Mingst, K. A., and M. P. Karns (2000), *The United Nations in the Post-Cold War Era*, 2nd ed., Oxford: Westview Press.

Mirga, A. and N. Gheorghe (1997), *The Roma in the twenty-first century: A policy paper*, Princeton: PER.

'Miroslav Lacko v. Slovak Republic' (2002), Committee on the Elimination of Racial Discrimination, Communication No. 11/1998, accessed 7 October 2002, available from University of Minnesota, Human Rights Library, http: //www1.umn.edu/humanrts/country/decisions/11–1998.html.

Misljija, Djuljisen, and Gasnjani Muharem (2002), *Report from local mediators from Kosovo housed in Macedonia with IDP status: Step back in the negotiations, 25th November,* accessed 3 January 2003, available from the RNN website, http: //www.romnews.com.

—— (2003), *Closing the camp of the Shuto Orizari*, accessed 10 March 2003, available from the RNN website, http://www.romnews.com.

Musisi, Christine (2002), *Advisory Mission for 'Your Spis' Programme, Spiska Nova Ves, East Slovakia: Brief Report by the Civil Society Empowerment Specialist, ECIS SURF*, (UNDP, 10th – 11th June), Document provided by Musisi.

Musisi, Christine, and Aron Cristellotti (2002), *Sustainable Community Development Project Field Mission to Spiska Nova Ves: Mission Report*, UNDP, Document provided by Musisi.

Myahofer-Gruenbuehel, Ferdinand (1978a-b), Special Assistant to the UN Secretary-General, Letters to Jan Cibula, 24 February (1978a) and 17 March (1978b), Archive 2.

Nazerali, Sean (2001), *The Roma – A Nation Without a State*, Paper delivered at the 'Democracy Unrealized' conference, Academy of Fine Arts, Vienna, 23 March.

Nesbitt, Jackie (1990), *Fourth World Romani Congress (Serock, Warsaw, Poland, 8th-12th April 1990): A report by the retiring secretary of the National Gypsy Education Council*, unpublished manuscript.

'News and Reviews: Give Equal Rights to Roma, U.N. Human Rights Commission's Call to Nations' (1977a), *Roma*, **3**, (2), 33–35.

'News and Reviews: World Romani Congress Delegation Meets the Prime Minister'(1977b), *Roma*, **3** (2), July, 32.

'News and Reviews: World Romani Congress Common Market Committee (Komiteto Romani Ande Evropaskero Ekhetane) (1978)', *Roma*, **4** (1), January, 44–46.

'News and Reviews: Romani Congreso – 3' (1981) *Roma*, **6** (1), January, 52–54.

'News and Reviews: Category II Status for the International Romani Union' (1994), *Roma*, (40), January, 45–46.

'News and Reviews' (1986), *Roma*, (24), January, 43.

NGO Committee on UNICEF (2001), *NGO Participation at the Third Substantive Session of the Preparatory Committee of the Special Session of the General Assembly On Children*, accessed 11 January 2003, available from the NGO Committee on UNICEF website, http://www.ngosatunicef.org/old/Special% 20Session/3rdPrepComReport.DOC.

—— (2002), *NGOs Helping to Make World Fit for Children*, accessed 12 January 2003, available from http://www.ngosatunicef.org/docs/SSC_final_report.doc.

NGO DIESA Office in New York (1979), Letter to Jan Cibula, 3 December, Archive 2.

Nimni, Ephraim (1999), 'Nationalist multiculturalism in late imperial Austria as a critique of contemporary liberalism: the case of Bauer and Renner', *Journal of Political Ideologies*, **4** (3), 289–314.

Nolan, Jim (1997), 'King of the Gypsies', *The Philadelphia Daily News – Sunday magazine*, 12 January, 18–20.

Noortmann, Math (2001), 'Non-State Actors in International Law', in Arts, Bas., Math Noortmann and Bob Reinalda (eds.), *Non-State Actors in International Relations*, Aldershot: Ashgate, pp. 59–76.

Noortmann, Math, Bas Arts and Bob Reinalda (2001), 'The Quest for Unity in Empirical and Conceptual Complexity', in Arts, Bas, Math Noortmann and Bob Reinalda (eds.), *Non-State Actors in International Relations*, Aldershot: Ashgate, pp. 299–307.

Novoselsky, Valery (2002), *2nd International Roma conference on Employment, Professional Education and Entrepreneuring 2002*, E-mail to the author, 17 October.

OHCHR (Undated), *Commission on Human Rights Membership*, accessed 20 February 2003, available from the OHCHR website, http://www.unhchr.ch/html/menu2/2/chrmem.htm.

——, *Permanent Forum on Indigenous Issues*, accessed 12 April 2003, available from the OHCHR website, 193.194.139.190/indigenous/forum.htm.

——, *Indigenous Peoples*, accessed 12 April 2003, available from the OHCHR website, 103.194.138.190/indigenous/main.html.

OSCE and UNHCR (1999–2003), *Reports: Situation of ethnic minorities in Kosovo*, Accessed 4 March 2003, available from the OSCE website, http://www.osce.org/kosovo/documents/reports/minorities.

Ott, Rudolf (1995), 'Zivot venovany cikanum, hudbe a leceni' [Life dedicated to gypsies, music and healing], Basel, 7 July, Article published in *Medikal Tribune*, Slovak translation, Archive 5a.

The Paris Congress or the true history of the false Warsaw Congress (WRC4) seen from the French side (Undated), File received from Jean-Claude Megret (Balval).

Parliamentary Assembly of the CoE (1969), *Situation of Gypsies and other travellers in Europe: Recommendation 563(1969)*, Strasbourg.

Passy, Florence (1999), 'Supranational Political Opportunities as a Channel of Globalization of Political Conflicts. The Case of the Rights of Indigenous Peoples', in della Porta, Donatella, Hanspeter Kriesi and Dieter Rucht (eds.), *Social Movements in a Globalising World*, London: Macmillan, pp. 148–169.

Perez de Cuellar, Javier (1991), 'Secretary-General of the United Nations Greeting the Romani Union', *Informaciaqo Lil e Rromane Uniaqoro*, (1–2), July-August, 4.

Perez Molina, R (1998), *Labour market discrimination against migrant workers in Spain, B. Discrimination against immigrant workers in access to employment in Spain: From worthless paper to effective legislation*, accessed 30 October 2000, available from the ILO website, http://www.ilo.org/public/english/protection/migrant/research/imp/09/b.htm.

Pietrosanti, Paolo (1994), *Project for a Non-territorial Republic of the Romany Nation*, Manuscript obtained from Paolo Pietrosanti.

—— (1998), *UN Commission on Human Rights fifty-fourth session, 16 March-24 April, agenda item 12 – Racism, racial discrimination, xenophobia and related intolerance, Oral Statement by the Transnational Radical Party, NGO in consultative status (Category I), Geneva, 23 March*, Accessed 29 January 2003, Available from the TRP website, http://www.radicalparty.org/ human-rights/gy_un.htm.

—— (2000), *UN Subcommission on the promotion and protection of Human Rights, Fifty-second session, Geneva, 31 July – 18 August 2000, Agenda Item 8 'Prevention of discrimination against and the protection of minorities,' Oral Statement by the Transnational Radical Party, a NGO with Status of Category I*, Manuscript obtained from Paolo Pietrosanti.

—— (2001), *UN Commission on Human Rights Fifty-seventh session – March-April, Agenda item 14, Oral statement by the International Romani Union, a non-governmental organization in Special Consultative Status*, Accessed 29 January 2003, Available from the TRP website, http://www.radicalparty.org/human-rights/gy_comm_57_pietrosanti.htm.

—— (2003), The Romani Nation: or "Ich Bin Ein Zigeuner", *Roma Rights* (4), available from the ERRRC website, http://www.errc.org.

Pinnock, K. (1999), 'Social Exclusion and Resistance: A Study of Gypsies and the Non-Governmental Sector in Bulgaria 1989–1997', unpublished PhD dissertation, University of Wolverhampton.

Pluim, Martijn (2001), *Study on Current Irregular Roma Migration to the EU Member States*, Vienna: International Centre for Migration Policy Development, February.

Pramod, Kumar (2001), *Forgotten Children of Mother India – Introduction: International Roma Conference, April 29,* accessed 10 December 2002, available from the Hindu Vivek Kendra website, http://www.hvk.org/articles/0401/138.html.

Prashar, A. S. (1990/91), 'Roma: light at tunnel's end', *Roma*, (33–34), July, 44–45.

PER (1994), *Countering Anti-Roma Violence in Eastern Europe: The Snagov Conference and Related Efforts*, Princeton.

—— (2001), *Leadership, Representation and the Status of the Roma*, Princeton: PER.

—— (2003), *Roma and the Question of Self-determination: Fiction and Reality*, Princeton: PER.

'A Permanent Forum on Indigenous Issues at the United Nations' (2000), *Yachay Wasip 'Simin': The Voice of Yachay Wasi*, **7** (2), Fall, 1 and 5.

Presidium of the Romani Congress (Undated), Archive 3.

Press Information Bureau Releases (2001), *PM's Assurance to IRU Delegation India Will Continue to Support Romani People's Struggle for Human Rihts* [sic], accessed 10 December 2002, available from the Press Information Bureau Government of India website, http://pib.nic.in/archieve/lreleng/lyr2001/rapr2001/14042001/r140420015.html.

PROROM (2000), *Los Gitanos y el Convenio 169 de la OIT, Presentation for 'Taller de Evaluacion de la Aplicacion del Convenio 169 de la OIT,' Hotel Bacata, Bogota, D.C., 9–10 August,* accessed 8 January 2003, available from the Fundacion Secretariado General Gitano website, http://www.fsgg.org/01docstcCOL02.htm.

Puxon, G. (1971), Personal notes from the First World Romani Congress, Archive 1.

—— (1973), *Rom: Europe's Gypsies*. London: Minority Rights Group.

—— (1975), *Road of the Rom*, Unpublished manuscript, Shuto Orizari, Skopje, Archive 6.

—— (1977a-c, 1978d), Letters to Raymonde Martineau, 5 October (1977a), 12 September (1977b), 12 December (1977c), 6 January (1978d), Archive 4.

—— (1977d), *Roma: The right to recognition as a national minority of Indian origin: An appeal to the UN Sub-Commission on Prevention of Discrimination and Protection of Minorities*, Archive 1.

—— (1978a), Letter to Barbara Webb, NGO Liaison Officer, 21 January, Archive 4.

—— (1978b), 'Task Before the 2nd World Romani Congress', *Roma,* **4** (1), January, 7–9.

—— (1978c), Letter to Czech Romani delegates inviting them for the Second World Romani Congress. 24 February, Archive 1.

—— (1978/79), 'Romano Kongreso 2: Second World Romani Congress', *Roma,* **4** (2–3), July and January, 32–72.

—— (1981a), 'Romani National Movement: Decade of progress 1971–1981', *Roma,* **6** (1), January, 10–12.

—— (1981), *Romano Kongreso 3: Gottingen*, Archive 2.

—— (1986), 'Yul Brynner Passes into History', *Roma,* (24), January, 17–18.

—— (2000), 'The Romani Movement: Rebirth and the First World Romani Congress in Retrospect', In Acton, Thomas (ed.), *Scholarship and the Gypsy Struggle,* Hatfield: University of Hertfordshire Press, pp. 94–113.

—— (2001), 'Rudko Kawzcynski', Message forwarded to Aven Amentza newsgroup (AvenAmentza@yahoogroups.com) by Ariel Eliyahu, 31 October.

—— (2003), 'Empowering Roma is aim of the new UN programme', Ustiben Report, 14 January, E-mail messages posted to the Patrin list (patrin-roma-culture@igc.topica.com).

—— (No date), Letter to Ian Hancock, Archive 1.

'Press release' (1991), *Informaciaqo Lil e Rromane Uniaqoro,* (3–4), September-October, 3–5.

Rajandran, Marty (2000), UNICEF regional office for Central Eastern Europe, the Commonwealth of Independent States and the Baltic States, *UN special session on children: September 2001,* accessed 12 January 2003, available from *Roma Rights,* (3), http://www.errc.org/rr_nr3_2000/education.shtml.

RANELPI (2001), *Project of a Frame-Statute (Moral Charter) of the Romani People in the European Union*, Archive 3.

Reece, G.M. (1979), NGO/DIESA Section, Letter, Reference OR 340(1064), 12 February, Archive 2.

Regional NGO Network for Children (2002a), *The Regional NGO Network for Children Inaugurated in Sarajevo: Regional 'Leave No Child Out' campaign launched,* accessed 15 January 2003, available from the VPF website, http://www.vpu.lt/socpedagogika/file/pressngo.doc.

—— (2002b), *Statutes of the NGO/UNICEF Regional Network for Children in Central and Eastern Europe, Commonwealth of Independent States and Baltic States,* Accessed 2 January 2003, Available from the VPF website, http://www.vpu.lt/socpedagogika.

—— (2002c), *Report of the NGO/UNICEF Regional Network for Children in Central and Eastern Europe, the Commonwealth of Independent States and the Baltic States: The RNC is born, Sarajevo, Bosnia and Herzegovina 27 – 29 June,* Accessed 15 January 2003, Available from the VPF website, http://www.vpu.lt/socpedagogika.

Reinalda, Bob (2001), 'Private in Form, Public in Purpose: NGOs in International Relations Theory', in Arts, Bas, Math Noortmann and Bob Reinalda (eds.), *Non-State Actors in International Relations,* Aldershot: Ashgate, pp. 11–40.

Reinalda, Bob, Bas Arts and Math Noortmann (2001), 'Non-State Actors in International Relations: Do They Matter? in Arts, Bas, Math Noortmann and Bob Reinalda (eds.), *Non-State Actors in International Relations,* Aldershot: Ashgate, pp. 1–8.

Reinalda, Bob and Bertjan Verbeek (2001), 'Non-State Actors in Foreign Policy Making: A Policy Subsystem Approach', in Arts, B., M. Noortmann and B. Reinalda (eds.), *Non-State Actors in International Relations,* Aldershot: Ashgate, pp. 127–144.

Remmel, Franz (1993), *Die Roma Rumaeniens: Volk ohne Hinterland,* Vienna: Picus Verlag.

'Report of the Third World Romani Congress, Gottingen (West Germany), May 15–21, 1981' (1981/2), *Roma,* **6** (2–3), July and January, 43–85.

Reyniers, Alain (1998), *Tsigane, heureux si tu es libre!* Paris: UNESCO.

RFE (2003), 'UN Report: Central-East European Roma Live Under African Standards', *RFE/RL NEWSLINE,* **7** (11), Part II, 17 January.

Riggs, R. E., and J. C. Plano (1994), *The United Nations: International Organization and World Politics,* 2nd ed., Belmont, CA: Wadsworth.

Ringold, Dena (2000), 'NGO Coordination with the Bank and the Annual Meetings,' E-mail to the IRU office in Prague, 3 May, Archive 3.

Rishi, Weer Rajendra (1978/9), 'Amongst Roma', *Roma,* **4** (2 and 3), July and January, 1–25.

—— (1980), 'Roma! Keep United', *Roma,* **5** (1), January, 3–19.

—— (1981a) 'Upre Roma!' *Roma,* **6** (1), January, 5–9.

—— (1981b), Letter to Grattan Puxon, 29 October, Archive 1.

—— (1986), 'News and Reviews: Fourth World Romani Congress', *Roma,* (25), July, 50–51.

—— (1987), 'Unity – Need of the Hour', *Roma,* (26), January, 3–6.

—— (1990), 'Roma! Keep United', *Roma,* **5** (1), January, 3–9.

—— (1992), 'Interest in the Roma', *Roma,* (36 and 37), January and July, 105–182.

RNC (1998), *Roma in Europe: Status Regulation through Self-Determination.* November, Paper prepared for the OSCE ODIHR, Archive 3.

RNN (2001), RNN Exclusive – Rudko Kawczynski to be imprisioned [sic] in Germany, Message posted to Romano Liloro newsgroup (romano_liloro @yahoogroups.com) by Ariel Eliyahu, 5 November.

—— (2002a), 'Protests in front of the residence of UNHCR', English translation of 13 August article from *Dnevnik,* a Macedonian daily, entitled 'Around hundred Roma from Kosovo are asking to leave Macedonia', accessed 10 November 2002, available from the RNN website, http://romnews.com.

—— (2002b), *Report from the local mediators, Refugees from region of Kosovo with status P.H.Z.L. – in Macedonia, 12 September,* accessed 10 November 2002, available from the RNN website, http://romnews.com.

—— (2002c), *Refugees (Kosovo and Macedonia), 31 July 2002,* accessed 12 November 2002, available from the RNN website, http://romnews.com.

Roma [Special issue on W.R. Rishi] (1992), (36–37), January and July.

Romani CRISS (2000), *United Nations Committee on the Elimination of Racial Discrimination, Fifty-seventh session, Special thematic discussion on Roma issues, Statement on behalf of Roma Center for Social Intervention and Studies, 15 August,* accessed 20 November 2002, available from the GHM website, http: //www.greekhelsinki.gr/english/reports/uncerd-criss.html.

Romani thematic commission (2001), *Recommendations for the NGO Forum Declaration*, accessed 27 September 2002, available from the Icare website, http://www.icare.to/wcar.

Romani Union (1989), Invitation to Congress, from 9th to 11th December in Bellevue-Hotel in Bern, Archive 3.

'Romani Union (Romani Ekhipe) Granted Consultative Status by UN' (1979), *Roma*, **4** (4), July, 1.

Roma India Task Force, Back to the Roots, OSCE Conference – Side Events (2001), accessed 5 November 2002, available from the National Office for the Roma of the Romanian Government website, http://www.rroma.ro/info_osce_events.htm.

Romapage (2002), *Kosovo refugees Roma protest to UNHCR: Report of month-long protest by refugees in Skopje based on material from Asmet Elezovski and Zenelj Berisa*, accessed 20 December 2002, available from the Romapage website, http://www.romapage.hu/English.

Ronit, K., and V. Schneider (eds.) (2000), *Private Organizations in Global Politics*, London: Routledge.

Rooker, M. (2002), *The International Supervision of the Protection of Romany People in Europe*, Nijmegen: Nijmegen University Press.

Rose, Romani (2000), Central Council of German Sinti and Roma, *Statement for the UN CERD 57th Session,* 15 August, Geneva, Archive 3.

Rose, N.A. (1973), *The Gentile Zionists: A Study in Anglo-Zionist Diplomacy, 1929–1939*, London: Frank Cass.

Rromani Baxt Albania (Undated), *A Bird's Eye-View of Our Activities*, Tirana, Document obtained from Marcel Courthiade.

Rucht, Dieter (1996), 'The impact of national contexts on social movement structures: A cross-movement and cross-national comparison', in McAdam, Doug, John D. McCarthy and Mayer N. Zald, (eds.), *Comparative perspectives on social movements: Political opportunities, mobilizing structures, and cultural framings*, New York: Cambridge University Press, pp. 185–204.

—— (1997), 'The Transnationalization of Social Movements: Trends, Causes, Problems', in della Porta, Donatella, Hanspeter Kriesi and Dieter Rucht (eds.), *Social Movements in a Globalising World,* London: Macmillan, pp. 206–222.

Ryan, S. (1995), *Ethnic conflict and International Relations*, Dartmouth: Aldershot.

Sankey, John (1996), 'Conclusions', in Willetts, Peter (ed.), *'The Conscience of the World': The Influence of Non-Governmental Organisations in the UN System*, London: Hurst & Company.

Save the Children (2001a), *Denied a future? The right to education of Roma/Gypsy and Traveller children in Europe*, Vol. I: South-eastern Europe, London: Save the Children.

—— (2001b), *Denied a future? The right to education of Roma/Gypsy and Traveller children in Europe – International legislation handbook*, London: Save the Children.

Save the Children Scotland (2001), *A summary of a consultation with children and young people by the Save the Children Scotland Programme on the United Nations General Assembly Outcome Document 'A world fit for children'*, accessed 2 March 2003, available from the Save the Children Scotland website, http://www.savethechildrenscot.org.uk/pages/whats_new/pdfs/world_fit_for_children.pdf.

Secretary of the European Human Rights Commission (1969), Letter to Rudolf Karway, 25 March, Archive 1.

Sharma, M. K. (1986), 'Yul Brynner the Baro Rom 'King' Passes Away', *Roma*, (24), January, 12–14.

Siklova, Jirina (1999), 'Romove a nevladni, neziskove romske a proromske obcanske organizace prispivajici k integraci tohoto etnika [Roma and Non-governmental, Non-profit Romani and Pro-Roma Civic Organizations Contributing to Integration of this Ethnie]', in Lisa, Helena (ed.), *Romove v Ceske republice: 1945–1989* [Roma in the Czech Republic], Prague: Socioklub, pp. 271–289.

Simma, Bruno (2002), *The Charter of the United Nations – A Commentary*, 2 ed., Oxford: Oxford University Press.

Smith, A. (1983), *Theories of Nationalism*, 2 ed., London: Duckworth.

Sobotka, Eva (2001), 'They Have a Dream: The state of Roma affairs in the Czech Republic', accessed 10 July 2002, available from the *Central Europe Review*, **3** (18), 21 May, http://www.ce-review.org/01/18/sobotka18.html.

'Standardisation of Romani Language' (1990/91), *Roma*, (33–34), July, 26–43.

'Statutes of the Romani Union' (1991), *Informaciaqo Lil e Rromane Uniaqoro*, (1–2), July-August, 5–7.

Stavenhagen, Rodolfo (ed.) (1994), *Double jeopardy: the children of ethnic minorities*, Florence: UNICEF International Child Development Centre, November.

Suy, Erik (1978), 'The Status of Observers in International Organizations', *Recueil des cours de l'Académie de droit international*, **160** (II), 75–179.

Tamir, Yael (1991), 'The right to national self-determination', *Social Research*, **58** (3), Fall, 565–590.

Tarrow, S. (1994), *Power in movement: social movements, collective action and politics*, Cambridge: Cambridge University Press.

'Timeline of Romani History' (1998), accessed 25 February 2001, available from the *Patrin Web Journal*, http://www.geocities.com/Paris/5121/timeline.htm.

Tipler, Derek A. (1968), 'From Gonads to Nation', *Midstream*, 61–70.

Thorup-Hayes, Helene (Undated), *Evaluation – plotting the course*, accessed 12 October 2002, available from the UN website, http://www.un.org/dpi/ngosection/evaluation.htm.

Tuzla Roma Association 'Sa e Roma' (2002), Roma monthly bulletin for the culture and information, (32), August, Forwarded to Roma Daily News newsgroup (Roma_Daily_News@yahoogroups.com) by Ariel Eliyahu on 5 September.

UN (2001a), *Press briefing: Headquarters Press Conference By International Romani Union, 5 June*, accessed 10 November 2002, available from the UN website, http://www.un.org/News/briefings/docs/2001/ROMANIPC.doc.htm.

—— (2001b), *Fact Sheet No. 27 – Seventeen Frequently Asked Questions about United Nations Special Rapporteurs*, accessed 7 February 2003, available from UNHCHR Office website, http://193.194.138.190/pdf/factsheet27.pdf.

UNDP (2003a), *Roma Regional Human Development Report*, accessed 20 January 2003, available from the UNDP website, http://www.ocean.sk/undp/.

—— (2003b), *Avoiding the Dependency Trap: The Roma Human Development Report*, accessed 22 January 2003, available from the UNDP website, http://hdr.undp.org/reports/.

—— (2003c), *Outline of a project idea for sustainable vocational education and employability improvement for Roma youth*, Draft document provided by Christine Musisi.

—— '*About Civil Society Division*', accessed 8 February 2003, available from the UNDP website, http://www.undp.org/csopp/CSO/NewFiles/about.html.

—— '*Policies and Procedures*', accessed 8 February 2003, available from the UNDP website, http://www.undp.org/csopp/CSO/NewFiles/policies.html.

—— *Indigenous Peoples*, accessed 10 January 2003, available from the UNDP website, http://www.undp.org/csopp/CSO/NewFiles/ipindex.html.

UNECE (2002), *First Regional Forum on Youth: Security, Opportunity and Prosperity*, accessed 12 December 2002, available from the UNECE website, http://www.unece.org/operact/meetings/documents/y20.pdf.

UNESCO (2001), *Non-Governmental Organizations Section of NGOs and Foundations: Cooperation*, accessed 5 October 2002, available from the UNESCO website, http://erc.unesco.org/ong/en/cooper_inter.htm.

UNHCR (2000), *Roma Asylum-Seekers, Refugees and Internally Displaced*, Geneva, October 2000, Document distributed at the OSCE Human Dimension Implementation Meeting in October 2000, No. 178.

—— (2001), *Report of the Seminar Housing and the Roma Community: What can we do to avoid ghettoization?* Brno, 3–4 October.

—— (2002a), *UNHCR Prague's activities for the Roma community in the Czech Republic*, December, Internal document.

—— (2002b), *Note: Operation of the Emergency Social Fund in Usti nad Labem and Ostrava*, Prague, 26 November 2002, Internal document.

UNHCR Briefing Notes (2000), *Kosovo: concern at Roma deportations from Germany, 4 August,* accessed 22 October 2002, available from the UNHCR website, http://www.unhcr.ch.

UNICEF (1995), *Children of minorities: deprivation and discrimination*, Florence: UNICEF International Child Development Centre.

UNICEF Albania (Undated), *Networking*, accessed 14 November 2002, available from the UNICEF Albania website, http: //www.unicef.org/albania/networking/ngo.htm.

UNIHP (Undated), *Brief Administrative History of UNOG*, accessed 20 October 2002, available from the UNIHP website, http: //www.unihp.org/UN.Archives.Gen.htm.

UN Off the Cuff (2001), *Durban (Kingsmead Cricket Stadium), South Africa, 30 August 2001 – Transcript of Q&A session after Secretary-General's address at NGO Forum, (unofficial transcript),* accessed 6 January 2003, available from the UN website, Off the Cuff section, http://www.un.org/apps/sg.

UN Press Release (2000a), *Subcommission on the Promotion and Protection of Human Rights, 52nd session, 14 August, Afternoon,* accessed 5 October 2002, available from the OHCHR website, http://www.unhchr.ch.

—— (2000b), *Subcommission on the Promotion and Protection of Human Rights, 52nd session, 14 August, Evening,* accessed 5 October 2002, available from the OHCHR website, http://www.unhchr.ch.

—— (2000c), *CERD 57th session, 16 August, Afternoon, Adopts Conclusions on Report of Netherlands*, accessed 10 October 2002, available from the OHCHR website, http://www.unhchr.ch.

—— (2000d), *CERD 57th session, 15 August, Afternoon*, accessed 8 October 2002, available from the OHCHR website, http://www.unhchr.ch.

—— (2000e), *CERD 57th session, 16 August, Morning, Several Experts Advocate Equality and Identity for Roma*, accessed 8 October 2002, available from the OHCHR website, http://www.unhchr.ch.

—— (2001), *30 July, Subcommission on Promotion and Protection of Human Rights opens fifty-third session, Hears Address by High Commissioner for Human Rights; David Weissbrodt Elected Chairman*, accessed 22 November 2002, available from the UN Office in Geneva website, http://www.unog.ch/news2/documents/newsen/sc0102e.html.

Ulster University (2002), *UN High Commissioner Mary Robinson Calls for 'Joined Up' Approach to Human Rights, 20th May*, accessed 12 January 2003, available from Ulster University News Releases, http://www.ulst.ac.uk/newsreleases/2002/490.html.

van Baalen, H. (2000), *The Position of the Roma and Sinti in an Integrating Europe: Rethinking National Identity*, 14 July, The Hague: Liberal International.

van Boven, Theo (1978), Letter to Jan Cibula, 1 March, Archive 5a.

—— (1980), Letter from the Director of the UN Division of Human Rights to Grattan Puxon, 22 September, Archive 1.

—— (1981), Letter to Grattan Puxon, General Secretary of Romani Kongreso 3, 17 March, Ref. No. G/SO211/1(5), Archive 1.

van der Stoel, Max (1993), *Roma (Gypsies) in the CSCE Region: Report of the High Commissioner on National Minorities (HCNM)*, accessed 20 May 1999, available from the HCNM website, Meeting of the Committee of Senior Officials, 21–23 September 1993, http://www.osce.org/inst/hcnm/recomm/roma/roma93.htm.

Van Roozendaal, Gerda (2001), 'The Influence of Trade Unions on the Social Clause Controversy in the International Labour Organisation and its Working Party', in Arts, Bas, Math Noortmann and Bob Reinalda (eds.), *Non-State Actors in International Relations*, Aldershot: Ashgate, pp. 161–176.

Vermeersch, Peter (2001a), 'The Roma in domestic and international politics: an emerging voice?' *Roma Rights*, (4), 5–13.

—— (2001b), 'Advocacy Networks and Romani Politics in Central and Eastern Europe', accessed 10 May 2002, available from the *Journal on Ethnopolitics and Minority Issues*, Special Focus 1/2001, http://www.ecmi.de/jemie/download/Focus11–2001Vermeersch.pdf.

—— (2002), 'Roma and the Politics of Ethnicity in Central Europe: A comparative study of ethnic minority mobilisation in the Czech Republic, Hungary, and Slovakia in the 1990s', unpublished PhD dissertation, Catholic University of Leuven.

Vertovec, Steven, and Robin Cohen (2002), 'Introduction: Conceiving Cosmopolitanism', in Vertovec, Steven and Robin Cohen (eds.), *Conceiving Cosmopolitanism: Theory, Context, and Practice*, Oxford: Oxford University Press, pp. 1–22.

WB (2002a), *Roma Page*, accessed 1 November 2002, available from the WB website, http://www.worldbank.org/eca/roma/about.htm£current.

—— (2002b), *Briefing on its involvement in Romani issues*, accessed 24 October 2002, available from the WB website, http://www.worldbank.org/eca/roma/data/briefing.pdf.

Webb, Barbara (1978), Letter to Grattan Puxon, 13 January, Archive 4.

Weber, Max (1947), *The Theory of Social and Economic Organisation*, New York: Oxford University Press.

Wiklund, Daniel (1969), *Report on the Situation of Gypsies in Europe*, Strasbourg, Council of Europe, Document 2629.

Willems, Wim (1997), *In Search of the True Gypsy*, London: Frank Cass.

Willetts, Peter (1982), 'The Impact of Promotional Pressure Groups on Global Politics', in Willetts, Peter (ed.), *Pressure Groups in the Global System: The Transnational Relations of Issue-Oriented Non-Governmental Organizations*, London: Frances Pinter.

—— (1996), 'Consultative Status for NGOs at the United Nations', in Willetts, Peter (ed.), *'The Conscience of the World': The Influence of Non-Governmental Organisations in the UN System*, London: Hurst & Company.

—— (2000), 'From "Consultative Arrangements" to "Partnership": The Changing Status of NGOs in Diplomacy at the UN', *Global Governance* (6), 191–212.

Wilmer, Franke (1993), *The Indigenous Voice in World Politics: Since Time Immemorial*, London: SAGE Publications.

'World Congress for Peace at Sarajevo' (1994), *Roma*, (41), July, 3–8.

'World Romani Congress Activities of its Presidium' (1980), *Roma*, **5** (2), July, 28–39.

World Romani Congress Preparatory conference (1971), London, April, Leaflet, Archive 1.

Zigeunermission Statutes (1968), English Translation, Archive 1.

Zolo, Danilo (Undated), *What is Globalization? Some Radical Questions: Danilo Zolo interviews Ulrich Beck*, accessed 2 May 2003, available from the National Chiao Tung University website, http://www.cc.nctu.edu.tw/cpsun/zolobeck.htm.

'IV World Romani Congress, Serock, Warsaw, Poland, 8–12 April, 1990' (1990/91), *Roma*, (33–34), July and January, 3–53.

Personal, Written, Electronic and Phone Communications and Interviews[1]

Abtahi, Massoud, Chief of UNESCO Section of International Non-Governmental Organizations and Foundations.

Acton, Thomas, Professor of Romani Studies at the University of Greenwich.

Atchebro, Daniel, Desk officer for the UN Special Rapporteur on Racism, Racial Discrimination, Xenophobia and Related Intolerance.

Baran, Ales, SRPS Secretary.

Bauboeck, Rainer, Researcher at the Austrian Academy of Sciences Research Unit for Institutional Change and European Integration.

Black, Mary E., Programme Coordinator, UNICEF Belgrade.

Blukacz-Louisfert, Blandine, Chief of the Registry, Records and Archives Unit, UNOG Library.

Cahn, Claude, ERRC Researcher.

Cohen, Robert, Regional Communication Advisor, UNICEF Regional Office for CEE/CIS/Baltics.

Concolato, Jean-Claude, Director of the UNHCR Prague Office.

Courthiade, Marcel, IRU's plenipotentiary to UNESCO.

Daniel, Marciella, UNHCR headquarters South-Eastern Europe Operation Senior Protection Officer.

Day, Radha, Officer for the OHCHR Focal Point on Roma, Sinti and Travellers.

Fedoroff, Michele, NGO/DIESA Section.

Ferrier, Neda, Chief of UNESCO Section of International Non-Governmental Organizations.

Flynn, E.J., Coordinator of Europe and North America Team of the UN Office of the High Commissioner for Human Rights.

Gheorghe, Nicolae, Former IRU Vice-President.

Hancock, Ian, Former IRU representative at the UN in New York.

Ivanov, Andrey, UNDP Officer.

Kappenberger, Marco, Former IRU representative at the UN in Geneva.

Kashiwa, Fumiko, UNHCR Office in Prague.

Kempf, Francoise, Specialist Group on Roma/Gypsies of the CoE.

Kenrick, Donald, London Institute of Romani Studies.

Lacroix-Hopson, Eliane, IRU ECOSOC representative between 1985–2000.

Liegeois, Jean-Pierre, Centre de recherches tsiganes.

Maguire, Mairead, Assistant to the Director of the UNESCO Liaison Office in Geneva.

Main, Lynnaia, Author of a master's thesis on the interaction between the IRU and UN.

Mandallaz, Francoise, NGO Liaison Bureau at the Director General at the UN Office in Geneva.

Matras, Yaron, Former RNC activist.

Moserova, Jaroslava, Director of the UNESCO Czech National Commission.

Nazerali, Sean, Assistant of the IRU's Secretary General.

Nirnberg, Jud, Former Assistant to the IRU General Secretary.

Nistorescu, Diana, Chair of the NGO/UNICEF Regional Network for Children in Central and Eastern Europe, Commonwealth of Independent States and Baltic States.

Olomoofe, Larry, Human Rights Trainer at the ERRC.

Pietrosanti, Paolo, IRU's Commissar for Foreign Policy.

Pralong, Sandra, UNDP Officer.

Puxon, Grattan, Former IRU General Secretary.

Rajandran, Marty, UNICEF regional office for Central Eastern Europe, the Commonwealth of Independent States and the Baltic States.

Reidbauer, NGO Information Officer in Vienna.

Scuka, Emil, IRU President.

Spinelli, Santino, IRU Parliament member.

Thomas, Constance, Section Chief of the Equality and Employment Branch, International Labour Standards and Human Rights Department, International Labour Office.

Trehan, Nidhi, PhD candidate in Sociology at the London School of Economics.

UN/SA Reference Team, United Nations Library, New York.

van Boven, Theo, Former Director of the UN Division for Human Rights and Member of the Commission on Human Rights, Subcommission on the Prevention of Discrimination and Protection of Minorities, and the Committee on Elimination of Racial Discrimination.

Whitaker, Benjamin, Former Member of the Subcommission on the Prevention of Discrimination and Protection of Minorities.

Yoshida, Yuko, Office of Public Partnership, Office of Executive Director, UNICEF New York.

List of Archives Used[2]

Archive 1 – Private archive of Grattan Puxon, Colchester (UK).
Archive 2 – Private archive of Jan Cibula, Bern (Obtained from Bernhard Schaer).
Archive 3 – Private archive of Nicolae Gheorghe, Warsaw.
Archive 4 – UN Archive in Geneva, Registry No. G/OR 340(118), Organisation, Consultative arrangements and relations with NGO, Romani Union.
Archive 5a – Museum of Romani Culture in Brno, the Czech Republic, Dossier 51/98 Jan Cibula – Osobni materialy [personal materials].
Archive 5b – Museum of Romani Culture in Brno, the Czech Republic.
Archive 6 – the Romani Archives and Documentation Center, University of Texas at Austin.

Notes

1 Dates are indicated throughout the book. For a more detailed bibliography with dates and types of communication specified see Klimova 2003: Bibliography.
2 This bibliography does not include full references for UN documents, which are cited throughout the text under the UN documentation number (UN Doc.). Full references for these documents can easily be found via UNBISnet on the basis of the UN documentation number. Their full list can also be found in Klimova 2003: Bibliography.

Index